D1314418

The Chance

The Chance

The Chance

*The true story of
one girl's journey to freedom*

**Lisa Cheng
and
Bruce M. Baker**

Soonershoot Press
Oklahoma City, Oklahoma

ISBN: 978-1-7361995-0-3

All events portrayed in this book are true.

Details expressed are a combination of memory along with gleanings from historical writings from and about the period. Some time frames were compressed, particularly during Muoi's early life for ease of reading. Quotations are English representations of the Chinese spoken by Muoi and her family. Due to her age at the time and translation difficulties, some dialog may be representative rather than exactly what people said.

The Chance

Contents

Part III

Part IV

Introduction and Dedication

This book is for my children and their children yet to come. It is also for my brothers and sisters and their children. We all encountered the same perils when we left Vietnam. That shared experience has brought all of us closer, and for that, I am truly blessed. This book is so none of us ever forget the struggle of how we came to the United States and that you will share our story with your children as well.

I was a normal girl. Nothing special. Nothing that set me aside from the others. Not unlike you, I loved to play with my friends, especially the rougher games that the older boys played. My parents loved their children very much and took care of our needs to the best of their ability. Life outside of my city was a mystery I had only begun to unravel; life outside my country was totally unknown. Although I often dreamed of leaving, I had no way to envision what going would encompass.

Fate stripped away my innocence and my ignorance one night when it selected me to board an escape boat in the place of a girl who didn't show. If Father hadn't dragged me away from my game, if I had not gone to Billy to get the few pennies he had, my story would be radically different. My life changed forever that night. From that moment to this day, I was no longer the girl trying to get out of her chores. I now had to jump through hoops I never knew existed, trying to adapt and change to my ever-shifting environment. I often found the steps on my journey nearly impossible to keep pace with. I had to face the real world, not my dream land. My changing and adjusting have never stopped. I am still on a continuous learning curve as more and more obstacles have and will race to meet me head-on.

More than ever, I feel that God has guided me every step of the way. I know that I never ceased praying for help, and somehow Billy and I survived. I am humbled and amazed by the graces we received. Even though I sometimes look back on those days at sea in disbelief, there was never a time when I doubted that we would survive. I have kept that attitude with me every day. Every time I face a significant change in my life, I remember that evening on the dock, close my eyes and take a step into nothingness — a leap of faith.

I wanted to write all of this down so that you, my children, would know about my path. You need to know how amazing people can be. We would not be here today without the crowd of family, friends, and chance acquaintances that helped us on our way. You cannot face life alone without others. Life requires us to take chances with no guarantees of the outcome, and the sharing of the experiences with others is sometimes the only thing that gets us through. There are no free rides.

I wanted to remind you of my mother, Xu Huynh. Her gentle spirit was the perfect counter to the explosiveness of my father, Quyen Quan. She was the perfect combination of perseverance and courage. I recognize now how hard she worked and am amazed how she remained so kind to everyone. The things she did were selfless, never about herself. She was a great cook, not just with food – with life as well. I know, beyond any doubt, that her presence is with us, flowing through all of us, keeping our family close today and in all the days to come.

If your quiet courage comes from my mother, then your willingness to adapt and change quickly comes from my father. He was a go-getter, a dynamo. He was quick with ideas, and during the turmoil of the post-1975 years, changed continuously with the times to provide for us. Mother and Father's spirits are with us. Look no farther than your parents' faces to see their influence on yourself.

In our family, we always talk a lot. Every time we travel together, a cruise or a special destination, I always make a point of reserving a meeting room for the family. Everyone meets at a specific time where we have fun and play a game. Sometimes we have small prizes to spice things up a little.

While we are together, I talk to the kids about the family. Other adults and youth as well join in and share their stories too. We share how important the journey was, how our parents took the chance and made a better future for us all. Their dream is our reality. We hope that you, our children, will remember this as you continue to grow. Then, we have a moment of silence to remember those who are no longer with us. We never forget where we came from, how we got here, how we continue to grow. We never fail to praise the kids, too, and show how proud the entire family is of their work, their achievements, and the respect they show each other. I pray that you will continue this practice long after this generation is gone.

Always appreciate everything in life. Good and bad. Don't be afraid of trying things. Everything happens for a reason, so embrace new things. Fate may throw you seemingly impossible things at the time but remember that everything in the world was impossible once. Work hard and be patient. Once you get past the problem, you are stronger and more aware of new directions available to you and can appreciate what you have accomplished. Remember always how proud I am of you.

Lisa Cheng (Mom)

The Quan Family

Quyen Quan, Father, Escaped from Vietnam with rest of family in 1982

Xu Huynh Quan, Mother, Escaped from Vietnam with rest of family in 1982

Hung Quan, (Billy). Brother, Age 17, escaped with Muoi in 1979

San Quan (Sandy), Sister, Age 16 at the time of Muoi's escape

My Quan (Amy), Sister, Age 15 at the time of Muoi's escape

Muoi Quan (Lisa), Age 12 at the time of Muoi's escape in 1979

Nguu Quan (Steve), Brother, Age 9 at the time of Muoi's escape

Phuc Quan (Jay), Brother, Age 8 at the time of Muoi's escape

Ly Quan (Scott), Brother, Age 7 at the time of Muoi's escape

Le Ouan (Ashley), Sister, Age 5 at the time of Muoi's escape

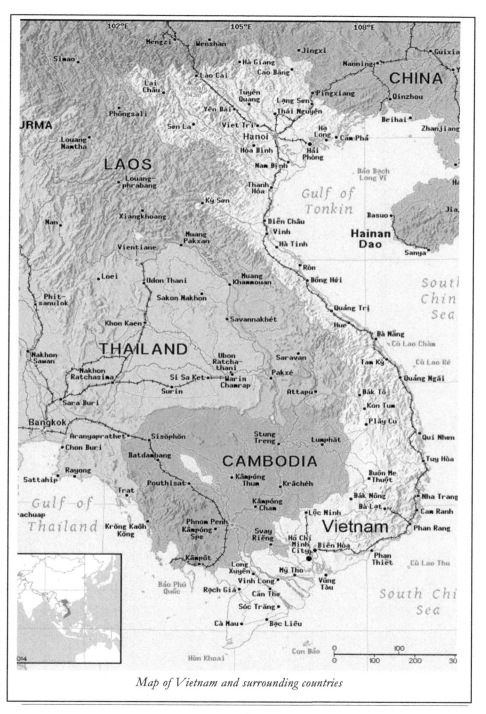

Map of Vietnam and surrounding countries

Chapter 1

A day in my life

Figure 1 Incense burner outside house

The sun never rose at my house in Cho Lon. For us to see the sun's first rays as it peeked over the horizon, we had to go to Vũng Tàu, a beach that was several miles away and much different from where I lived. Here, a honeycomb maze of walls, streets, and alleys with houses almost touching each other, stood just tall enough to keep the sun from making its formal appearance until mid-morning. Suddenly, its rays would explode onto the concrete and asphalt walkways of my hamlet or neighborhood. Its white brilliance often forced us to turn our heads or cover our eyes. Sometimes, we would rush into the shade formed by the surrounding walls for a small respite. Of course, by that time, our day would be half-done.

A typical day found me getting up with the chickens. Many families in the hamlet raised them for food, and, as a result, we never needed an alarm clock. A solitary rooster started his crowing while darkness still filled the alleys, and the only hint of the day to come was the thin streak one could see by looking straight up. Another rooster soon joined in the serenade. Then another, and so on until their sharp "cock-a-doodle-doos" ricocheted off the concrete canyons of the neighborhood so loudly that only the genuinely deaf could feign sleep.

My name was Muoi Quan. The day was October 20, 1974, 9-6-4672 on the Lunar calendar, the year of Jia Yin, the Tiger, and the month of Jia-Xu, the dog, and I was eight years old today. Although our country was currently at peace, the war remained fresh in our minds. It had not affected us personally in almost six years. That time, over the TET holiday, mortar rounds had taken the top two floors of our house and turned them to rubble. I was only two at the time, so I don't remember any of it, only what my parents have shared with me. On this day, my city was relatively quiet. Only the military's presence on the streets accompanied by the strange-looking American GIs trolling through the shops indicated how fragile our peace was.

The home I shared with my parents, five siblings, and assorted relatives was at our hamlet's far end. The house was made from concrete blocks and stood five levels high, the tallest one around, very impressive until you realized it was also very narrow. Homes in Cho Lon were typically one room per floor, and my immediate family shared the room on the third one. In Cho Lon, houses grew up, not out. Eight of us currently shared a twenty by twenty foot room. Our limited available space demanded that we respect each other's privacy and compromise for the family's good.

There were only two beds in the room, my parents' bed in the corner and the bunk bed. My parents' bed was a wooden panel held up by a headboard and footboard. A plastic curtain and a few inches of space were all that separated my parents from the rest of us. My sister, San, and I slept on the top of the bunk bed nose to feet to allow enough room for both of us. Even though it was not a bed in the traditional sense, we felt lucky to have the bunk bed.

There was no mattress. Where it would have been was a sheet of steel with exposed holes perforating the surface. At night when we slept, the holes gave us ventilation below our bodies. Unfortunately, this same surface resulted in red "checkerboard" marks all over us when we peeled ourselves off it in the morning. Since we were in the tropics, we didn't require any covers on the bed other than a thin mosquito netting. It never got cold this far south. The bottom bunk didn't have a permanent occupant. My father reserved it for guests. Of course, if no guests were around, my older brother, Hung, would snag it so that he didn't have to sleep on the floor with my other brothers in one of the corners. I always checked below before jumping out of the top bunk. It was better to be safe than jump on one of the boys. The baby, Le, slept with my parents. Privacy was not a word we ever used.

Today, I allowed myself the luxury of being the last one up. Occasionally, I liked to stay in the bunk staring at the ceiling for a short time while my older siblings got ready to go and cleared the room. On her way out, San would take my brother, Phuc, and my baby sister, Le, to the second floor where Grandmother Quan would take care of them. Hung would sprint for the door and bounce down the ladder-like steps so he could join his friends on their way to school, while my four-year-old brother, Nguu, begrudgingly slinked upstairs, complaining all the way. His place was with Mother and Father. He stayed out of the way while they worked in our family business, making Chinese medicines for the doctors and apothecaries in Cho Lon. The job was a vital one and one that our family took great pride in doing.

As the chaos of the morning gradually lessened, I groaned and flopped myself out of bed and onto the concrete floor. Being last would mean that I would have to walk by myself to school. I didn't mind. It wasn't unusual for me to go alone; after all, it was only a mile away. While I washed my face in the basin, I heard my father and mother talking as they began their workday. Their work filled the house with the glorious aroma of the herbs used in medicine making.

Only a matter of seconds later, I heard Father explode angrily at Nguu. I smiled. Nguu was a magnet for trouble. He learned his name at an early age for no other reason than everyone used it so much to yell at him. The boy just could not behave. Dad's outburst of temper was quickly followed by Mother's quiet, calm, soothing response. Mom was the peacemaker of our family.

I quickly finished combing my hair and dressed in my white shirt and blue skirt that made up my school uniform. I checked my appearance in the lone mirror located at the end of the cabinet attached to my parents' bed. My mother's appearance was somehow always perfect, and I longed to be like her in all ways, especially in how I presented myself at school. I would not want to embarrass her.

As I headed for the steps, our neighbors' radio duel started up just outside my window. Our windows contained no glass. We did not need it. Instead, they were metal grates that kept out the larger bugs but allowed the air to enter freely. Despite the heat, there was no air conditioning in the Quan house or, for that matter, any other place in the hamlet. The open grates allowed the sounds to come in loud and clear. One neighbor played Vietnamese music, the other Chinese. Each of them battled for speaker superiority as they ratcheted the volume louder and louder. Soon, the melee of noise would progress to the point where even the roosters would surrender to its unrelenting audio attack. Despite it all, the rest of our neighbors seemed to love the music. Most of them did not own a record player or radio of their own. They found this barrage of sound a delightful, if not soothing, way to start their day.

The last thing I did every morning was to grab my daily allowance of coins from the cabinet. Mother made sure that each of us had his or her allocation placed here every day. This money had to purchase everything I needed for that day, including breakfast, which I would grab from a street vendor on my way to school. I was free to spend it as I chose, but when it was gone, it was gone. There was no point in going back and asking for more. Father would refuse any such request. He and Mother expected their children to be responsible with our belongings, and that included money. On the small landing outside our room, I carefully stepped over the well-used "necessary pot" blocking my way. Our only bathroom was on the first floor. The pot allowed us to relieve ourselves without having to negotiate the steep stairs in the dark.

I flew down the staircase past the second floor where my Grandmother, Aunt, and Cousin Tran lived. They shared their space with some of our semi-permanent visitors who stayed with us. Some of them might remain for months at a time while they completed school or looked for work. I stopped abruptly on the landing outside their room and gave a short bow of respect to my grandmother. I couldn't see her inside, but I bowed every time regardless. I don't know how, but she would know if I didn't. Grandmother Quan was a force to be reckoned with, and I did not want to incur her wrath.

As I started down to the first floor, the clock began tolling the half-hour. I smiled. I loved that clock. The gentle chimes often reassured me during the night. Now, the old wall clock reminded me that my time was indeed short. I needed to move faster, or I would be late for school. Our kitchen and living area on the first floor were empty of people at this hour. The only occupants being my father's moped and assorted bicycles that the family stored there overnight.

With speed and agility, I snaked my skinny body through them, trying not to knock any of them over in my escape. I bowed in the direction of my ancestor's altar as I raced through the sliding grate into the alley.

Calling the walk space an alley was an exaggeration. In truth, it was barely more than a footpath, so narrow that Hung could stretch out his arms and almost touch both walls at once. Of course, he was fourteen and a lot bigger than me. I imagined myself doing it when I was his age as I swayed back and forth, bouncing off the walls of the homes on either side.

A few doors down, I made a right turn into a slightly larger alley. Here two mopeds could pass side by side if they were cautious, and the drivers weren't very fat. This path dead-ended at an even larger alley, almost a road that formed the entryway to my neighborhood. It was almost big enough for a small car. This road opened onto Hoc Lac, one of the main streets in Cho Lon. Its traffic, and its associated noise, were the heartbeat of our community in that it connected us with the capital city of Saigon via Hong Bang road.

On Hoc Lac, I spied a food vendor standing at his cart. I hardly slowed as I dropped some of my precious coins into a cardboard box and grabbed a sweet potato with the other hand. Then, I raced toward my school - munching away.

The Chinese School was a private school that catered to us of Chinese descent in the area. There I studied the Chinese language and customs as well as mathematics and science. Classes began promptly at nine in the morning and ran until noon. After a two-hour break for lunch and rest, classes continued from two to four in the afternoon.

I ran swiftly, artfully dodging foot traffic on the sidewalk. When I saw the large iron gate that marked the entrance to my school grounds looming ahead, I accelerated so that I was moving at full speed when I sprinted around it. I secretly prayed that there would be no teachers in the open courtyard. If there were, they would command me to stop, present myself, and bow. All of that would take precious seconds away from my on-time arrival for class.

Just as I turned the corner, my gaze suddenly snapped into focus. I saw something much worse than one of the teachers. My blood ran cold. There stood the headmaster not twenty feet away, and I appeared to have his complete and undivided attention. I was late. Much worse than being tardy, it was the headmaster who caught me.

Behind him stood some of my fellow students, other offenders I guessed, all standing at attention, none daring to breathe, let alone move. The look of fear on their faces told me volumes. After he determined that I was the last one, the headmaster scolded us for our tardiness. He stressed the importance of managing our time better, that we could not expect to succeed in life if we were slackers who showed up late. His steely, authoritative voice then ordered us to report to this same gate at the end of the class day. At that time, he would supervise the administration of the punishment. He did not have to say what our sentence would be, nor did he have to stress being timely for our arrival. I knew what my penance would be, and the thought of it caused my heart to sink.

The rest of the day was tortuous. Seconds dragged on for an eternity as I awaited the end of the day. I was usually a good student, but now I had a hard time concentrating on even the simplest things. Just thinking about what waited for me later made me forget everything I knew. We had a two-hour lunch break where we would go home, eat, and play. Typically, I was excited about this time. I would eat quickly and then play with my friends while the adults napped during the heat of the day. Today though, I was pretending to play, not really getting into it at all. My friends from the Catholic school wondered what was wrong with me, but my Chinese school friends advised them to leave me alone.

After lunch, I arrived back to school early, walking as one of the dead. The anticipation of what was to come even spoiled my writing lesson, my favorite class. When the end of the day finally came, my fellow truants and I marched toward the iron entry gate. We seemed like prisoners going to our execution - not a bad comparison, actually. Once there, we stood in a straight line. Without waiting for instructions, we squatted down, hips to heels, and held our fully-loaded book satchels out in front of us at arms' length. Then we waited, frozen in place, as every single student in the school slowly paraded past us. It was so humiliating! I was positive that the happy laughing of the passing students targeted me and me alone. I couldn't wait for the time to end. My bag only weighed about twelve pounds when I started, but it seemed to add five pounds for every minute that I held it out in front of me. When we finally watched the last student pass by, my arms nearing the breaking point, the headmaster slowly approached and had us lower our bags. Before he dismissed us, he said that he hoped we had learned our lesson and would not be in this situation again. I could not speak for the others, but I knew that the punishment had made its point with me. I, for one, would never be tardy again!

That afternoon, with my book satchel safely on my back where it belonged, I made my way home. My friends, now all aware of what had happened, played with marbles in the alley and told me to hurry up and join them. I went into the house, said hello to San and Mom as they prepared food for our dinner, ran upstairs, and changed into my rags that passed as play clothes. The day's pain was ebbing away with each step I took. Now was not the time to painfully dwell on past offenses. Now was the time to enjoy life, and I intended to do just that!

Playtime was my time. San claimed I was a tomboy, and I guess that was true. I loved adventurous things much more than she did, and when I tried a new game or activity, the riskier, the better. I always gave one hundred percent. Because of my love for adventure, I enjoyed playing the more competitive boys' games. They were a better fit for my active lifestyle, especially when it involved throwing, hitting, or being hit. Anything the boys would try, I would be there right there by their side.

I quickly snagged my collection of marbles from my cubby on the third floor. I was now prepared to engage the enemy when I launched myself into the alley. The game was in full swing when I joined them. It was the perfect thing to take my mind off the events at school today. I had almost convinced myself that nothing could ruin this moment when I heard my father's moped as it entered the main gate off Hoc Lac.

There weren't many mopeds in our neighborhood, and his bike made a unique sound. I could easily recognize it, even while it was still far away. Today, the sound reminded me that I had not done my afternoon chores yet. I shouted hasty goodbyes to my friends and hurried back inside the house. Mom and San, still in the kitchen, gave each other looks, obviously knowing what was going on. They laughed at me and rolled their eyes as I flew up the steps to our sleeping room, dropped off my stuff, and then shot up to the fifth floor, the roof, to retrieve the day's laundry. That was where Father found me, folding and stacking the day's wash. He seemed pleased that I was busy at work – a dutiful daughter. I was happy that he was pleased because if he found out about what happened at school, I would need all the positive thoughts I could get.

Thankfully, after chores and dinner with no one telling of the day's "adventure," it was time again for play—no running and shooting this time. I was in the mood for something a bit more sedate. I went next door to Nhi's house. Nhi was my best friend in the whole world, and together we had a lot of games that we both enjoyed. Of course, the boys called them all "girls' games," but, after all, I am a girl, and I certainly didn't want people to think I was a boy!

Nhi was already in the alley with our other friends, Yenlinh and Hue Hinh, engaged in a hopscotch game, which I happily joined. Yenlinh and Hue Hinh attended Sunday School with Nhi at the Catholic Church located just around the corner, on Hoc Lac. That was where I met them while accompanying my cousin to Mass.

After a bit, we switched over to Chopsticks. Chopsticks is a little like the American game, jacks, only with a tennis ball and, well, chopsticks. I ran into our kitchen and grabbed some for the game, at which my mother shouted that "they [chopsticks] are made for eating, not for playing!" She laughed after saying it, though, so I figured it was OK to go ahead.

In the afternoon, the sun disappeared in the hamlet as suddenly as it rose that morning. With school tomorrow and the alleyways growing darker by the second, I said goodbye to my friends and went home. San was in the common room on the first floor with my parents as I entered. Hung was not around, probably running around with his friends. He was able to go about pretty much as he pleased. I climbed the steps until, once again, I found myself in our sleeping room. I glanced over at my little brother and sister, already asleep and quietly prepared to join them. All in all, it hadn't been too terrible a day. As I drifted off, my dreams looked forward to great days ahead.

The Chance

Chapter 2

Meet my family

Figure 2 Quan family @1976

I am a first-generation Vietnamese citizen. My parents were born in China and came here with my grandparents when they were young. Their departure was all courtesy of Mao Zedong and the hold of Communism on China in the late 1940s. Mao's intentions told my grandparents all they needed to know. It was apparent to them that this "new" China would not be the right place for them or their children. They had few options available to them, and speed of the essence. They decided to risk everything to go to a place where personal initiative was still valued. They needed a place where work would produce success and where they would have control over their own lives. They had heard of a Chinese town - Cho Lon, near Saigon. In that place, people would welcome them, and opportunities would abound. They set their sights on this haven and set out.

There was one flaw with their plan. Vietnam's government would only allow one son per family group, and my father's parents had three. After consulting other families and much consideration, my grandparents found a solution. The middle son, my Uncle Ling, accompanied my grandfather under his last name of Ly. My grandmother took my father, the youngest boy, and his sister under her maiden name of Quan. A family friend named Phung "adopted" the eldest son, my Uncle Ho. They had no sons and were more than willing to complete the adoption to help my grandparents through this little technicality. Although the method may seem unusual, at the time, it was not. Many families made similar "trades" to get their children out of China. Once in Vietnam, the government required the boys to use their legal surnames throughout their lives. Even so, they remained family in blood.

My mother's family also immigrated from China around the same time. Instead of Cho Lon, they settled in My Tho, a much smaller community located far south of Saigon near the Mekong River's mouth. My mother was from there and would have stayed there her entire life if fate had not stepped in.

That single fortuitous event happened when she was a young woman in need of employment. She and her sister both found work at a small candy factory in My Tho – a candy factory that happened to be owned by my Uncle Ho. His factory was not large. It only occupied the back portion of his house on the first floor like many others in Vietnam. Small though it was, that factory turned out the best hard candy ever – all kinds of flavors and colors. I can taste them even now.

My father often took the bus from Cho Lon to visit his brother in My Tho. That is where, quite by accident I'm told, my mother, Xu Huynh, and my father, Quyen Quan, met and fell in love. My father began visiting his brother more and more under the guise of helping with the work, but he actually just went to see her. Ho even began dating her sister, and he and his brother often double-dated after work. In the end, Mother's sister, To, married my uncle, and of course, my mom married my dad.

Mom was perfect. She could do anything. A Chinese saying said, "She could be out in the living room and in the kitchen at the same time." The expression meant that she was a fantastic cook but also a well-versed conversationalist. Mom lived this saying every day. She could adapt to any situation, domestically or socially. She was also a natural beauty who could brighten any room with her smile. She was also adventurous, which I guess is where I got that side of me. She would tell me stories of when she was a little girl. One of them was about how she would dive off the river bridge in My Tho, fifteen to twenty feet into the water below to swim and cool off on a hot day. She took every opportunity to encourage me to be the best I could be at everything. In her spirit, I tried everything available to me. I loved her, and I envied her. She was magnificent, and she was the woman I wanted to become one day.

My father was as handsome as my mother was beautiful. That isn't just a daughter talking. He stood tall, even around those whose height was greater. He had a presence that required respect. He was fiercely proud of the business he had built and the family that the enterprise supported. My father's only fault was his temper. It was fiery and intense - withering the strongest people with just a glance. It was not a pleasant experience when his temper turned on us. We avoided angering him at all cost.

Hung was the firstborn son of our family. In my culture, this meant that he could do no wrong. He was the golden child. He was also four years my senior, a fact of which he often reminded me. He was so stuck up and arrogant! He never looked out for anyone but himself. Once, he tricked me into going up to the fourth floor with him for no other reason than to have me turn on the lights. As it turned out, my big, bad brother was afraid of the dark. Our paths rarely crossed. As a rule, he was far too busy with his friends and never seemed to have much time for me. Most nights, he was still out running around long after I went to bed.

My sister San was a miracle. She was three years older than I and, because of that, had far more responsibilities in the household than I did. At times she seemed like a second mother as she ordered me about pointing out mistakes I had made and jobs I needed to do. At other times, she became an insightful older sister. She knew just the right thing to say and the right secrets to keep. San was the best.

Chinese culture considered having a second son to be most fortunate for the family. Fortunate was not the adjective I would use to describe Nguu. He lived to be in trouble and succeeded most of the time. If Mother and Father weren't scolding him, then the rest of us were getting on to him for one thing or another. To say that Nguu was impish would be an understatement. Yet, his boyish charm meant that none of us could stay angry with him for very long.

My other sister, My, was born two years before me. Unfortunately, she was a sickly child and needed much care. She required so much attention that my parents decided it was best to send her to live in My Tho with my maternal grandmother and aunt. There, my grandmother could give her the individual attention she required. A few years later, my younger brother, Ly, joined her. He also needed extra care after his premature birth.

Rounding out the Quan children would be Phuc and Le. Phuc was another son and Le, a daughter. In 1974, Phuc was only three, just beginning the ordeal of potty training, while Le was only a few months old. My Grandmother Quan was their caretaker. On any given morning, I could find Le sitting in the small wicker infant chair, complete with a bar to keep her in place. Looking past her, I could see Phuc running around the room naked with Grandmother watching him closely. Here in Vietnam, cloth diapers were only for newborns. Children of Phuc's age ran around naked.

Whenever it looked like they were going to go to the bathroom, their caretaker would snatch them up and put them on the potty chair. This process continued until potty training was complete.

My Grandmother Quan was a powerful personality. My grandmother didn't get respect; she commanded it. My father's mother, Quan Nhuan, was the matriarch of our house, and she ruled it like her own personal kingdom. Even neighbors and distant family members referred to her as "boss lady," and most, if not all, feared her wrath. My father inherited his temper from her, but as wicked as his temper could be, it paled in comparison.

Even with her white hair tucked neatly into a bun, her persona quickly reminded everyone that she was not a shy and retiring grandmother. She wasn't a large woman, but her presence made her appear like a giant to the rest of us. Maybe it was because she had the voice of a lion and was not afraid to use it that made her such an enormous presence in the home. For whatever reason, everyone knew that the house had one head - and she was undisputed for that task.

Along with my grandmother, my aunt lived on the second floor. She was relatively short and had been born with a cleft lip. Even with this deformity, she was not a shy person. Instead, she was quick to share her opinions with anyone who would care to listen. Every morning, she prepared her supplies for her large pushcart of sweet drinks, which she would strategically place right outside the Catholic Church gate. There she would sell cold drinks made from mung beans, red beans, and coconut juice to the passersby.

The last permanent resident of our house was my cousin Tran. Although she lived on the same floor as my aunt, she was not her daughter. If my mother had the most significant influence on my life, my cousin Tran would be a close second. Even though she was twelve years older than me, older than any of my siblings, her inner strength impressed and inspired me so much. She had contracted polio when she was four, but she never let it slow her down. Like me, Tran was willing to try anything, and when her polio-wrecked body failed her, she would simply laugh and try again later when she felt stronger. I cannot think of a single time where she could not succeed in something she wanted to do.

In Chinese tradition, the family was everything, and there was little doubt that despite being born in Vietnam, it was a strong, vibrant, Chinese blood that ran in my veins. Together, my family stood against every adversary and faced every problem, every difficulty, that life tossed our way. I felt that we were invincible. They were my rock, my anchor in the maelstrom of life, and I loved them for it.

The Chance

Chapter 3

Services rendered

Figure 3 Market scene in Cho Lon

I don't remember exactly when I became Tran's official assistant. I only know that I was relatively young. Perhaps I became her "sidekick" because Tran needed help, or because I was the youngest girl at the time, or maybe because of our similar temperaments. Perhaps my parents just needed someone to keep an eye on me. Whatever the reason, I became Tran's companion. I went with her whenever she left the house. I was her door opener and her partner in crime. Our new arrangement was a fantastic stroke of luck for both of us. So many opportunities came to me that I might have missed otherwise, and in me, she had someone who wouldn't tell her that she couldn't do the things she wanted to do. We even had the same sign in the Chinese Zodiac – the horse. My mother always told me that "the horse never stops galloping." I guessed she was right. Tran and I never stopped. The adventures just kept on coming.

Most of my duties were straightforward. I would accompany Tran to Mass every afternoon. She was a devout Catholic, and even though I was Buddhist, I respected her faith very much. I would also run errands for her around the hamlet and in the surrounding area.

Early one morning, we walked together to the open-air food market about a mile from the neighborhood – she on her crutches and me dancing around her. Someone from our house had to do this every day since we had no way to store perishable food. The food we bought this morning, Mother and San would prepare this afternoon. We all would then eat it for our evening meal. Today was Tran's and my day to shop, and experience had proven that the earlier you arrived, the better the produce you took home.

Tran and I often stopped on the way to look at all the things offered by street vendors and shop keepers along the way. Cho Lon, loosely translated, means "Big Market," and nowhere was this more apparent than on its streets. Vendors extended out from the storefronts almost into the traffic. We both loved to shop, so shop we did. Today we might look at jewelry, tomorrow maybe baskets. Next week? Who knew? Every trip was different and, in its own way, unique. We did mostly "window shopping" this early, but it still counted since we didn't have any money to spend on such things anyway.

Before you could see the market, you sensed it. The smells and the sounds were unmistakable. We traveled up and down every row of vendors, drooling at each stall as we passed. Food vendors came here from all over the city. They filled their stalls with so many products that they spilled out onto the walkways. Each vendor rushed to sell his or her wares as soon as possible. Wait too late, and they would begin to spoil.

Today, we bought rice and some vegetables, along with some fresh fish for the evening's soup. When the time came to pay, we haggled. No one ever paid full price for anything. I loved to watch Tran go back and forth with the vendors over the cost and learned some valuable tricks from her. Sometimes, she would allow me to do the negotiations by myself. Afterward, she would critique my efforts to improve my style and technique.

The vendors and we were satisfied by the end of our trip. We had paid a fair price, and the vendors received a reasonable price. We loaded all our purchases for the day into our bags, ready to begin the journey home. By this time, Tran was exhausted and could not walk all the way back, so we hailed an *xe lam* for the trip. A *xe lam* is hard to describe. It was kind of like a bus or maybe more like a glorified wagon. The front resembled a Volkswagen beetle with the driver sitting in a narrow front seat and the cab's sides open to the elements. The back looked like a long truck bed with two wooden benches with backrests running the body's length. There would be a tarp-like canopy over the passenger area, but the sides were open to the elements. At the very tail end of the *xe lam*, there was a step up for passengers. Because of her polio, we had to ensure that Tran sat at the end closest to the back so she could exit easily. Having to inch her way up to the front was too tedious and painful for her.

After we got home, I took our daily food to the kitchen area while Tran started upstairs to begin the daily laundry. She would take all our dirty clothes out onto the narrow second-floor balcony. There, Tran filled the washtub with a short hose attached to a standing faucet. Using a washboard, she washed and then rinsed each piece by hand before running it through a hand wringer to get as much moisture out of the articles as possible. Then she took the clean laundry up to the roof to dry in the sun. The job would be tough for anyone, but for Tran, living with the aftermath of polio, it was particularly difficult.

Watching her struggle was painful to see. She crawled more than walked up the stairs pulling the basket of wet laundry behind her. I would have loved to step in and help her but knew that she would firmly refuse any assistance. Tran never complained about her work and absolutely would not accept help or pity from family or friends. In her opinion, the family required everyone to do his or her part, and this was her way of helping daily life in the family. She defended her right to do it with a fierce intensity.

Chapter 4

A day at the beach

Figure 4: Sand beach on the Condao island in Vung Tau, Vietnam

Being the enterprising young person I was, I did not take much time to realize that being Tran's assistant had advantages. One of them was that having a spontaneous adventure of my own suddenly became much more manageable. Mid-November presented me with such an opportunity. The torrential monsoon rains of September and October had finally stopped as if a benevolent god turned off his heavenly faucet. The sun majestically reappeared, claiming its rightful place in the Vietnamese sky. Today would be a perfect day to go to the beach!

I approached Tran cautiously. We were friends and companions, but I had always accompanied her. I had never tested that relationship from the other side. I asked her what she would think about going to the beach for the day. Fortune was on my side. She was more than agreeable. She felt that getting out of the house for the day sounded terrific. Before she changed her mind, I ran next door and convinced Nhi's mother that she had to come along with us. Then, the three of us snagged a cab to downtown Saigon where a charter bus was loading up to go to Vũng Tàu, a gorgeous peninsula surrounded by beaches on all sides. In my soul, I knew today was going to be an epic day - and it was, that is...until it wasn't.

The first disaster occurred to Nhi. Unbeknown to us, she was susceptible to car sickness. Her illness wasn't her fault. How could she have known? After all, this was her first trip by bus, and she had been fine in the cab. Now, this wasn't the "I feel woozy" kind of car sickness. This was the "throw up your guts" kind. She was miserable the entire trip out, and by the time we arrived, the rest of the passengers weren't doing too great either. When we finally reached our destination an hour later, everyone was more than ready to get off the bus. In fact, people were tripping over each other, trying to get off.

Both feet on solid ground once again, Nhi recovered quickly. She seemed fine, happy even, ready for a day of adventure and fun. Looking into her now smiling face, I didn't have the heart to tell her that we would have to take the bus back that afternoon. I did, however, make a mental note. Nhi should not eat before we left and that I should carry a plastic bag - just in case.

The rest of the day was indeed magnificent. Nhi and I played in the surf while Tran rested comfortably in a chair surrounded by shade. The gentle ocean breezes made the air around us so pleasant compared to the heat in the city. The day was perfect. We ate the food that we had brought along and then played some more. After over two months of almost constant rain, the sun once again warming our bodies was blissful indeed. When at last the time came to reload the bus, three tired yet happy people trudged back for the return trip home. Fortunately for all of us, Nhi went right to sleep, which kept her nausea at bay, while Tran and I casually chatted as we returned to Saigon.

Not until we got out of the cab back at the house did the second disaster happen. As I peeled my back from the car seat, my skin felt as if it were on fire. I had the occasional sunburn, of course, but this one was one for the record books. Nhi seemed to be OK, so she and Tran made their way back toward the house while I gingerly walked over toward the Catholic Church. I wasn't feeling particularly religious; I had another motive for going in that direction. First of all, I knew that there was almost always something going on in the churchyard. Secondly, I was hot and tired, and I hurt. I desperately needed something cool to drink, and I knew just where to go. Spying my aunt's drink cart at her usual location on the sidewalk, I put on my most pathetic look and approached her. To my relief, my aunt didn't take too much begging and cajoling before taking pity on me and giving me one.

With the drink firmly in hand, I already felt much better. As I stood at the gate, I noticed a group of older boys playing a pick-up basketball game in the large paved area that made up the churchyard. Watching basketball seemed like an excellent way to enjoy my drink, so I went inside and moved over toward one of the goals, one where the pole was mostly in the shade, and I sat down. The metal pole felt delightfully cool against my pained back. The feeling was heavenly. I allowed myself to relax just a little and decided to watch more of the game before going home to do my chores.

As usual, the boys were all trying to outdo each other with their jumps, leaps, and dunks. The game was fast-paced and loud. All the action and noise drew many more spectators from the street. Of course, their attention only caused the boys to get more outlandish in their attempts to amuse the group. Out of the blue, one of the players tripped. He was attempting a layup during a fast break at my end of the court when it happened. I watched as the action appeared in slow motion. His body launched itself into the air toward me. I clearly saw the look of disbelief on his face. I was about to get creamed, and there was nothing he or I could do about it. Right before he slammed into me, I closed my eyes tightly, hoping that alone would let me avoid the inevitable. It didn't help. I felt his body crushing my already tortured back into the metal pole and sending the remains of my drink flying out of my hand. I had never experienced such pain. The fall was an accident, of course, but that didn't make it hurt any less.

Suddenly, things moved at regular speed again. The embarrassed player bounced up quickly. He was so sorry and kept asking me if I was OK over and over, to which I kept responding through gritted teeth that I was fine, no harm done. I put on a brave smile for him and the others as I painfully pulled myself off the ground, not for a moment showing any of the anguish my bruised body felt. I made a conscious effort not to cry; after all, only little girls cried. Besides, they were older boys. With my dignity more or less intact, I limped home.

The walk back to my house was slow and painful. I wasn't sure what hurt worse, the sunburn on my back or the injuries sustained in the fall. I mentally brushed them off as I gingerly walked up to the fifth floor and began doing my chores. Just as I was close to finishing, the ache on my back reignited into a blaze of searing pain. The agony I was experiencing seemed much more than just a sunburn reminding me of my stupidity at the beach. This was different. I tried my best to shrug the pain off, moving around the roof to loosen the tight skin a bit.

After several futile attempts to do so, I went downstairs where Mother was preparing dinner and begged her to have a look. She was busy and told me that she didn't have time for such nonsense. Then Mom looked up and saw my face in agony, and the tears welling up in my eyes. She knew then that something was terribly wrong. San took over the cooking duties while Mother came over, turned me around, and lifted the back of my shirt. Her scream froze me in place. "What happened? Where have you been? Who did this to you?" Her questions fired past me so fast that I had no time to respond before she threw the next one my way. I didn't understand. I had done nothing wrong. I just had a sunburn, right? Now, the tears started to run like rivers down my cheeks, both in pain and in fear. I could not imagine what would make my mother react this way.

It seemed that the tears weren't the only things running. Blood and pus were flowing down my back too. That was what freaked her out. Through my tears, I blubbered the short version of the events of the day. I had come back from the beach, gotten a drink, and gone to watch the basketball game. As an afterthought, I might have added that one of the boys had fallen on me.

Wow! That had been the wrong thing to say. I had no chance to take it back once I said it, or for that matter, say anything else before she dragged my father away from his work, showed him my back, and repeated what I had told her. She added a bit about how she was confident that the boy had been responsible for this damage to her little girl.

That did it. The fuse had been lit. Father's eyes blazed up in a fit of rage. I had seen him angry before, but never THIS mad! He picked me up and half carried half dragged me back to the basketball court where he sat me down, looked me in the eye, and demanded, "Which one? Who did this to you? Which boy did you get into a fight with?"

Fight? What fight? There had been no fight. By this time, the game had broken up, and only a few of the players still milled around the area. Father began to interrogate the remaining boys and men aggressively. They had no idea what the problem was. Who had hurt his little girl? Who had attacked her? They knew nothing about an attack. All they remembered was that one of the other players had fallen into me during the game and that I had seemed fine when I got up to leave.

An eternity later, his anger finally spent. Father took me back to the house, where he relayed what had really happened to my mother. Mom then took me aside, peeled off my shirt, and painted my wound with red medicated water (mercurochrome). Later in life, I heard that medicine referred to as "the fiery spit of Satan," which, in retrospect, seems to be a reasonable comparison. You knew the medication was working when it hurt. Well, it was working great that day! I swear that the cure stung worse than the damaged skin did, but even that pain was not as bad as the scene in front of the boys. What an embarrassing moment! I had stood there in tears, snot running out of my nose, unable to make a coherent sound, while my father ranted and raved at them like a crazy person. I saw no way that I could face those boys ever again!

The Chance

Chapter 5

If at first you don't succeed...

Figure 5 Dai Tong Lam Pagoda

A few painful weeks and about a gallon of mercurochrome later, Tran wondered if I would like to go back to the beach with her and some of her friends. She didn't really need any help but thought that I might want to come along anyway. What else could I do? I had told my parents that I would shadow Tran, right?

My mother took the news with caution. She did not want a recurrence of what had happened in November. After repeated warnings from her and San followed by my assurances that I would watch my time in the sun, she relented. Tran and I set out. When we got to the charter bus, her friends were already there. Typically, I like being around older kids, but this was different. They weren't kids. Tran's friends were her age, and that meant that they were fifteen years older than me. That put me off a little bit. I wasn't sure how to act or what to say around them, so instead, I simply sat quietly and listened to their conversations intently. Her friends were so smart! I was so impressed by what they knew. The trip to the beach seemed to take no time at all.

One of the things they went on and on about was the recently completed Buddhist pagoda, a kind of temple, on *Nui Lon*, the Big Mountain. In particular, they were fascinated by its statue of the Sleeping Buddha. Side trips like this were not usually my thing, but the others' excitement was contagious. So, after we arrived, we were off to *Nui Lon*. The beach would wait for later.

Although the climb only took thirty minutes, it was long and steep, with hundreds, maybe thousands, of steps marking the way. Fortunately, there were many level places where Tran could rest, although she still required help from her friends. While we walked up, the view of the surrounding area was breathtaking.

I could plainly see the water surrounding the three sides of the peninsula. The sea breeze was strong here, making the air cooler, more comforting than down below. Even the sun seemed less harsh here, though one of Tran's friends told me that was not true.

Once we got to the park itself, I was glad we came. Everything was larger than life. Everywhere were statues of the Buddha, depicting him at various stages of his life. Some of them were gigantic! The pagoda itself was the most beautiful place I could ever imagine. I walked forward in silence and listened as the others discussed the works of art in hushed voices. When we finally reached the reclining Buddha, we stood in awe at the vision before us. The statue was twelve meters long. He seemed so life-like that I was positive that he could wake up at any time.

The hike down was nothing like the one up. With gravity's aid, we quickly made the descent. Going down, I was not quite as shy and asked a lot of questions that I thought were intelligent. The group answered each one of them respectfully, although I often got a sly smile and a wink included with the response. All in all, the day had exceeded expectations. Never in my life felt had I felt so grown up.

In short order, we were back at the beach, where we changed into our swimsuits, and I got ready for play. The beaches at Vũng Tàu are golden sand surrounded by the South China Sea's azure blue waters. I immediately busied myself by jumping in and out of the surf. At the same time, Tran and her friends ventured farther out, towing Tran in an inflated tube to keep her safe nearby. Occasionally, I would look up from my play and watch them frolicking in the water just out from shore. Everyone was having such a wonderful time.

Only a minute later, I realized what a difference a minute made! I had just seen Tran waving to me from her inner tube as she playfully splashed a friend. Then, I looked up and couldn't find her anywhere! I saw her friends gesturing wildly and shouting things that I could not hear over the waves. Others joined in the shouts and frantic hand gestures. Lifeguards came flying down the beach to where we were.

I didn't understand. What was going on? Where was Tran? Time stood still. An eternity later, reality reached me. My heart went into my throat as I watched the lifeguards pull her still form from the water and onto the beach. I screamed her name as I rushed down the shoreline to where she was. The lifeguards and friends were gathered around her so tightly that I could not see a thing, nor could I break through the surrounding crowd. Why were they just standing around? My cousin was dying or was perhaps already dead! They should be doing something. What would I do without her? As I prayed to anyone who would listen, I finally dropped to my knees and crawled between the ring of legs surrounding her. I had just broken through when she sat up. She noticed me at once and weakly waved in my direction. That was all I needed. She was alive. She was going to be OK. I threw myself across the open space between us and hugged her as hard as I could. I dared anyone to try and pull me away.

Her friends were all talking at once, trying to explain what had happened. From what I could understand, there was a large wave that had come out of nowhere and overturned her inner tube. Before she could catch her breath, another wave tumbled her over and pushed her inner-tube far out of her reach. Her friends had been involved with their game when the wave hit. The strong undercurrent had pulled their feet out from under them and forced them under the water. As they attempted to regain their balance, none of them happened to notice Tran floundering in the water about twenty feet away. Fortunately, someone walking along the beach had seen her thrashing and sounded the alarm.

That evening, as we boarded the bus going back to town, we were a sober, somber crowd, much different from the happy crew that had set forth that morning Our exhaustion and fear of what might have been replaced the idle chatter from earlier in the day. There was no laughing and joking. Gone was the peace and tranquility I had felt in the presence of the Buddha. Now, Tran was sitting next to me, still and quiet. Her face seemed frozen in place. Her friends indicated that she was in shock. I was afraid that the water might not have taken her life but stolen her spirit instead. I realized that I feared that more than death. I needed Tran back, my Tran.

I didn't know what else to do, so I just huddled close to her, willing my strength into her. I asked myself, *What if she were never the same? What if her vibrant light never shone again?* I put my fears to rest on our cab ride home. She bent down toward me, her sharp, severe gaze focused on me, as she whispered, "We had better not tell anyone about this, or the family will not let us go again!" She followed that with a laugh - a little laugh, not a hearty Tran laugh like before. Nonetheless, it was genuine, and I happily joined in with her.

For the first time since the accident, I began to relax. My Tran was back.

Chapter 6

The family business

Figure 6 Cho Lon House - Fourth floor kitchen/workshop

Today was medicine day – not a day for taking medicine, instead a day for making it. As much as I loved waking up to the smell of herbs in the morning, I believe I loved working in the family medicine business more. Making our medicine was an involved process, and the work required all but the youngest of us to assist in its manufacture. Working alongside the rest of the family made me feel good. It made me a part of our success.

Earlier in the week, Father, Hung, and Mother had put all the ingredients in a fifty-gallon barrel, filled it with water, and then turned on the large propane burner under it and waited for the right time. The herbal soup would cook for a day or two with Father constantly checking the mixture for consistency. Finally, Father would declare the mix ready to process. He and Hung would then carefully drain the liquid from the barrel, revealing a black, rough, doughy substance at the bottom. This material would be scooped out and placed into smaller, sealable containers so that it would stay fresh. Now, the rest of us could do our part.

We all gathered on the fourth floor, along with all the necessary equipment and materials. San would take the dough from the containers and knead it by hand, just as though it were a loaf of bread. When she felt the texture and consistency were correct, she passed the dough off to Tran. She fed it into the top of an electric meat grinder. This step gave the dough the texture of ground beef and made it easier to do the next step. One of our houseguests or a visiting family member grabbed the ground material, placed it between two sheets of plastic, and shoved it through a hand-powered laundry wringer flattening the mixture out and making it extremely thin. Another worker carefully removed the plastic sheeting from the dough and placed it on a flat metal table. At this point in the process, I came into the picture.

I took a circular, cookie cutter-type mold and made perfectly round wafers out of the flattened dough. Then, I took the finished discs and carefully placed them on a tray made from chicken-wire framed by wood allowing the air to circulate on all sides of the disk to assist the drying process. I gathered all the scraps of material from my cutting and returned them to the wringer person who combined them with the next batch. We did not waste anything. When the drying tray was full of wafers, I took it to the fifth floor and set it on a large metal sheet to bake in the sun and air dry. The last step in the process happened when all the discs were dry. The whole family would then take the finished wafers and package them in small plastic bags that Father would deliver to his clients around town.

Everything was going smoothly and efficiently that day. I thought we might finish early for once, and I could play some with my friends. The relaxed mood and the lively conversation focused on my Uncle Ho's family coming to visit the next day. Their visits were always a big event. He would bring his big car, and all of us would get to ride around town inside – a huge treat.

In the middle of our chatter, the unthinkable happened. I have no idea how, but somehow Tran became distracted – just for a second. Such a simple thing. Her right hand slipped ever so little from its position at the top of the grinder and suddenly found itself in the gnashing teeth of the spinning blades below. My first indication that something was wrong was her scream piercing the overall rumble of noise. My head snapped up along with everyone else's to the reason for the cry. Our search did not take long.

Tran, sitting on her stool, held the remains of her bloodied hand in front of her. Shreds of flesh trailed down from where her index and middle fingers had been only a moment before. Blood had spattered everywhere. All I could see was blood - lots of blood. I remember thinking, "How could someone lose so much blood and still live?" At that moment, everyone froze. No one knew what to do.

A fraction of a second later, my father grabbed a rag from the counter and quickly wrapped the cloth tightly around Tran's wound as he applied pressure – hard. In what seemed like the same moment, not wanting to waste any time, he grabbed her, picked her up while still maintaining pressure on the wound, and carried her down the stairs at a breakneck pace. Outside the entryway, my grandmother, who was too old to participate in the assembly, sat perched on her usual throne. She caught just a glimpse of the wound as Father and Tran flew by with the rest of us in fast pursuit. One glance was all she needed. She passed out cold and fell off the stool. A few of us stayed behind to take care of Grandma, but I stayed focused on the back of my father. I was not going to leave Tran for anything.

We raced for the local hospital on foot; there was no time to hail a cab, my father showing no sign of fatigue. Tran's screams were now a quieter wailing. Once there, however, there the doctors could do little for her. They surgically removed the ragged pieces of skin trailing from her injured hand, which left a pair of stumps where her fingers had been. They stopped the bleeding and stitched up the wound, but there was no replacing the lost fingers. Finally, their work finished, the doctors gave her something for the pain and released her to go home.

Silently, in my nine-year-old naivete, I wished that the disaster had happened to me and not Tran. She suffered so much every day just getting by. For this to happen to her was beyond my childlike understanding. It just wasn't fair.

One of the few things Tran could do unaided was writing. She was a regular contributor to our Chinese newspaper, and her calligraphy was legendary. Her skill was so great that Tran taught calligraphy to students of the craft. She taught those skills to me as well! How would she be able to continue after this?

Weeks later, I realized that I shouldn't have been so concerned. Tran treated this injury as she did any other obstacle in her life – she galloped past it. She indeed was unstoppable. In a short amount of time, she painstakingly re-taught herself to write and draw, using only the remaining three digits on her hand. In the end, her painstaking efforts had paid off. Her writing was as beautiful as ever. This new disability hadn't stopped her at all. It had only been a speed bump that slowed her down for a bit. She once again wrote and taught as if nothing had happened. Her spirit remained indomitable, and I adored her for her tenacity.

I observed her as she struggled to regain her abilities, and I took all her efforts into my heart. I decided that if Tran could overcome obstacles like this, I could too. I would be unstoppable in my pursuits as well. Whatever challenges faced me, now and in the future, I would gallop past them just as Tran had done. After all, we were both children of the horse; how could I not?

Chapter 7

My artsy side

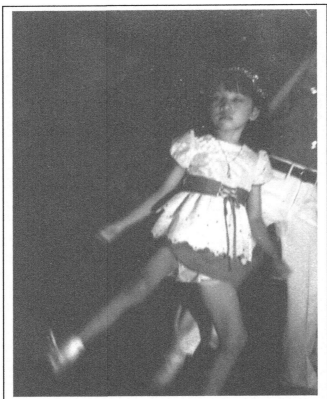

Figure 7: Photograph of Muoi in a dance program pre-1975

I loved to play, and I loved to write. These were not just things I enjoyed. They were my passions, my reason for living. Playing competitive games got my blood going just as intricate calligraphy with Mother or Tran calmed me and forced me to focus. I thought that my life was complete. My world was perfect. I would naturally tolerate the chores, but they were only a means to get what I needed to write and play. Then, unexpectedly, I discovered something exciting and new, something that made me realize my world had room for something more.

The change in my life started innocently enough. My father often allowed students from outside the city to stay with us while they did their studies. They might be relatives or friends of relatives. All were welcome. These young people came and went without much notice from me until a young woman, Thuy Anh, came to live on the second floor as one of our student borders.

Along with her studies, she was an accomplished dancer and joined a Chinese dance troupe that practiced nearby. I would stand in the corner and watch her in envy as she dressed in some of the most beautiful clothes I had ever seen to perform her dances. When she practiced, I attempted to imitate her moves as best I could while standing out of the way. After all, I didn't want to intrude. The way her body flowed to the music entranced me. She was perfection in motion. I was positive that I had kept my admiration a secret until one evening when she called me over and invited me to tag along to practice.

I loved it! There was nothing about dancing that I didn't love. The movements, the costumes, the music were all so perfect, so elegant. Dancing was nothing short of magnificent. I guess my enthusiasm made an impression because the rest of the troupe invited me to return and join their children's group. I couldn't believe my luck. I was so excited that I could hardly wait to get home and tell my parents the good news.

As we walked home, my enthusiasm waned as I began to worry about what my parents would say. What if they didn't see my dancing as good news? The group would require a lot of practice time. Some time would come at the expense of play, but some would have to come from chores and studies. Performances would require a lot of new clothing. In my world, where you did not buy clothes at the store, they would be clothes that my mother would have to make. What if she and my father said no?

I had a cold feeling in my heart as my new friend and I asked my parents about joining the troupe. I held my breath as I waited impatiently for their response. When their "Yes" came, I was overjoyed! My mother was ecstatic and gave the idea her total support. She was confident that making my clothing would not be a problem for her. My father was also pleased that I was committing to something worthwhile, especially if that something would use up some of my excess energy. Hung and San didn't seem to care one way or another, and the younger children were completely oblivious.

I put all my heart and soul into my dancing. If I had planned to practice for thirty minutes, I pushed for an hour instead. I analyzed every move, every gesture. I was my worst critic. My dances had to be as perfect as I could make them. Like everything else, I gave one hundred percent to be the best dancer I could be. Finally, when the time came for my first public performance, all that practice paid off. Dancing gave me a thrill like no other. Adrenaline rushed through my veins when I danced, and that feeling made me seem invincible. We moved as one as we danced. We bowed, and the audience applauded. My parents applauded! Performing had to be the best feeling ever.

I can only remember one time that my dress wasn't ready on the day of the performance. Mother had simply not had time to finish the stitching before the date was upon us. When she told me, I was crestfallen, and I am embarrassed to say that my disappointment reflected on both my face and in my manner. The dress was a beautiful polka-dotted polyester. It was gorgeous, and I was so looking forward to dancing in it, but Mother simply hadn't had the time to finish the hem.

Mother, seeing my disappointment, tried a different solution. She grabbed the dress and a candle and rushed over to the table in the dining area. What was she doing? Was she going to burn it! I watched with questioning eyes while she carefully held the hem of the dress and slowly passed the fabric over the candle's flame. Using her fingers, she took the cloth, now melted with the heat, and fused it between her fingers; that way, the fabric would not unravel. With that trick, she saved my performance. My mother was my hero, still and again.

My newfound interest in the arts opened other opportunities as well. One night, Tran invited me to accompany her to the opera, and I, being her trusted assistant, had to go. I wasn't even sure what an opera was, but Tran was excited, and that was enough for me. That evening we dressed up in our finest outfits and took a cab to the opera house. The building was stunningly beautiful. I had often seen it as I passed by and loved the French architecture, especially the statues at the entrance. Tonight I got to go inside for the first time. The excitement was electric. We pretended that we were princesses as we climbed the stairs and entered the lobby amid so much finery. So many people surrounded us, all dressed in their finest clothing. I was so confident that the evening would be perfect, and it was - until Tran got lost.

I didn't know where she could have gone. She was right beside me only a few seconds earlier. I became frantic as I swept my eyes across the lobby in search of my friend. I couldn't see more than a few feet because of the crowd. The people around me were so tall compared to me that I felt invisible down here. No one noticed me. No one seemed to care that I had lost my cousin! My whimpers soon transformed into full-fledged crying with loud sobs and tears flowing down my cheeks and onto the floor.

This got some attention. A security guard came over to see if he could help. I explained haltingly through my sobs how I had lost Tran and didn't know what to do. He comforted me and kept me by his side while we waited, not too far from where I had lost her. Sure enough, within a few minutes, a teary-eyed Tran, retracing her steps, found us. She and I stood in the lobby for the longest time, crying, laughing, and hugging. I am sure we were quite the spectacle for the rest of the crowd, but we just didn't care.

About the same time, my aunt began inviting me to attend plays at the Chinese Theater with her. Her invitation surprised me as she and I were never very close; nonetheless, I welcomed the opportunity and jumped at the chance to go. She explained that there was one small thing I would have to do, which I discovered would require some of my playground toolset to accomplish.

My aunt was very frugal. She worked hard for her money and hated parting with even the smallest coin without good reason. She would stand in line at the theater and purchase a ticket, one ticket, for the standing section – the cheapest ticket available.

My job was to wander over and wait by the theater entrance watching the attendees until I saw a couple of patrons deep in conversation preparing to enter. I pretended as though I were with them and walked into the theater using them as a barrier between the usher and me.

Once inside, my job was to find a seat in the section reserved for season ticket holders. I would sit there as if I owned it, daring anyone to challenge me. If by chance, someone did come to claim the seat as their own, I would humbly apologize for my mistake and move on to a different one within the section. The season ticket holders who were coming to the performance tended to arrive by the end of the first act. By then, I would have latched onto a couple of "spare" seats and fetched my aunt. Then we sat and enjoyed the rest of the play.

My deception wasn't stealing exactly, and I never felt guilty about the ruse. After all, the season ticket holders had paid for the seats in advance. That those people had simply decided not to be there that night wasn't my fault. My actions didn't harm or cheat anyone. No payment changed hands. I truly believed that letting the seats go to waste would have been more of a crime. Frankly, I found the whole escapade kind of exciting – a real-life game where sneaking into the building was the challenge. For the record, no one ever caught me.

In this way, a new side to my life evolved – one outside of play and school. My dance classes went well, and my performances continued to improve. I never grew tired of the stage. My mother tirelessly made new outfits for me, and my sister tried hard not to be jealous that I was getting new clothes when she did not. My life was now complete.

Chapter 8

Happy New Year!

Figure 8: Chinese New Year Celebration, Oklahoma City 2017

During the fall and early winter, the Chinese and Vietnamese cultures celebrated a whirlwind of holidays - not counting my birthday. This string of celebrations started with the Moon Festival. For the Chinese people, this was the second most important holiday in the Chinese calendar and always occurred during the new moon at harvest time. As was our custom, I gathered with my immediate and extended family from around the region. The festival was overall a quiet one. Because we were Buddhists, we would begin by making food and incense offerings and placing them upon the small altar on the first floor, the one devoted to our ancestors. Afterward, we sat together and ate moon cakes. Moon cake was appropriately named because it had an egg yolk cooked in the middle that looked very much like a full moon when we cut it open.

December was for Christmas, of course. I wasn't a Christian, but Tran and many of my friends were, and I was always up for fun and parties. Weeks ahead of time, my Christian neighbors began putting up distinctive star-shaped lanterns on their doors. These made the alleyways come alive with colored light after dark. I accompanied Tran to extra plays and services at the Catholic Church, where we sang specific songs for the holiday called carols. The highlight of the season was the special Mass held outdoors at midnight Christmas Eve. It was magical. The singing, the pageantry, the Christmas story were breathtaking to behold.

The biggest holiday of them all, though, came in January or early February. Since we used the western calendar, we celebrated January 1st along with the rest of the world. Yet, after the first day of the Western new year was long past - long after those parties and celebrations ended,

Chinese New Year or TET, as the Vietnamese referred to it, took center stage. In my world, there was no comparing the Western and Chinese new year. The Chinese New Year was the best. It was Christmas, birthday, and...every other day all rolled into one. Typically, the festival fell in late January, but in 1975, it was later, on February 11th. Waiting the extra two weeks was brutal.

Why was it so great? To start with, the New Year wasn't just one day. We celebrated the New Year for a whole week, seven days! We would start preparing months ahead of time. Each of us received seven new TAILOR-MADE outfits, one for each day of the celebration. True, those outfits, along with our old clothes and any hand-me-downs from family or friends, had to last for the entire year, but that was fine by us. As far as I knew, I was the only exception to this rule, and that was only because of dance, and mother made those. Each day of the celebration, I would dress in my new outfit for that day. As a special treat, my mother allowed me to wear some of her jewelry when we attended the dragon dances and other public events. I felt like royalty.

There were many events planned for each day, but the third day was incredibly wonderful. That day, Uncle Ho would bring his car up from My Tho, which was always an event in itself. We would all pile into his car and go to other relatives and friends all around Cho Lon and Saigon. At each house, the hosts would give us red pockets. Red pockets were made from a stiff red paper into envelopes. They were special because they each contained money. The significance was so that the recipients could start forth into the new year with prosperity and joy. There might be only a few coins inside, but our anticipation was overwhelming. The hosts decorated each envelope festively for the event. We LOVED getting our red pockets.

The rest of the seven days followed suit—seven days of parties and dances with no worries and little work. There was no medicine made during that period and no unnecessary chores assigned. The New Year was a time filled with food, laughter, fun, and joy. When the week finally ended and celebrations turned into memories, we reluctantly returned once again to our everyday lives. Our minds raced with what this exciting new year of 1975 would bring.

The year began with so much promise, so much hope. How tragic it was that our dreams transformed into nightmares far too soon.

Chapter 9

Bad things happen to good people

Figure 9: Ho Chi Minh Poster

I didn't realize...I guess I was just too young to understand what was happening. I had been taught in school that the Americans and the South Vietnamese Army had defeated the North. The danger was gone. All parties had signed a peace treaty in Paris just before TET in 1973 that officially ended the long war and guaranteed us peace at last. The Americans had promised to aid us in the event of a North Vietnamese attack. We felt safe and secure in that reassurance.

That peace turned to ashes only a year later, in December 1974, when the North Vietnamese forces attacked and defeated our men at Phước Long, around 150 kilometers north of Saigon. Following that 1974 attack, other skirmishes broke out. While we had been celebrating Chinese New Year with laughter and joy, the North's soldiers had prowled through our borders via Cambodia and reignited the flames of war. The promised help from America never materialized. We were in this alone.

Later, as is often the case, I realized that Father and Mother spoke in hushed voices a bit more than usual during that time. In my innocence, I had just dismissed the secrecy. I thought they were just coy about the upcoming New Year festivities. About that same time, Father began quietly selling some of the other properties that he owned. Now, Father was buying and selling things all the time, so I never gave the sales a second thought. The reality of what was happening around me did not dawn on me until a few months later, in April. Even so, I was only nine and had little idea of how much these events would affect my life in the future.

Then, on April 29th, 1975, the unthinkable happened. I am not likely ever to forget that day. Father and Mother had gathered all our family together on the roof of our house.

Even for a family as close as ours, that was extremely unusual. We were rarely all together. Someone was always off wandering somewhere in the evening, especially Hung, but this evening was different. We had not gathered by choice. This morning, the government had imposed martial law on its citizens that forbade any civilian travel out on the streets tonight. The police and military officers had orders to shoot any violators of the curfew on sight. There were to be no exceptions.

From here on top of our house, I had a clear view of the surrounding area, and Hoc Loc, Hong Bang, and the other main roads were eerily empty. Now, in place of the hordes of private and commercial cars, bicycles, and mopeds, I could only see an occasional armored military vehicle flying down a vacant avenue honking its horn incessantly. Those trucks and cars usually had white flags flying from their radio antennas. I had no idea why. In the distance, I heard firecrackers going off, but Mother swiftly corrected me. The sound I heard was gunfire, not fireworks. We couldn't tell if the shooting was men battling in the city or people shooting into the sky. Where the sound came from didn't matter. I was old enough to realize that this was a scary time. The war had suddenly been reborn and had come home to us, and that realization filled my heart with a dread of what might come next.

We slept on the roof that night. We sometimes did so when the night was hot and there was little breeze. Often, the top floor was the only place one could catch a rogue draft. Tonight, our being together just felt right, here on the roof under the stars. Somehow, cradled in my mother's arms, I managed to fall asleep.

When I awoke the next morning, April 30th, the area around our house was eerily calm. With nothing else to do, I went about my chores. Why should this day be any different from others? About mid-morning, my mother interrupted my sweeping to report what she had heard on the radio. It seemed that our country had given up...quit. After fifteen years of almost continuous civil war and countless lives lost, we had surrendered to the North. The broadcast had continued with the news that our president, Nguyễn Văn Thiệu, had fled the country like a coward two days before. His successor, Dương Văn Minh, officially turned over the government to the North Vietnamese forces that very morning.

The curfew from the previous day expired with the night. Slowly at first, the people, our people, warily came out from the shelter of their homes and began to roam about in the streets. There was still that eerie quiet surrounding us. No one spoke except in whispers. No one needed to talk. Everyone wondered the same thing, "What was going to happen next?" Out of fear, everyone kept close to their homes. Hoc Lac, usually brimming over with vehicles this time of day, was unnaturally silent. No traffic today.

Hung and his friends, unwilling to stay put any longer and eager to prove their courage, had taken off about nine o'clock. They wanted to see for themselves what was going on in the surrounding neighborhoods and on the main streets. The boys wandered about as far as the now deserted food market in their search for answers. Whereas our hamlet had been quiet, the farther the boys ventured, the more people they encountered. In fact, as they crept into Cho Lon's business district, they found a surprising number of people in the streets, and to Hung and his friends, all of them seemed possessed by demons.

When he returned, he related all the things that he had witnessed. The stories he told did not seem possible. People were looting businesses and homes, searching for valuables. When the boys asked the looters why they were doing this, they found the looters knew little. It seemed the former residents had been either in the government or working with the Americans. Because of that association, the families had run in absolute terror from the Communists. They knew very well what would happen to them if the invaders captured them. In a mad dash to escape, they only took with them what they could carry – precious little of their belongings, leaving their homes and businesses behind.

The scavengers arrived shortly after and took everything they could lay their hands on from the newly abandoned structures. "If we don't take it, the Communists will get it" was their common cry, and so they took everything. Everything was up for grabs. Men who would have never thought of theft two days ago grabbed furniture, televisions, refrigerators, clothing, and even carpet off the floors. Looters then set their new-found fortune into motion down the streets and alleys of the city. on the backs of vehicles sometimes, but often on the heads of the looters themselves. Of course, the men didn't consider themselves thieves. The owners were gone. They were either already out of the country or looking frantically over their shoulders as they tried to stay one step ahead of the new government. Whether they escaped or the Communists captured them would make no difference. They would not be returning for their things now or ever.

One of the questions Father asked Hung was, "Where were the police during this?" I was confused when he said that there were no police anymore. The policemen and South Vietnamese soldiers feared for their lives. They had stripped themselves in the streets, leaving their uniforms behind so the invaders could not identify their association with the previous government. Then, they ran, practically naked, back to their homes, praying that they could remain anonymous. For them, the temporary embarrassment was nothing compared to the peril of being found out. None of the looters dared to grab the discarded clothing either. They also dreaded the association the uniform held. Our new rulers, the Communists from the North, were already sweeping the city, looking for any military holdouts. Occasionally, we could still hear the static bursts of gunfire informing us when they found some. So far, our new masters had not had the opportunity to think about dealing with civilians. There would be time for that later.

My world had truly gone insane.

Later that day, my mother gave my siblings and me a written message containing our name, address, plus her and Father's names. She told us not to be afraid but to stay with family or close friends whenever we went outside the hamlet. I wondered, "Why do we need to do this?" I stopped myself short of asking her aloud. I could see the wildness in her eyes that I had never seen before. When combined with the weirdness happening around me, that told me not to question her or her judgment.

Every hour, outrageous new stories came to our ears. Our neighbors and we lived in fear of doing anything or going anywhere. Now and then, gunshots rang out, their loud retorts echoing through the streets. Gradually, the need to do something overrode the fear. We began the process of restarting our lives. Companies reopened for business. People went back to work. We could once again hear traffic on the streets, each day growing in intensity little by little. At home, we began manufacturing medicine again. The fresh food market reopened along with the shops and vendors on the streets. In the alleys, my friends and I once again played with reckless abandon.

When the government announced that school would restart, I had a shock coming. They had closed my Chinese school. Closed was not the correct word. The government had moved in with their bulldozers and razed the building and gates to the ground only a few days after the South's surrender. The school was closed for good.

I could not understand why all of this had to happen. What threat was my school to the government? With its closure, I would go to the newly created public school instead. Since the government had outlawed the Catholic Church, Catholics no longer assembled. Its clergy were now in hiding or exiled, working to the government's advantage. They "appropriated" the Catholic school and rededicated it as a public school. That would be the school I would attend. Even though losing my old school saddened me, the new school allowed me to go to classes with Nhi and all my other friends. Some of my previous teachers were even there. Other than the change of venue, not much seemed different.

Even though the presence of armed soldiers patrolling the streets bothered many older people, I didn't see how our lives had changed that much. There wasn't much difference between the Northern Army and the old police force except for uniforms – or in the Viet Cong's case, the lack of uniform. Of course, we had all heard the rumors of mass arrests and executions around Saigon, or Ho Chi Minh City, as our new masters called it. Still, nothing like that was happening here. Slowly, hesitantly, almost reluctantly, the residents of Cho Lon took a deep breath and began to relax – just a little. They seemed to be taking the time to gather their energies to preparing for whatever this next chapter in their lives would bring.

Chapter 10

The new normal

Figure 10: The Fruit Peddler

Amazingly, after all the doom and gloom of April, the sun did come out. Summer seemed to go on as always. The ever-present sun remained glaring in the sky as it beat down unmercifully in its trek across the heavens. The comforting moon still went through its phases. The months passed, and discipline and order soon replaced the public unrest of May. In my house, we continued to make and deliver our medicines. I attended school. Mother and San prepared our meals. Life went on as it is prone to do.

As the school break progressed, as hot became hotter, and the doldrums settled into place, Nhi and I found ourselves restless with the monotony and routine. We decided that we needed an adventure, and we knew just the place. The mission was to be top secret. Only she and I and our selected invited friends knew what was going to happen. No one else, including our parents – especially our parents - were informed about our plan. They couldn't know anything about it. As our planning grew from an idea to a reality, we could feel the old excitement simmering and beginning to grow in us. This was going to be great!

Why all this mystery? Well, our adventure was easier to prepare and a whole lot more fun this way. I, for one, saw no need to bother my parents with our plans. My philosophy was and has always been, "If you don't ask, no one can tell you no." I doubted that they would care anyway. We had fifteen to twenty people living in our house at any given time. People were coming and going at all times of the day and night. The odds were in my favor that they wouldn't even miss me. My presence at the house would be more of a distraction than my absence would be. Anyway, even if they knew, they wouldn't worry about me. I had wandered

floor, where I quietly changed into my clothes. I pushed on the sliding door, but it didn't budge. I tried again, harder this time. My heart nearly stopped when the door let out a horrendous squeal as it inched open. I continued until there was just enough space to squeeze myself through. Success! Freedom was mine!

I ran down the pathway just as the first murmurings of life started up from the surrounding houses—sleepy voices whispering as they prepared for the new day. The narrow splinter of sky peeking between the rooftops seemed clear. The stars were starting to fade away, leaving behind only the promise of a beautiful day to come.

I turned into the alleyway and found Nhi and my other cohorts already on their bikes waiting, none too patiently, for me to hurry up. We had to ride a good five miles to our destination through heavy traffic, and we needed to get going soon. I leaped onto the back of my friend's bike, and off we went!

We negotiated the remaining alleys of our hamlet with a practiced hand and then careened haphazardly onto Hoc Loc. The morning traffic was still light, mostly bicycles like ours, with some mopeds, motorcycles, and cars thrown into the mix. Still, there was nowhere near the bumper to bumper free-for-all that would soon occur. As a group, we snaked in and out of traffic as more and more vehicles joined in the parade until we all became a single creature moving as one down the street.

As more vehicles joined, the creature grew both in size and volume. The first roundabout appeared suddenly. The snarls of traffic going all directions at once were both frightening and challenging. Without a thought, we launched ourselves into the melee without hesitation, daring the traffic gods to stop us if they dared. Seconds passed, and somehow...miraculously...the roundabout spat us out on the other side unharmed.

I laughed wildly; my short black hair blew back in our man-made wind as we gained speed and merged onto even busier streets; our bikes were weaving back and forth with the precision of seasoned dancers. We had little concern for our personal safety. After all, we were young. Nothing bad could happen to us. We felt that we were invincible in our youth. We were free.

At that precise moment, I did not care that Saigon was no more and that Ho Chi Minh City had taken her place. I did not care that the Communists now ruled and that democracy had failed. I wasn't concerned that uniformed soldiers stood with weapons readied on the street corners that we passed. Some of the soldiers were nice. They returned our happy waves with smiles, but more often, the men scowled at us as we flew by them, as if to say, "Why should you get to play while we work?" None of this bothered me. I didn't care about any of it. There was nothing that could dampen my good mood. The pool was straight ahead, and we were going swimming!

Not long after this perfect day, my world did experience change.

A slow change.

An unrelenting change.

And, suddenly I cared...I cared a lot.

Since the fall of 1975, the new regime had subtly altered much that made Cho Lon special. My community had become a twisted reflection of its previous self – an alternate reality. In some ways, the place I called home was unrecognizable as the old Cho Lon at all. The needs of the government had forced the destruction of many of our temples and palaces. If they didn't destroy them outright, they repurposed them for offices and schools like they did with the Catholic Church and school. Every exposed wall and bridge now displayed bright red murals or posters. Each of them proudly showed the omnipresent hammer and sickle of Communism accompanied by patriotic slogans and cautions. Seemingly overnight, loudspeakers had popped up on almost every street corner in the city. They now blared non-stop recordings of political speeches and patriotic music. They began their tirade at six in the morning and continued droning on until time for bed. The endless rants praised people for their attempts to remove all foreign influences from our country. There were necessary changes that were the only way that Vietnam could move forward, unencumbered by their presence. They designed the speeches to give people a new sense of purpose, a common direction in their lives. Mostly, my friends and I just ignored them. After all, they didn't affect us. They were just an annoyance — bees buzzing in the background of our lives.

When the changes affected our food supply, the government's interventions became personal. One of the first things I noticed was that the rice was different. I realized that this was such a little thing, hardly worth mentioning, yet our rice had once been pure white, and now the kernels were laced with brown rice as well. It was indeed a small thing, yet these little things sometimes point toward more extensive, more significant changes to come. For me, that small change was the rice.

Other things began showing up on my almost daily trips to the market. Meat was scarce since Reunification, and what little was there was substandard and had exorbitant prices – far more than what we had to spend. At first, this didn't concern my family a great deal. We adjusted. We ate less meat and more vegetables, but then as time went on and the problem worsened. It was almost necessary to eliminate meat from our diet.

Work at home wasn't getting any easier either. We had always been comfortably middle class. Our family business had provided for all our needs, along with a few extras on the side. Now, there simply wasn't any money for extras. Our costs had increased significantly, as had the taxes we paid. Our clientele were as hard-pressed as we were. They were often unable to pay for what they needed. Many had closed their doors.

Everything we made went toward paying for our basic requirements. We weren't the only ones affected either. My friends reported the same things happening in their homes. It appeared that the government would not be happy until they strangled our community out of existence.

One of the chief causes of our strangulation was the currency exchange. As a ten-year-old, I required some time to think this through. I thought changing money was no big deal. People just swapped their money for other money. The paper just looked different. Later, I realized that I had no idea what was happening. When I saw my parents' and older siblings' worrying about an exchange, I asked, and they explained it to me. What I had not realized was that the "exchange" wasn't a one-to-one swap. The government required five hundred dong in the old South Vietnamese currency to get one – only one dong in the new one. There would be only one day allocated to complete the exchange, and after that date, the only thing the old money was good for was fires and mattress stuffing. Now I saw the problem. No wonder they were so upset!

In theory, even though everyone knew the exchange was coming, no one knew the exact day. That date was a tightly held secret. No one outside a tight circle could know the day; otherwise, people might want to cheat. The concept was a good idea in theory. However, the reality was that some government minister would tell his wife, in the strictest confidence, of course. She, in turn, felt terrible for her sisters and cousins. She couldn't have them miss out, so she told them. After all, that's what family does for family. They, too, promised not to tell a soul. Unfortunately, at this point, the secret wasn't a secret anymore. Someone would tell someone else in confidence. Someone else would overhear the conversation and would then tell their entire neighborhood. An hour or so following the minister's whispered secret, pretty much everyone knew the substance of their conversation. The word flew through the streets like a raging flood. Tomorrow was the day.

Now, losing money is never a good thing. So, when providence provided us with something we could do, we did it. Armed with our knowledge, we, along with our neighbors, launched a coordinated attack on the marketplaces. Enmasse, we frantically tried to purchase food, supplies, or anything else we might potentially need before our money became virtually worthless in the exchange. Of course, vendors had also heard the unofficial "announcement." They raised their prices, knowing full well that people would have no choice but to pay the inflated amount. No haggling today! No one was in the mood. While my parents and siblings went to their own assigned places to shop, I took my bicycle to the food market with money in hand. My instructions from my mother were simple. I was to buy whatever food I could get with the money I had. I wouldn't be buying much.

There was, of course, another side to the exchange coin. From the government's point of view, the exchange was an equalizer. They planned to treat all people the same and allow all to share in future prosperity. This plan penalized the rich by setting a maximum amount for a single person to exchange while allowing an increased amount for businesses. Any amount exceeding that threshold number was forfeit.

Along with so many other government plans, this one was flawed. As always, the rich people found a way to get around the situation. They hired poor people for a small amount. Their job was to exchange the rich person's money. Once the transaction was complete, the rich took half of the new money that the poor person received. I suppose the poor did benefit a little, but the rich came out on top once again.

When the dust settled from the turmoil of the day, we found ourselves in even worse straits than before. The exchange had been at 500 to 1. We had expected a similar change in prices, but the prices afterward did not go down proportionately. The purchasing power of the new currency was not enough for many people to survive.

These economic tsunamis occurred at least three times between 1976 and 1979. Each time the chaos repeated itself, and each time the results remained the same. The government and the wealthy were richer, and the rest of us were poorer. The only way to not lose in this monetary shell game was to have gold. Many Chinese people, including my father and mother, had taken our surpluses during good years and bought gold bullion. Hundreds of years of Chinese and Vietnamese political history and personal experience with the governments made Cho Lon citizens have little trust in banks for their savings.

There were other exchanges, as well, that disrupted our lives also. I came home from school one day to find my father hard at work on the fourth floor. He was moving the kitchen from the first-floor common area to the fourth-floor workshop because he could no longer purchase propane. He had already removed part of the wall and put in ventilation for a wood stove. From that day forward, we used charcoal or wood instead.

Since everyone was in the same position, more and more people did the same in their homes. The demand for wood overwhelmed the supply until that became too expensive as well. When we could no longer get wood, we burned sugar cane husks or anything else disposable and flammable for fuel.

Even the process of getting food changed. We were used to buying everything we needed at the market every day and storing little food aside from rice in our home. Now, we had a food commissary where the government distributed staples like rice and beans to every household once a month. The center designated each neighborhood a specific time and day to receive their share. There was no discussion. If you were there, you got food. If not, you were just out of luck. Worse, there was no guarantee there would be enough for everyone. The center often ran out of items before it ran out of people to serve. This required us to queue up in the pre-dawn hours to get a good place in line.

I was the designated line placeholder for my family. While the day was still dark, I proceeded to the distribution center to save a place in line for my aunt, our designated head of household. She was the only one who could collect our allocation. I was not alone in my task. Many other families did the same thing. To ensure we still got a good place, I would get up even earlier to get there first. I was exceedingly good at my job. We might not be first, but we always had a great place in line. Waiting for my aunt was the hard part. I had to do what I dearly hated doing – stand still, patiently waiting, doing nothing, until she joined me just before the commissary opened.

My aunt presented our card to the official in charge. It indicated that we had thirteen permanent residents in the home. My older sister My and my brother Phuc returned to us from my grandmother's house in My Tho. Simply put, we needed their allocation much more than my grandmother did. After the official signed our card, he sent us to a row of tables with rice, beans, and other dried food. Here my family received our share.

We thought that the food should have been much heavier than it was and guessed that the scales used were not accurate. Even with being cheated this way, we could have dealt with the situation if the food had been OK. The fact was that the food was terrible. Rice, for example, would include the husks and even small rocks in addition to the food grain. Every time the officials weighed out our rice with their faulty scales, they cheated us even more by including inedible parts in the food. There were rumors that officials took the good, white rice and sold it on the black market where a steep price would be paid by the wealthy. I would not have been surprised if that were true.

When we got home, we had to separate the rice from the trash. The task was not as easy as it sounded. We had to pick out the edible rice one grain at a time. There was no quicker way, and it took forever to complete. Out of necessity, sifting out the rice became a family activity; all of us gathered around the table. Sometimes, when the food was more corrupted than usual, we threw out as much as half of what we had received. That meant we had to replace our missing rice with noodles when we could or barley when we couldn't. We would add these to the soup pot along with whatever vegetables we could buy at the market or manage to raise on our own.

Naturally, we tried different things to work around these limitations. Yet, whenever we tried something new, it seemed that an official would magically appear to shut us down. The government seemed to frown on personal initiative. They even came and confiscated the ducks and chickens many of us raised to supplement our meager meat rations. As they hauled them away, the officials told us that the birds would help ensure that the government could equally feed all people. Somehow, we never seemed to enjoy any of that "sharing among all."

The government also restricted our freedom of movement from one area to another. Local party officials required that anyone changing their residence, permanent or temporary, had to report to the neighborhood leader immediately regardless of the time of day. Anytime someone went to visit relatives, he or she had to report to the local committee when leaving. The relatives would, in turn, report to their committee upon the visitor's arrival. The local committee held a mandatory neighborhood meeting once a week, and the chairman ordered the head of household for each family to attend. The number of committees and departments in each community increased rapidly. With that growth, so did the need for places to keep them all. The homes vacated during Reunification, either voluntary or otherwise, became official meeting places. Every aspect of our lives seemed to be under a microscope from our overlords.

Stories still raged through the neighborhood about the military invading homes and arresting people in the middle of the night for supposed crimes against the state. There was no need for proof, they said. Accusations resulted in convictions and sentencing of individuals and whole families, some of whom I knew. They disappeared into thin air. The word was that officials still had public executions every day in Ho Chi Minh City proper. The message we received was clear. The police were not our friends. We lived in fear of them now.

School, after its easy beginning, took on its own change. Our teachers removed everything that even hinted at being Chinese. They only taught Vietnamese customs and language now. Not long after school resumed, our Chinese speaking teachers were all replaced by Vietnamese ones. We didn't know where our old teachers had gone. They just were not there anymore. The new teachers weren't even from around here; they were from the northern part of the country. They don't speak the same way up there as we do in the South. The language sounded similar but had many differences in nuance. For those of us who didn't use Vietnamese at home, this made the instruction incredibly difficult. Many students, including one of my dear friends, simply could not adapt and had to drop out in frustration.

With that in mind, along with a good deal of fear and worry, I began my first formal lessons in the Vietnamese language and the teachings of "Uncle Ho." Understand, this was not MY Uncle Ho! This was the country's Uncle Ho, Ho Chi Minh. He had been the founding father of North Vietnamese Communism back during the French Colonial Period. The amazing thing was that his lessons made perfect sense to me, and I was proud that I was the first in my group of seventy to memorize them! I only wished that everyone, adults included, obeyed them.

The Five Lessons of Uncle Ho
Love your country.
Love your compatriots.
Learn well, work well.
Take really good care of your sanitation.
Be modest, honest, and brave.

Life would have been simple, almost pleasurable if all we had to do was live by these five lessons. I discovered that governments do not like things simple. These five rules evolved into many, many more. Our teachers pounded these rules into us repeatedly, requiring us to repeat them over and over in class. Our "lessons" became little more than brainwashing. We would repeat the lesson until the teacher was confident that we had permanently stored the required material in our memory. Our instructors also interrogated us with questions about our parents, their loyalty, and our homes.

"Do your parents have valuables hidden in the home?"

"Are your parents secretly meeting against the government?"

"Are there secret hiding places around your home?"

"Uncle Ho loves you more than your parents."

"Uncle Ho wants all of his children to be happy and well-fed. He can't do that if your parents are keeping things from him. Would you help?"

Our teachers hammered us with these and other questions while we sat captive in our classrooms. They told us that reporting on our parents would be an excellent thing for the country and our own future. No one would harm our parents. They were not at fault. The Party would reeducate them to find their place as contributing members in the new society.

The Party made the goals of Communism seem so good. It stressed that many people, maybe even our parents, could not see the greater good for all the people. I saw this line of questioning for what it was, an attempt to pull families apart and enrich the government in the process. I don't know of any children personally who betrayed their families. Still, I am sure that some did; the young ones seemed especially eager to please their new teachers.

After school and often in the evening, my friends and I attended Communist Youth meetings with others our age. Such sessions were not optional; I had to go. I was astounded to discover that I had fun while I was there. We played lots of games. Most of them aimed at making us work as a unit, which made them entertaining as well. We even got to participate in special groups according to our talents. Here too, the group leaders carefully formed questions and statements. They insisted our parents hoarded wealth, that they denied other citizens basic needs, and, as such, were criminals against the state.

I knew that was a lie!

These meetings weren't just for our age group, of course, everyone had to attend some sort of group activity or work detail. There were even special activities for the aged like my grandmother. They would put younger adults, like Hung and San, into service repairing buildings, cleaning streets, or some other type of hard labor – all for the benefit of the state. Naturally, no one received payment for this service; service to our country was, after all, considered to be a person's patriotic duty. If anyone failed to participate, that person was subject to punishment, if not arrest, for his or her unpatriotic behavior. For Hung's efforts working on the city sewer system, he received a signed piece of paper. If an official challenged him, he had to present that paper. That could be his boss at his new job at the cannery or just some official on the street. The form proved his patriotism and his participation in building a new Vietnam.

Of course, with the criminalization of all things non-Vietnamese, they condemned my old Chinese dance troupe, as well as anything else that reflected Chinese history or customs. Fortunately, the Communists provided an opportunity to continue my dance, this time, along with my friends, as one of the Communist Youth Organization's special activities. The dances had quite a different style, though. Gone were the flowing, gentle dances I had learned with my Chinese troupe. The new music was more strident, more military, and the dances more rigid and unified. Our leaders allowed us to practice during and after club meetings. They then had us perform for special occasions like Reunification Day, Uncle Ho's Birthday, and things like that.

The performances still excited me. The thrill of standing in front of an appreciative crowd was addictive. The crowds we drew now were much larger than before, and the people's response was loud and enthusiastic. The government used the loudspeakers around the city to announce the dates and times of our performances. At the appointed time, all the people would gather. We would dance for our part of the program, but others in our age group would recite patriotic poems or sing songs. The state required that everyone had some role to play. I didn't find out until much later that the Party mandated adult attendance at the performances along with their enthusiastic response to our work.

Even as the group leaders and teachers attempted to brainwash us, our parents would charge us to "Never listen to what the Communists say, watch what they do." I did as my parents said, and I didn't like everything I saw. All around the city, the Communist Party was doing plenty. At every turn, I saw them destroying our heritage, our history. They converted some of the buildings into office space and museums, with much of their structure intact. The rest they razed to the ground and put new construction in their place. One by one, they erased all things that reflected the old ways, Chinese and South Vietnamese, and they did so with a vengeance. I was sickened as I watched them purge so much of our culture and history in the name of progress.

The authorities even ruled over what we wore. They banned all Western styles, especially denim jeans, from the country and restricted many others. As a result, pretty dresses turned to rags overnight. The same thing went for hairstyles.

Long haircuts for boys, once popularized by Western television, were no more. Our rulers' appeared to think that if we all looked the same, we would be the same – be equal. My siblings and I didn't fare too badly. My family had not been into the pre-Communist era's fads, but that didn't keep Hung from having to get a new haircut.

Throughout all the ups and downs of that first year, my family's life in Cho Lon continued, not precisely as life had been before, but close enough to bring some comfort to us all. We provided a gentle cocoon that surrounded us and protected us from the ever-growing evil around us. Blissfully, I rested comfortably in my family. I decided to shut out the real world and to live here in my own little one instead. I played, went to school, attended youth meetings, and danced. Innocently, perhaps naively, I had never thought of us, Chinese though we were, as "foreign influences." Were we something they would need to eliminate?

Chapter 11

Things that go bump in the night

Figure 11: Alligator at Con Phung Island, 2017

One of the many unexpected things our new government provided was random rolling blackouts. These were times when they turned off all the electricity in an area. These happened with little or no warning and would generally last a solid forty-eight hours. In our tropical climate, this effectively turned our homes into steaming ovens. There was nothing, not even a fan, to break the misery. When a blackout happened, the residents of my neighborhood headed outside - out onto the narrow alleys and paths that connected our homes in an attempt to catch even a hint of a breeze. Everyone kept their movements to a minimum because even a slight exertion would generate more heat. Those who were not out on the pavement hung from their narrow balconies eight to ten feet above. Everywhere, hand-held fans buzzed like a thousand bees, each hoping to generate a single breath of air that would somehow make the situation more bearable.

One activity did not generate additional heat. People would often pass the time telling stories and singing songs. My friends and I knew the exact place where we needed to be. We swarmed around Nhi's mom in the intersection where the two alleys joined. The sky darkened with the only light coming from the few faint stars shining above and an occasional candle. Batteries had become a scarce commodity, so we used our flashlights sparingly. We all grabbed stools and chairs where we could find them and sat close so we could hear every word as she spun her enthralling tales of the supernatural.

The first one was my favorite, the headless woman. Though I had heard the story many times before, I never grew tired of hearing it again. I also loved hearing the gasps from the first-timers who had never listened to the tale before.

Although I couldn't make out who they were, I could sense their shivers of fright at what might be waiting at the end of the neighborhood, in the public toilet that many of them still used. That was almost as good as the story itself!

The woman was a local ghost who haunted the fountain in front of the public toilet. As the tale spun around me, I observed the story unfold in my mind. The time was sometime after midnight in the small courtyard around the fountain. Out of the surrounding blackness, a young woman of about twenty appeared just at the edge of the light. She seemed to be pretty and carried herself in a dignified manner. Her hair was long and black as night. She silently approached the small rock ledge around the water and sat demurely on top of the curved border. She glanced furtively around, looking for others, not wanting a crowd to observe her, but mine was the only face she saw. She smiled knowingly at me, her face shining a radiant white. Then, she leaned down toward me while placing her hands firmly on either side of her head like she had a secret that she wanted to share with me.

All at once, in one deft move, she jerked her head completely off her shoulders! Her eyes still watched me as her body carefully dipped her head into the fountain's waters. With practiced hands, the woman washed her hair. I noticed how she was so careful in the way she caressed each strand between her fingers. When she finished the task, she carefully combed her long tresses with her fingers slowly and gently, taking care to remove all the tangles from the dark black tresses.

Finally, her evening ritual complete, she matter-of-factly slid the head into place on her body with hands that had obviously performed the same task a thousand times before. Her nightly job finished, she stood as if to leave. Before she walked away, she turned her head toward me, tilted it, gave me a sly, knowing grin, and then vaporized as abruptly as she had come.

As the story ended, I felt a sharp chill in the air that had nothing to do with temperature. I have never heard a name for the woman. No one knew it, or at any rate, no one would tell. As I shook off the effects of my reverie, I swore to myself that if I ever saw her for real, I was not going to be the one to ask for it!

Nhi's mother went on to tell stories of the ghosts haunting her kitchen. Since Nhi lived next door to me and was my best friend, this grabbed my attention right away. I had never known that my neighbor was haunted! How exciting! She told us that many nights after everyone had gone to bed, she heard people cooking in the kitchen. Pots rattled, and utensils fell to the ground with a crash. An eerie glow came from the kitchen area. Our group sat silently in the alley, straining to hear any strange sounds coming from the house located just a few feet away. She fell silent, too, as if she were also intently listening.

Then, Nhi's mother told of creeping up to the kitchen's entryway, fully expecting to find intruders inside, and no idea what to do with them when she saw them. She paused in her tale for effect. She said, "When I peeked around the corner, there was no one there!" She looked around the kitchen area carefully and found everything in its proper place. She scolded herself at reacting so over what had to have been a bad dream. The next night, though, it happened again, and the night after that as well.

By then, she realized that spirits were involved. I could feel the hair on the back of my neck stand up.

She went from there to the stories of the hauntings at the Catholic Church next door. Many of us played there after school and at night. Although we had never seen anything supernatural while we were there, we wanted to know what to expect. She went on to tell us that she had often seen lights late at night glowing in the now deserted classrooms. The building remained locked with no one allowed inside since the priests' exile shortly after reunification. On other occasions, she and other witnesses saw people in white garments walking around the meeting rooms having conversations. A short time later, they disappeared into thin air. I shivered at the thought. Suddenly the night wasn't so hot after all.

These stories were excellent fuel for our imaginations. The night after the blackout was over, we went to the churchyard and played hide and seek. We dashed among the buildings, trees, and statues there, all the time keeping one eye open for the ghosts of dead priests and nuns who might be out roaming the grounds. We taunted the spirits to show themselves and then ran when a loud fluttering sound from the church startled us. Bats trailed out of the bell tower. Bats, the traditional omen of zombies! The fact that bats nested around the church and had more of a right to be there than we did had no meaning for us. Their presence only made our game more exciting.

We flew in and out of the dark spaces with heightened senses looking for great places to hide and maybe pull a prank or two on our fellow gamers. I loved getting up close behind someone and jumping out. I would scare the daylights out of them! Such fun! Later, I carefully climbed a palm tree at the edge of the square. I nestled in among the branches and patiently waited for an unaware victim to walk below me so I could jump down on top of him or her.

I wasn't paying close attention to the others in the group, so I didn't notice that another friend had positioned herself a short distance behind me on the sidewalk. She looked up at my tree and mistook me for a ghost's head. She shrieked at the top of her voice! The noise caught me off guard. I frantically grabbed for a limb to regain my position and failed miserably. I tumbled to the ground in a graceless pile. The resulting combination of our laughs and howls echoed against the church walls.

Chapter 12

A trip to grandma's house

Figure 12: River scene on the way to My Tho, 2017

Of all the things we overcame during the late summer of 1975, the greatest was a personal tragedy. My Grandmother Quan died. One day she was with us, and the next, she was gone. There was nothing really to understand, I guess, but when she died, she left a massive hole in our family tapestry with no obvious way to replace her. My grandmother and I were never close; I honestly tried to stay as far away from her and her temper as my duties would allow. She could be a terror when she was in a bad mood, which seemed to be a lot of the time. I think what I missed most was her solidness, her ability to stand in any storm. She had been our family's rock, and now that rock had disintegrated into dust. What would happen to us now?

The events that followed pushed us past what we had thought were our physical limits. There was now a funeral to prepare for - not a small thing in Chinese tradition. Contacting our local family was not a problem. We went to each house personally and told them. Notifying the family in My Tho, mainly my Grandmother Quynh and Uncle Ho, was the difficulty. Neither household had a telephone, and a letter would take far too long for them to come to Cho Lon in time for the funeral. Someone had to go to My Tho to get them, and my father elected me for the job.

Some people may find it strange that he chose me for this trip. It wasn't that I was some kind of special messenger or anything. Dad and Hung had to keep the business going. Mom, San, and My had to prepare for the funeral and the hordes of people they would have to feed in addition to everything else involved in running the household. I was simply the only person left who could go. Anyway, this would be no problem. I had been to My Tho several times.

Granted, not by myself, but how hard could the journey be? Get on a bus and go. Dad gave me the money for the ticket and sent me off to the bus depot where I purchased a ticket on the next bus to My Tho.

The four-hour bus ride was uneventful. People got on, and people got off. I stayed to myself, and people ignored me. As we left the outskirts of Ho Chi Minh City, rice paddies and thatch huts of rural Vietnam gradually replaced the concrete walls and buildings of the city. Villages came and went past my window. At long last, My Tho was the next stop. Now, My Tho was not as nearly as large as Cho Lon and Ho Chi Minh City, but the town was large enough that I had to think a bit before setting out from the downtown bus station. I wandered around the village until I came across the famous bridge from which my mother used to jump. The bridge's appearance did the trick. I knew where I was. From there, I was able to rush to my grandmother's house to share the bad news with her and my aunt. She then sent me to my Uncle Ho's home while she and my aunt prepared to leave. Uncle Ho had everyone loaded into his car in no time, and we headed back to Cho Lon.

The funeral was to be at our New House. My father had bought the New House shortly after the arrival of Nguu. At that time, he had grand plans for it. My father, feeling blessed with a second son, made renovations to the house to accommodate his growing family and to reflect our prosperity. Ironically, we were not living in the new house because Grandmother Quan had forbidden our move, and my father had given in to her. After all, she was the head of the household. Now we used the house for get-togethers and a place where my mother could quietly rest after giving birth.

At the New House, other women would pamper her for about a month before she would return with the child into the chaos that was our home.

Anyway, let me get back to the funeral. Buddhist funerals are much different from Christian ones, more of an event than anything else. Everyone Grandmother had known showed up – and she had known a lot of people. We in the family all had white cloths draped over us to honor grandmother. All her family and friends gathered around her to say goodbye and wish her well in the next life. There was lots of incense, of course. Its fragrance floated through the three floors of the new house until its aroma impregnated every nook and cranny. While everyone sat silently, reverently attentive, my father and uncle spoke at length about my grandmother's life and how wonderful she had been. I thought of several things that they left out, but I guess that was OK. After all, funerals should reflect the good things, right?

A Buddhist monk, hired for the occasion, danced around the casket for what seemed like hours burning even more incense, chanting, and casting blessings with rattles and whistles. Later, he placed seven roof tiles on the floor around the casket, each one with a different Buddhist demon painted on its face. As he danced around them, he took a steel post and smashed the tiles one by one. After the ceremony, the demons safely banished, men picked up grandmother's casket. They carried her remains out to the main street with all the mourners following closely behind.

There, they loaded her remains into a funeral bus along with many of the family. With the bus leading the way, we formed a long procession through the streets. By design, the procession passed by our hamlet's entrance. According to tradition, they did so that her spirit could say goodbye to the place where she had lived. From there, the group went on to the cemetery for burial. Music played over speakers all the way there, and local traffic paused its way to let us pass. As we went by the hamlet, they dropped the younger children and me off to go back to our home. I got to babysit. Everyone else accompanied Grandmother to the cemetery.

After the burial, all the mourners came back to our house where they ate and played games late into the night. Some even gambled. Most of them spent the night on the floor wherever they could find a place to lay down. Gradually, their numbers dwindled until, after the third night, we were once again by ourselves.

The third night had special significance to us. The spirit world had a strong presence in my Buddhist world. We believed that the third day after burial, his or her spirit returned to visit the house where he or she had lived and died. On that night, everyone in the family returned to that place and spent the night. The next day the family would talk about how noisy the spirits were and looked for signs of his or her passing. When my grandmother died, we lit a candle on the third day and put out some rice to show that the family was doing well. The candle fluttered uncontrollably with no breeze to disturb the flame. In the morning, someone had scattered the rice all over the tabletop. I did not doubt that she had been there.

This occurrence of the spirit world interfacing with ours was extremely special to me. I had not realized that I needed closure on my grandmother's death until that night when she scattered the rice. When I saw the grain flung across the table, I knew everything was alright with her and that I would be OK too.

Chapter 13

Market day

Figure 13: Fresh food market frequented by the Quan family, 2017

Time continued to move forward. Days passed into months and months into years. As I celebrated my twelfth birthday, I found it hard to imagine that the Communists had been in charge for over three years. Every day, we found our life here to be more demanding and less rewarding. We all felt the strain. The currency exchanges and further crackdowns on Chinese customs had left indelible marks on the Cho Lon community. Still, for the most part, the Communist powers had left us alone. Our experience was completely different from what was happening in old Saigon. The government seemed to treat the two communities as if we were two separate entities, even though only a few blocks separated us from them.

As I have mentioned before, one of my greatest pleasures was walking to the market every day. The trip gave me some one-on-one time with my mother, cousin, or big sister, which, as a pre-teen, was very important to me. It also allowed me to run free and explore my community's wonders that we passed in route. The market was only about a mile away, but there were hundreds of small shops and stalls lining the road from home to there. Each one seemed to grab at our heels, attempting to snare our interest as we passed. The journey often took a long time.

This morning, San accompanied me. We left in the morning, not long after the sun was up, but still while the buildings' shadows held some of the cool from the overnight hours. As was the custom, we carried our empty shopping bags to contain our future purchases. I didn't particularly want to be grown-up that day, so I skipped down the sidewalk, hugging the buildings and running my fingers over the grates of the still closed businesses. San walked calmly beside me. She tried to appear dignified as befit a young lady while desperately pretending that she didn't know the immature child beside her.

I paused for just a moment in front of the midwifery where I had been born twelve years ago and wondered if any new babies came into the world today. Occasionally, sidewalk proprietors, setting up their stalls, shooed me out of the way, requiring me to dodge in and out of the traffic that buzzed by on the already busy road. A few stores were already open, and those provided many things to gaze upon while I chatted idly with the owners.

About a block from the market, we passed by the tall concrete walls of the state-run orphanage. Inside the courtyard, out of view, children were laughing and playing. Their sounds were so natural, but I knew that there was nothing natural about their circumstances. Most of their parents had died either in the war or in the political consequence of reunification. I felt so sorry for them. What would my life be like, I thought, to be utterly alone with no family to guide me on my path? That thought was beyond my imagination. I needed my family so much that I could not see a time when they would not be there. At the same time, there were so many children lost in the world. One moment, they had been part of a family, and the next, they were alone. Their struggle was tragic.

At long last, we reached our destination. The open-air market spread out in a blaze of color before me. The proprietor's stalls still occupied more than a city block with vendors lining both sides of the street and a line down the middle. Here, in a flashback to pre-Reunification times, stall owners sold all the foods that one could imagine. There were vegetables and fruits brought in from the country on trucks, fresh fish from the harbor and river, and sometimes, rarely now, even pork or chicken. Of course, there was nothing in our budget for meat today. The expense was far too great for us now.

As we strolled up and down the makeshift aisles, we jostled for position with other purchasers vying for the best produce. We used our trained eyes to examine the spectacular choices spread out before us. We slowly began our search for the foods that would best serve our needs today. The stall owners looked at us expectantly, wanting to make a quick sale so they could move on to the next customer before their produce spoiled. When we reached the far end of the marketplace, there was a stall offering manicures and pedicures. Though such a pampering would have been nice, we had no time or money for such luxuries today. We had to make the most of the meager funds that we had before hurrying home.

Haggling the price was the way of life in Cho Lon and Vietnam in general. Whether one was at a street shop, a market, or an emporium, the asking price was only the starting point. Only tourists or the very wealthy ever paid the full price. Few of those people frequented our district anymore, preferring the relative luxury and choices of District 1 where the affluent Vietnamese Communist Party members now lived. Here, haggling was still the norm, making the purchase more of an event than a transaction. Even if the haggling did not get you a lower price, bargaining usually resulted in a little something extra, some cilantro, or green onion, instead. Haggling made shopping fun for both the buyer and the seller, a contest between worthy adversaries who were still friends and neighbors when money changed hands.

I was a born haggler, and I played this game with all the intensity I could muster. After all, I had learned from the best. Tran had finely honed my abilities on our many trips here. I was not beyond using any advantage to get the best price or the most extras. I was a small, some would say scrawny girl, so I used that to my advantage. I looked young for my age. I used that too.

Additionally, I had the grit and determination born from playing with the bigger boys on the streets of my hamlet. That helped me the most. Not backing down in the face of a determined merchant was often the best way to go. Where others withered, I stood firm. Of course, most of the market's vendors had been around for years and knew me and my ways. However, we still enjoyed playing the game, and, in the end, I got what I needed for a fair price, and the seller got what he or she had expected to get. Additionally, we both got a bit of entertainment for our efforts in the process, and everyone usually left the deal with smiles on our faces.

San and I were in the middle of negotiations over a piece of fish for today's soup. We offered a low amount, much less than we were ready to pay. Simultaneously, the vendor, looking indignant, praised his catch's quality and how we were insulting him by offering so little. We were well on our way toward middle ground when a loud shout followed by cries of anger went up behind us. Many people gathered in the market this morning, shoulder to shoulder, not unusual for this time of day, yet everyone else around us seemed calm and composed and, like us, looking around for who was shouting.

Suddenly, a blur out of nowhere, a boy exploded from the crowd. He artfully dodged past San and me. He impressed me as I watched him move in and out of the mass of people like a fish swimming against the current. He furtively glanced over his shoulder with a wild terror in his eyes as he hurried forward. I traced his gaze back until I spied a uniformed member of the Vietnamese police force in pursuit. The policeman was the one doing the shouting, and he ruthlessly shoved people out of his way while his eyes remained fixed on the back of his target.

How exciting! I lived for adventure, and here I was in the middle of an actual police chase! I could see everything as the situation unfolded right here, right in front of me, almost within arm's reach. San grabbed me by the arm and pulled me back, attempting to get me out of harm's way. Of course, I immediately moved back to my original position, not all the way back, just enough to get a better view of the proceedings without causing her any alarm. Entertainment like this did not happen every day, and I did not want to miss a moment of it!

The boy continued to plow his way through the crowd with the sweating policeman not that far behind. He was using the path formed by the boy's push to gain on him until the boy's luck finally ran out at the next intersection. I instinctively followed them while San tried to catch me and pull me back. The policeman tackled the boy to the pavement, their bodies' momentum carrying them forward several feet before they stopped. Some of the food that the boy had secreted in his shirt cascaded out onto the street. There was no gasp from the crowd when this happened. No one was surprised that the boy was a common thief. Thievery was becoming all too common these days. The more the government squeezed the currency, the more those on the lower end of the economic food chain suffered. For them to survive, theft became a necessity.

The arresting officer, still panting from his unexpected exertion, pulled himself slowly from the ground while grabbing the thief by the shirt collar. Once standing, he jerked the thief to his feet. The thief found himself dangling in front of an angry cop who then dragged the boy's body to the major intersection about a block and a half away. The boy, who now appeared to be about the age of my brother, Hung, was helpless in the officer's iron grip. He could not escape. Fear shone in his eyes.

Another policeman appeared out of nowhere. He pulled a bullhorn to his mouth and quickly silenced the chattering of the crowd. He ordered all of us to proceed to where the officer had taken the boy, so we could personally witness Vietnamese justice in action. This was not a request. He did not ask us to go; He commanded us to go. While he spoke, his free hand never left his sidearm. His face remained a firm, stoic mask. The crowd, including San and me, did as he instructed. We proceeded obediently and fearfully toward the intersection as he followed behind us.

This intersection, like most of the major ones here, was a roundabout. Vietnam learned how to route traffic from the French colonists in the nineteenth and early twentieth century. Consequently, every major intersection mimicked those in Paris - a roundabout or traffic circle. The center of this traffic circle was a huge light pole with five separate lights ringed around the top. The number of lights made this pole unique among all the others in the area.

The first officer dragged the boy to the pole and slammed the thief into it. The impact of the boy's head hitting the light pole caused it to ring like a bell and reverberate for some seconds afterward. His eyes rolled back into his head. He appeared barely conscious as the officer secured him to the pole with his handcuffs. The policeman showed no gentleness or mercy during the process. I and others winced more than once in sympathetic pain for what the thief was experiencing.

Not long after, other officers arrived and blocked traffic on the roads in and out of the roundabout. They ordered the people to leave their vehicles and come forward to witness the proceedings. The crowd was now huge stretching out in all directions.

When everyone had assembled, the officer with the bullhorn again commanded us to silence. At the top of his voice, he preached to us about the need to obey the country's laws. He shouted, "All of us cannot share in the growth that is to come if selfish men like this thief steal from us. All the children of Vietnam should be happy and content." He rambled on and on for some time until his voice faded to a toneless drone in my ears. I managed to tune him out like I did with the loudspeakers and began to daydream, wondering when we would be able to go home.

I guess part of me must have continued listening because his last sentence snapped me back to reality and forever seared itself into my brain. He shouted, "My fellow people, this is what happens to a person who steals and gets caught!" When he stopped, and the last echo from the bullhorn faded, a quiet hush fell over the assembly. What was going to happen?

Then, everything went into slow motion as the officer pulled his pistol from his belt holster. His face twisted with hatred and disgust as he leveled it and then shot the thief multiple times with all the compassion one would have shooting a snake. Each shot sounded like cannon fire and reverberated for some time as the explosion echoed through the city streets. The criminal's body shuddered violently with every bullet's impact. It slid farther and farther down the pole until it finally lay in a heap at its base. The sheen of his blood was an angry red against the cold grey metal.

The policeman stood quietly, the smoke from his gun spiraling upward from the barrel like incense at a shrine. Yet, the pungent aroma I smelled from the blasts were not like incense. The shooter holstered his weapon, turned coldly to the silent masses surrounding the circle, and smiled a cold and cruel smirk. His eyes scanned the crowd allowing them to pause on every face as he did so. Speaking slowly and deliberately, he said, "This is how we deal with those who break the law."

The execution shook San and me beyond words. We slowly and silently began to find our way home, the rest of our purchases forgotten in the face of what had happened. There would be no fish in tonight's soup. Unfortunately, to go home, we needed to walk directly in front of the now dead, lifeless flesh still sprawled on the platform. The body was cuffed to the light pole, although there was no reason for that now. His once wild eyes were still open, but now, they stared vacantly into nothingness. I wanted to shift my gaze but found that I could not look away. His eyes seemed to follow me as I walked around him. San and I, stunned and shocked, did not speak the rest of the way home.

Later, when we told my mother what had happened, she told us to avoid that intersection for the next few days. She said the police would allow his body to remain there. It would provide food for scavenger birds and rats and a further reminder to the people of the price of crime in the new Vietnam.

I was in shock. My world had just been violently profaned - my twelve-year-old innocence gone. A boy had died. I had watched him die. I had seen his blood spilling into the street, and his eyes glaze over as he passed over from this life. The remaining piece of bread he had stolen had fallen from his bullet-riddled clothing soaked red in his blood.

What kind of world would allow this to happen? Was he a criminal? Yes, he was a criminal - a thief probably stealing food for his family. What I could not reconcile was the punishment. In whose idea of justice would death be the sentence for stealing food. Of course, I knew my answer before the thought ever crossed my mind. It was this world, this country's justice. Here any offense could be a death sentence. The idea sent a series of shivers and spasms running down my spine. I felt terribly cold even as the sun beat down in the tropical heat of the late morning.

That night, as I folded the laundry on the roof, I thought about the world around me. A slight breeze gently moved my hair and cooled my forehead. Piece by piece, I took my time removing the laundry from the drying place and folding each piece of clothing carefully before putting it away in my basket. As I worked, I allowed my eyes to scan over the rooftops of Cho Lon, my home.

The Catholic church, with its towering steeple, still sat off to one side. The government had silenced its bell, yet even in its quiet emptiness, its presence somehow comforted me. The church stood like a silent sentinel standing watch, waiting for the tides of history to change again. The church's grounds had borne witness to the assassination of President Ngo Dinh Diem when he died on its courtyard in 1963. It had stood in shock as mortars destroyed the outer wall during the TET offensive of 1968 - the same explosion that had damaged our home as well. When we spoke about the church, Tran and my Catholic friends assured me that the building could not remain silent forever. The people were the church, not the building. The government had silenced the building, but the faith of its people remained.

My mind randomly flashed back to that carefree day with Nhi and my friends riding aimlessly through the streets on our way to go swimming. How happy we had been! Not a care in the world. That day would indeed be one of my favorite childhood memories. The irony was that the "great adventure" had occurred less than two months after the old republic had fallen and the new regime had taken over. Three years ago, I was too young to understand. I could not realize how a change of government could alter my life and my family's lives. How could I have laughed so much with so much evil surrounding me?

I changed my focus and gazed again upon my neighborhood. One by one, I found the empty homes, homes where my friends had lived. People I knew - friends who I had played with during the day and who then simply disappeared overnight. Their houses sat abandoned while neighbors pounced upon them like vultures taking whatever they could before the government came in and took the rest. Here today and gone tomorrow.

Did my friends know they were leaving, or were they snatched in the dead of night? Did they escape – escape this country in the hope of a better one? If so, how could they go without saying goodbye? Did they not know people here would miss them – that I would miss them? I secretly prayed with all my heart that they had escaped. Having seen the new Vietnam's face of justice, I would not wish that on a friend.

Of course, there was no way to know how they had departed. Who had escaped, and who the military had taken to reeducation camps, or worse, sent to the new economic zones out west - an almost certain death sentence. Vast numbers of Vietnamese from the northern part of the country were now moving south. They were Party members, a status that those of us from the south found difficult if not impossible to attain. The government needed those northerners to fill the infinite number of administrative positions they had created - and they needed homes for them and their families. The few houses that still sat silent and vacant would soon have North Vietnamese families to fill them.

As I finished up the laundry, I gazed once more over the landscape, and a goal began forming in my mind. I was still young. I could not begin to comprehend the terrible dangers involved. My developing mind was incapable of even seeing them. Still, I longed with all my heart to escape this place and follow my friends into their great adventure. The taking of a young life had shattered the hopes and dreams I had held this morning. I did not doubt that the boy, like all youth, had felt immortal, that nothing could ever happen to him. I know that I had often felt that way. I smiled as I realized that part of me still did. Just the thought of leaving was liberating. These thoughts allowed me to think – to dream in ways that I could never dare to admit out loud.

I had no idea where my friends had gone or what dangers they had faced; I didn't care. I knew they were not here, and that was enough for me. I was done with here. I had heard fantastic stories about the West. The radio waves from Hong Kong painted a wonderful picture of a place full of plenty of food and fun. Tales of the United States, mostly obtained from people who had known the GIs, made the US sound like a magical place. It seemed to be a place of hope where all your dreams would come true and where an unlimited supply of food guaranteed that no one would go hungry, that no one would ever kill a boy for stealing bread.

I, Muoi Quan, wanted to go there as well.

Chapter 14

Night terrors

Figure 14: Birdcage behind barred door in My Tho, 2017

We had just finished our evening meal. My and I were washing dishes and putting them away with an occasional splash of sudsy water when Mother wasn't looking. Hung was…well off to wherever he ran off to most nights. San and my parents still sat around the table chatting while the younger children were in our sleeping quarters preparing for bed. There was a quiet joy in the normalness of the scene.

My aunt's shrill voice shattered the peaceful scene and sent shock waves throughout the house with her announcement. "They're coming!" was all she said. Not one of us asked who was coming. We didn't have to ask. We knew. The fact that the warning came to my aunt via the balcony told us more than enough.

The army was out looking for "volunteers."

We had been fighting someone for over thirty years. First, long before I was born, we had battled the French colonials to gain our independence. Next, they needed our men to fight a civil war between ourselves and the North. Now, rumors indicated that we were at war with our neighbors to the west, Kampuchea, over border violations, or some such thing. Of course, the one thing that all wars had in common was that they all required young men to fight them. That was the reason why the army came tonight.

They performed these searches regularly. They randomly selected a neighborhood and then searched from house to house, looking for able-bodied men to serve the country. If a man was at least eighteen years old and breathing, he was fair game, and they found him, the army would drag him kicking and screaming out of the house, to fulfill his "duty." Such were their "volunteers."

The houses closest to the main streets would always be the first ones. The squad would first deposit men at the hamlet's main entrance to catch any "escapees." The soldiers then worked their way inward along the alleys and pathways. Whenever people spotted them entering a neighborhood, the alarm would sound. Of course, no one was foolhardy enough to run up and down the streets screaming, so the warnings appeared in whispers across rooftops, through upstairs windows, and via balconies. Fortunately, our house was at the far end of the hamlet, which gave us the most time as a rule. Our location also meant we were at a "dead end" with nowhere to run. Luckily, this quiet notice was all Father needed. While other men ran across rooftops to escape, Father could hide in place and only needed a few seconds to disappear completely.

Within seconds of my aunt raising the alarm, my father leaped to his feet with my mother's voice urging him onward. He flew up the steep steps, his feet never seeming to touch them as he made his way to the second floor and the balcony. There, he found sanctuary. At the place where the edge of the balcony met the room's wall, there was a small space - an overlap. With practiced moves, he folded himself into that tiny area. I could never figure out how he got in there, let alone how he could breathe once he was inside. Once there, however, he was invisible to anyone in the house. The nook was the perfect place for him to disappear.

Not much later, the army arrived at my home, asking a thousand questions about the men of the house. "Were they here?" "Where had they gone?" "When would they return?" Our answers were always the same, "No" "We didn't know." "We had no idea." Of course, the soldiers wouldn't take our word for it. They began a top to bottom search of the house while leaving one soldier outside the front door to catch anyone foolish enough to flee the premises. I had to give them credit; they were thorough. They looked in every space, every cabinet, every cubbyhole they could find. They moved any piece of equipment or furniture that could feasibly hide someone behind it.

Finally…reluctantly… convinced that there was no one there, they left us and moved on to the last house. Still, my father did not leave his hiding place for a long time. He did not trust that the soldiers would not return. Hours later, when he was completely satisfied that the soldiers had left the neighborhood, he exited the nook. We all breathed a sigh of relief when he did.

My parents were more than happy that Hung was out of the house that night. True, Hung's papers showed him as seventeen, and that should be enough to satisfy the soldiers, but our family knew better. Even in the Republic days, the South Vietnamese army used the same recruiting techniques that the current regime did now. Since a father's greatest responsibility was to guarantee his children's safety, particularly his first-born son, Father did what he had to do. Just before the fall of South Vietnam, Hung gained a year of life.

Father asked a family friend to adopt him. This woman was the same friend who had sold us the new house and still had a small apartment on the property. Most importantly, she had no sons, and this was perfect for what Father had in mind. The law exempted those men who were the only sons of their parents from serving in the military. Once he became hers legally, the law protected Hung. Government bureaucrats were not the best at checking details, so while they were completing the adoption paperwork, my father took the liberty of altering Hung's birth date, making him a year younger than he was.

My father had just cause for being concerned about Hung's future. In a South Vietnamese raid in early 1974, the soldiers forcibly took my cousin, Quy, from his home. The warning had not come in time for Quy to get out, and the army grabbed him and took him away. They said nothing to the family as they left, no indication about where they would take him and no hint of how long his service would be. Quy's family watched in silence as their son walked away with the soldiers.

Naturally, Quy's mother was beside herself with worry. She wrote letters to him frequently but never received anything in reply. She then wrote to the Defense Department, begging for some news of her son. She just wanted to know that he was OK, but she got nothing from them either. Finally, after months of wait and worry, she showed up at the department's door in person, focused on getting an answer, and vowed not to leave without one. The guards bodily took her away with a stern warning to never return. She was heartbroken. It was as if her son, her Quy, had never existed. His family never heard from him again.

Quy's fate only made us more determined to hide our men when the army came. Yes, this was a new government, and the uniforms had changed, but there was one significant difference in their methods. The Communists were not so picky about taking only sons – particularly if they were Chinese sons. Also, for them, eighteen was a fluid number when determining eligibility. In the raids that followed, they drafted many Chinese/Vietnamese, some eighteen, some not. Few managed to return from their service.

There was another reason to beware of the military. Soldiers had patrolled the streets of Cho Lon since before Reunification. Still, now my friends and I noticed a lot more army men in our neighborhoods. Soldiers had once patrolled alone, now they moved in pairs or even larger groups, and they seemed to be everywhere. Every street bristled with armed guards. They had more than handguns now. Automatic weapons as well as armored vehicles lined up and down our roadways. All appearances indicated that we were at war again, and not just with Kampuchea. Soldiers had boxed in our entire district as if Cho Lon were under siege. None of us knew what was going on or why this was starting now. Our local Party officials were in the dark as well. They asked their superiors, but those officials gave no response. We had an uneasy peace.

Not long after the new year of 1978 began, soldiers returned to our home. This time there was no warning. They had a specific target in mind. They came for us during the middle of the night, while my family and I were dead asleep, so late that even the mosquitos had gone to bed. They shocked us awake with loud shouts and banging on our front door grate, demanding entry. My father shook himself awake as he dropped to the floor, bravely marching downstairs to face them while the rest of us cowered together in the dark.

I could hear a man's voice shouting harsh words echoed by my father's equally forceful reply. Then there was the sound of the front grate opening coupled with a loud crash as men shoved bicycles and mopeds out of their way. Heavy boots stomped up the steps, followed by the glare of flashlights splashing across the rooms, illuminating our faces. A man in uniform, who I took to be the one in charge, was shouting orders at us to get up and follow his men. They herded us downstairs and outside into the alleyway. They refused to allow us to take anything with us. What we wore to bed was what we wore outside. Once in the alley, my grandmother, aunt, cousin, and a few guests who were staying with us at the time followed us out.

An armed guard watched over us. His holstered gun was at his side, but his expressionless face left me little doubt that he could quickly get to the weapon and how well he could use it if provoked. I saw a few daring neighbors peek out through darkened windows, but no one ventured outside, even on the balconies, and no one said anything, even in whispers. No one wanted to draw the soldier's attention. I could sense the fear burning in their eyes, and I was sure that their questions were the same as mine. "Why were the soldiers here?" "What were they looking for?" "What would they find?" and of course, they would wonder, "Will I be next?"

The soldier in charge returned to my father and shouted at him. His Vietnamese words came fast and loud, so fast I had a hard time understanding him. He said that as head of household, my father was a criminal. Well, that was wrong. My father wasn't the head of household, and he most certainly was not a criminal; my aunt was the official head ever since my grandmother died.

They had already started to arrest him when my aunt came forward. At first, the commander did not believe her until she told him where to find the proof. He was not sure of what to do. This was unexpected. Women rarely held property.

At any rate, when my aunt presented the proof, he let my father go and arrested my aunt in his place. They tied her up and put her under armed guard in the first-floor room while the rest of the party scoured the house floor by floor.

The search seemed to take forever. We stood outside, afraid to move, while the men worked. What were they looking for? Who knew? We had little of value and had done nothing to warrant such treatment. My face burned with humiliation as our neighbors watched the soldiers treat us like common criminals. There had, of course, been rumors of such raids. The word was that they were looking for contraband. Somehow, the authorities had come to believe that we held valuables, maybe even gold, in our home. These men came tonight to catch us unaware and search for anything and everything that pointed to us as traitors to the state. There was to be no stone left unturned in their efforts.

What were we to do? There was nowhere to run. There was no place to go. We simply stood there, helpless as we listened to the men above us prowling about in our house. They did not speak as they went about the task, but the sounds from inside indicated they were taking our home and everything in it apart. There was the sound of heavy things moving around accompanied by the breaking of glass and pottery. The sound of tortured metal drifted down to the street. Finally, the noise stopped. With the search over and our ordeal at an end, the soldiers exited the house.

They escorted my aunt away with armed guards on either side of her. There was nothing we could do but watch her leave. They were taking her to the same place all the others went – the reeducation center. There she would learn the "error" of her ways before returning her to her home. Of course, even I knew that "reeducation center" was just another word for prison. I had heard the stories of others brainwashed and tortured into compliance with the Communist dogma. Even though she was in that awful place, I was relieved that they had not shown us what happens to "those who broke the law." No one died.

There was nothing we could do for my aunt. There would be no one to hear any complaint because there was no recourse available. She was beyond our help now. So, we did the only thing we could do. We went back inside the house and assessed the damage.

The house was a shambles. All our belongings that even hinted of Chinese influence lay in wreckage on the floor. Our record player, along with all my treasured records of Chinese music, shattered. My mother's vases, gifts from her mother, smashed beyond repair. The beautiful hand-painted wall hangings were torn to shreds.

Our clothing appeared to have been tossed in the air and then allowed to fall where it may. Dresses, shirts, and pants all spotted the concrete floor of our sleeping quarters. The soldiers had carefully pawed over each piece, searching for valuables sewn into the linings and then thrown them down. Boot prints showed that they had trampled on them as well. My clothes felt so dirty as I put them back in their place.

My father had gone upstairs to the kitchen/factory, and his cry caused us to fly up to the fourth floor as a group. All around us was devastation. They had scattered my father's Chinese medicine equipment and tools across the floor - materials gathered over a lifetime, mangled and destroyed. In only one night, we lost our family's sole source of income. We stood in silent shock as we surveyed the scene, a scene so unreal that we could not fathom its full importance. The government had made its point. There would be no old medicines, no old ways. The Communists would eliminate, no...purge everything Chinese from existence even here in Cho Lon.

The next morning as we cleaned up the mess to the best of our ability, our thoughts turned to our missing aunt. How could we help her? We knew that we could not go inside the reeducation center, of course. The authorities forbade any visitors at any time. The inmates were to have no contact with the outside world while they were being "treated." We heard from others whose relatives had suffered a similar fate. They told us that the inmates went out every afternoon on a work detail. The guards were very lax, and there was a possibility that we could see her and maybe even slip her some food at that time. We had no idea when they would come out or if the drill would be at the same time every day. So, some of us silently waited just outside the perimeter fencing until the door opened and the inmates came out.

At first, I couldn't see her. Had they kept her inside? No. Wait! There she was! She was OK! I was thrilled to see her unharmed and healthy. Every day, for the rest of her internment, one of us watched outside. Sometimes we brought food or other small items that we would carefully slip to her and that she could smuggle in under her clothes. At other times, we simply offered her the solace that we had not forgotten her. She was not alone.

A relatively short time later, perhaps a month, the center released her and allowed her to return to us. Words could not express the relief the family felt that day. Others in the neighborhood had not had as short or as easy a time. In fact, for some, reeducation turned into a life sentence. Maybe her treatment was different because she was a woman. After all, the Party did not consider women a threat, even propertied women. Women belonged in their homes. Honestly, I didn't care what the reason was. I was simply glad she was home.

Starting the day after the raid, my mother and father began dealing with the problem of our continued survival. My siblings and I knew that the situation was terrible but had no idea how bad it really was. The medicine business was gone forever; the equipment was beyond salvage. As a short-term solution, Father contacted an old acquaintance who owned a small sugar mill on the city's outskirts. He coaxed the man into selling us sugar at a wholesale price. We would then repackage and resell the sugar in smaller amounts at the market.

Every day after that, early in the morning, he and my mother would take the moped to the mill trailing an empty cart behind. When they returned, they had loaded down his cart with fifty to seventy pounds of refined sugar. Our job was to take this product and weigh it out into small bags. Those, we would take to the market to sell at a profit.

Being a middleman worked for a short while but was not a satisfactory long-term solution for the family. There was simply not enough money to support us. On his daily trips, he had the opportunity to observe how the mill worked and realized that the process was reasonably straightforward. He was optimistic that we had or could easily acquire the skills required to make our own sugar - and so we did.

With this new purpose in mind, my father collected the equipment needed to start our sugar processing operation. He installed the machinery at the new house, which then became our factory. Once everything was in place, he ceased buying sugar and began buying raw sugar cane directly from the fields. Our new enterprise had begun.

As before with the medicine, we all had a job in this as well. Even with a full-time job at the cannery, Hung had a part to play when he wasn't working there. Dad, Mom, and he would shuck and discard the leaves off the cane and soak them in water. After the sugar cane had absorbed the liquid and had softened, they squeezed it between the two rollers of a laundry wringer to force the juice out. I would take the cane juice to the centrifuge. A small motor would rapidly spin the liquid until it had removed almost all the liquid, leaving behind only a grainy slurry. Next, My and I took the still damp and heavy sugar to the roof so that it could dry completely in the sun. The final steps were to grind the sugar into even finer particles, package it into small bags, and take the finished product to market.

San was exempt from the sugar work, but her responsibilities changed as well. Father now needed Mother to help full time with the sugar, so San had to assume all of Mother's domestic duties. Therefore, fifteen-year-old San became responsible for the household, the cooking duties, plus responsibility for all her younger siblings. She became our second mom.

1978 was only half over, and our world had changed so much, so rapidly. My family and I did our best to adapt as each change came. We strove to rise above every difficulty. My father was a miracle in all this. He only knew one direction – forward, and he pursued every opportunity to push us there. We saw no point in complaining, although many other families did. There was nothing that we could do in the short term. For the long term, we waited. Our Vietnamese overlords seemed to have forgotten something important. For almost two hundred years, we, the people of Cho Lon, had been persecuted and forced to adapt to the winds of change. Throughout those centuries, we had survived, even thrived as our "masters" came and went. In our time, the political wind had changed directions more than once. Each time, the people of Cho Lon went with the flow of history and carried on. This time would be no different.

Toward that end, my aunt was always prompt at the neighborhood Party meetings. I went to school, attended youth meetings, and held our place in line at the commissary without complaining. We manufactured and sold our sugar with little interference other than taxes and bribes and somehow managed to make enough to keep our family going. We watched as the government took over vacant and sometimes occupied houses for various committees and public needs and never objected.

No one let on to the authorities that discontent was everywhere among the citizenry of Cho Lon. We shared a united view that the new government was an invader and an interloper. No one, man or woman, saw any hope for their future or their children's futures under the current regime. As the times were in my grandparents' day in China, more and more often, people sought a way out.

Chapter 15

A vacation in Đà Nẵng

Figure 15: DA NANG, VIETNAM - CIRCA AUGUST 2015:
Moc Son Mountain, Marble mountains, Vietnam

Tran and I had an incredibly close relationship, especially for two people so far apart in age. She had been going on and on about a trip that she and her brother, Tho, were taking - an extended trip to Da Nang to visit her friend Phung Tien. They were not going to be gone long, yet I would miss her terribly. The trip sounded so terrific; I had to admit that I was more than a little jealous. Imagine my surprise when, one morning, she asked me to go with her. I was numb with shock!

Would I like to go to Da Nang? I had never been farther than My Tho, and Da Nang was many times farther away – almost 500 miles! I had a difficult time containing my excitement, not just about going, but going by train as well! All I could manage to do was choke out a "Yes!" My answer made Tran giddy. She had hoped that I would want to go. Now that she had my approval, she needed to talk to my mother and get her permission.

Mother and Tran did not invite me to participate in their conversation. I was a little miffed at their ignoring me this way. At age twelve, I should have a seat at the table for something like this. Instead, I dutifully stood off to the side while straining my ears to catch a few words of what they were saying. Much to my dismay, their voices were just a low hum. I couldn't make out anything at all. I would have to wait to hear the decision, and they were taking forever. What was there to discuss anyway? Sure, the trip was long, but I would be with Tran and her brother, both trusted adults. Tran and I had gone alone all over the city together. What could be such a big deal?

A lifetime seemed to pass before Mom left Tran at the table and came over to see me alone. She bent down and looked me in the eyes. She was so serious, not like Mom at all. The closest she had ever looked to this was when she reacted to my bleeding back after the sunburn experience. She held my chin in her hand and continued to stare as she asked, "Do you really want to go?" Really? Of course, I wanted to go. This trip was the chance of a lifetime. I answered her with a resounding, almost shouted, "YES"!

Funny, my answer seemed to upset her even more. She wasn't angry, just upset. The next thing she asked confused me even more, "Would you still want to go even if going meant not seeing the family again?" What? Where did that come from? Now, I was the one confused and upset. Why would she ask such a question? Why would I not see the family again? In my confusion, I took her comments as just being concerned for my being so far away. I looked straight at her as I replied, "Yes, I want to go."

Mother slowly nodded her head and left me. She looked so sad. At first, I was concerned that I had said something wrong but, when I played the conversation back in my mind, nothing that I had said or done should have offended her. I guessed that she had something else on her mind, so I quickly put the matter out of mine. After all, I was going on vacation! What could go wrong?

Tran had waited until the last minute to include me, and now we only had a few days before time to leave. I felt stressed that there was far too much to do in such a short amount of time. Tran assured me that there would be no problem buying our train tickets at the station on the morning we left. There was no need for luggage. We only needed one or two changes of clothing since we could wash them at Phung Tien's home. When we had finished packing, it amounted to only a few things in some cloth bags, which I found to be a little disappointing.

My aunt took care of notifying the local Party officials of our departure. San and my mother put together a small package of food to sustain us on the trip. In the end, there just wasn't anything for me to do. All I could do was wait.

When the day of our leaving came, the day started as all the others did. Work could not stop because we were going. Hung had to go to the cannery for the early shift, and the rest of the family had to go to the new house to continue working the sugar mill. With my departure, there would even be more work to do. My and Mother would have to assume my responsibilities in addition to their own - something that appeared to disgruntle My more than a little. As everyone hustled around getting ready, Tran and I said our goodbyes. My mother had tears in her eyes when she kissed me. She hugged both Tran and me for a long, long time before sending us on our way.

We flagged a pedicab on Hoc Lac that took us to the train station in District 3, far on the other side of Ho Chi Minh City. I had never had reason to go there, so this was a new experience for me. When we entered the depot, the enormity of the place awed me. The building seemed to go on forever. Tons of people were hustling every which way to catch their trains. This station was the hub for all the southern rail lines and the main line north that we would be on. The crowds were enormous. Was everyone in Vietnam taking the train today?

Tho purchased our tickets, and we found our way to the Ho Chi Minh – Hanoi train, now called the "Reunification Railroad." Even though the North and the South both had rail lines, the long war had resulted in this one being the only one connecting them. When we got to the platform, Tho carried Tran onto the train car, and I followed behind with our meager belongings. Once on the train, we found a plain wooden bench seat in one of the rail cars with more than enough room for the three of us, and we began to settle in. I was so nervous with excitement that I bounced up and down on the seat, impatiently waiting for the train to start moving. My anticipation had built to a fever pitch when the train's whistle blew – loud! The noise scared me so badly that I nearly flew out of the seat altogether! Tho and Tran just laughed. Then I felt a vibration in my whole body as the train slowly inched out of the station, gradually picking up speed as the engine forged its way northward.

Train rides had been different in my imagination. They had been exciting adventures full of mystery and daring. Now, as I experienced the reality, I found the monotony boring to the extreme. The journey required a thirteen-hour train ride from Ho Chi Minh City to Đà Nẵng...thirteen long, grueling hours that this hyper-active twelve-year-old would have to endure with nowhere to run or to play. What was I supposed to do?

There were only so many times you could walk around the cramped passenger car. People, luggage, packages, and animals so filled the car that moving anywhere without stepping on someone was nearly impossible. Between the people shouting, the engine noises, and animals making their various squawks, honks, and barks, I had to struggle to hear myself think. Most of the time, I just resigned myself to sit, my face pressed against the metal grate that was my window, and watched the world slide past me.

We passed through many small villages on the way. I was amazed by how little space there was between the track and the buildings. In some cases, there was no right of way at all! Homes in those villages pushed right up to the tracks. I was confident that I could have grabbed laundry from one house's window if my arm had been just a little longer.

About an hour after we left the station, I discovered that our trip was not non-stop to Đà Nẵng. Some of the larger villages along the way had people and cargo getting off and getting on. There was usually no formal train station, just a slightly broader place in the right-of-way, a small space around the tracks that allowed the train to stop, load, and unload.

On these occasions, vendors magically appeared just outside the doors and windows. Some had carts, but others had their wares in baskets that they carried on their heads. They had all sorts of things for sale. One woman was selling bánh mi (bread), another with steaming pots of phở (noodle soup), and still another selling cold nuoc mia (a special drink made from sugar cane) and cà phê (coffee served with milk and sugar, iced or hot). All these wonderful things were bought and sold right through the windows of the train. We always browsed through the wares that the locals were selling, although we rarely bought anything. When the whistle blew, the vendors disappeared as quickly as they had come, and our journey began again.

The farther we pushed north, the more I saw new things out my window. The streams we crossed were much narrower here and far cleaner than the wide, muddy ones we had in the south. The broad flatlands of the river delta near My Tho had now become hills that led off into the distance.

They seemed almost like stepping-stones for the distant misty mountains whose silhouettes rose behind them. I found it increasingly hard to believe that this was even the same country.

The sun had long set over the mountains when we finally reached our destination at Da Nang Station. The day's journey had been exhausting. I was hot and tired, as I was sure Tran and Tho were as well. As we exited onto the platform, Tran once again took her place on her brother's back. I dutifully stumbled along behind them.

Suddenly, I found myself face to face with an angry-looking mob rushing toward the same door that I was trying to exit. What was happening? In my exhaustion, I panicked and started to retreat into the train car. Someone behind me grabbed me and made me stop. Then, they pushed me forward, out into the crowd, and kept going until I was through the mass of people. Afterward, I felt ridiculous at being afraid. No one had bothered me; they parted quickly to let me pass with no problems. They were simply ready to get on the train that we had just exited – presumably headed on to Hanoi. They were just anxious to go.

With that event behind me, I noticed that the station's crowd did not seem any friendlier here in the waiting area than the ones getting on the train. Some of them looked positively angry.

Just like back in Ho Chi Minh City, people were everywhere. Even though this station wasn't as large, the cavernous interior was still huge, and crowds of people were going every which way, even at this hour. We just stood around waiting for Phung Tien to show up. In my innocence, I thought, "What if she can't find us with all the people about?"

The thought had barely crossed my mind when I heard a thin voice shout Tran's name. Tran heard her voice as well and excitedly shouted back, waving furiously. Before a minute had passed, the two friends reunited amid much laughter, hugs, and hand-holding. We pushed toward the exit. When we were outside the station, we hailed a cab and went to her home on the city's outskirts. I don't think she and Tran stopped talking and laughing the entire way. I felt it best not to interrupt, so I followed Tho's lead and stayed quiet. This was their time, and I was happy they were enjoying themselves. I was ready for this vacation to begin, but first, I was ready for bed.

Our first day in Da Nang was close to perfection. Perfection was the only conceivable way I could imagine describing my surroundings. The weather was beautiful, clear skies feathered with marshmallow clouds with gentle ocean breezes tickling my neck. I walked to the crest of a small hill and watched the morning sun give life to the city, and then the town returning the light reflected from its multi-colored roofs and walls. The sea in the distance sparkled like diamonds, with fishing boats bobbing along like corks. Here, close to the mountains and the sea, the temperature felt so much cooler than back home - so refreshing! Paradise must be like this.

I had no idea what that first day had in store. Tran and Phung Tien had taken care of all the details. Tho and I, along with a few of Phung Tien's friends, were just along for the ride, and I was ready to ride. We walked to a bus station where we boarded a bus to Ngũ Hành Sơn, the Mountain of Five Fingers. We had talked about this place in my lessons at school, but I had never dreamed I would get to visit its secrets in person.

The history of Ngũ Hành Sơn stretched back to antiquity over a thousand years. Each finger on the mountain had the name of a different element: Metal (Kim), Water (Thuy), Wood (Moc), Fire (Hoa), Earth (Tho). This area had been a location for Buddhist monasteries and temples for centuries, and throngs of the faithful pilgrimaged here annually. In more recent times, especially since reunification, the place's art and beauty drew people more than religion. We, too, were not here for worship - the shrines and pagodas would have to wait. Our goal was far up the mountain – the caves.

Deep inside these magnificent hills lay an intricate network of tunnels that lead to elaborate shrines carved out of rock lit only by natural skylights. We had no such caves in the south, and I was anxious to see them. This excursion had the mark of an adventure, and I couldn't wait for our tour to start.

The steps leading to the cave entrance were steep - so steep that Tho and Phung Tien would have to help Tran climb them. We frequently rested as a result, which also allowed us to take in the breathtaking views. Here and there, seemingly suspended in air, were stunning golden pagodas hanging delicately from the sides of the mountain's fingers. So precarious were their placements, they seemed to defy gravity. Nestled down below them were clear pools of blue water with golden statues and intricate gardens surrounding them. The picture was a heavenly vision; a fairy tale scene come to life.

After our long and strenuous climb, we arrived at the mouth of Hoa Nghiem Cave. As we moved from light to darkness, our eyes took a few moments to adjust. At first glance, I had to admit that the opening underwhelmed me.

Granted, the space around me was gigantic, but Tran had led me to believe that the cave was also fancy, and this was not fancy at all. We followed the path farther inside to the point where the cave began to narrow. At this point, the narrowness of the trail forced us to proceed one at a time. When my turn came, I walked to the end of the passageway and through a narrow gate.

My jaw dropped. There, spread in front of me, loomed a fantastic cavern sparkling with marvels. My disappointment from the earlier room evaporated into amazement at the sight of this one. On two sides of the cavern were ornate altars pressed against the cave walls, and, on another, someone had nestled a small pagoda into a space carved out perfectly for its size. Statues of armed guards from a forgotten era stood on either side of the entrance, keeping watch over all who entered. As I turned my gaze upward, I saw twin natural skylights that sent beams of illumination to pools of water on the floor below. The water reflected the sun's rays and, in turn, illuminated millions of dust particles suspended in the air. Together they cast an eerie, otherworldly light across the room. My breath escaped me - I was astounded. This experience was well worth the walk up. I hated to leave when the others decided it was time to go.

Down the mountain from the entrance of Hoa Nghiem, we took a side trip into Am Phu. Am Phu was a completely different experience. For reasons I didn't know, this cave was much warmer, almost uncomfortably warm, and the art displayed on its walls was far more disturbing.

This cave represented the Buddhist hell, and both the increased temperature and the artwork reinforced that theme. Natural skylights also illuminated this space, but here, in place of pools of water and beautiful pagodas, demons and devils surrounded me. Some of the monsters were in the act of physically punishing sinners with canes and fire. Now, I realized that I had caused my share of trouble in my life, but there was no way I would submit to this kind of reconciliation. This time, I was more than happy to leave!

A tired and happy crew returned to Phung Tien's house at the end of the day. Quietly, we ate our evening meal, cleaned up, and unwound. Not being the type to rest, I was more inclined to snoop around the house and see what was going on. I was in the back of the place when I found Phung Tien's brother busy at a table working on some clothing. He was a tailor by trade, and like at home, work had to continue, even as others played. Watching him work didn't pique my interest either, so I went back to see what the others were doing. They were just sitting around the dining table talking. Talking - all they did was talk! Torn between two equally boring pastimes, I began to realize how tired I was and that there was a third option. As the exertion of the day caught up with me, I washed, went to bed, and slept very well indeed.

The next morning, our next adventure took us to the beach, or more aptly beside the beach. We passed long, beautiful beaches on the way, and I longed to stop at them. Perfect white sand and blue waters beckoned to me. The beaches we had down south were more golden and the water more brownish. I didn't own a camera, so I did the next best thing and tried to capture the image in my mind. I wanted to keep this view with me forever. Our bus driver finally delivered us to the day's destination, the shrine of the Sleeping Buddha. The legend was that the statue had drifted to this peninsula on the tide ages ago. The people of Da Nang felt that its presence was a sign from the Buddha himself and told how Buddha blessed the people here. They built a large pagoda on the spot to protect the statue from the elements. There, surrounded on three sides by the sea, he rested. We spent the entire day there before returning home.

Okay, so today wasn't all that exciting. Still, after the exercise the day before, today was exactly the kind of day I needed. So far, this vacation had been great! I loved everything we were doing. I loved putting the duties and problems in Cho Lon behind me and enjoy life a little. I did realize that all good things had to end eventually and that our real-life would be awaiting our return. Still, until then, I planned to relish every second of what remained.

A change in plans

That second night, I began to question some of what I was seeing. Tran and her friends had again left me to my own devices while they joined in quiet conversation. Boring – only made worse because they didn't invite me to join them. Not quite ready to go to bed, I decided that tailoring beat out conversation on the boring meter, so I sought Phung Tien's brother.

I found him exactly where he had been the night before, sitting at his worktable working away. Tonight though, he was making new buttons for his sister's clothing. Even though his activity was still dull, I considered it better than doing nothing, so I feigned interest as I watched from the side.

He was concentrating diligently on his work and never gave any indication that he knew I was there. As I looked closer into his efforts, I became confused by what his intent was.

The new "buttons" he was making were not plastic; instead, he constructed them from precious gems and gold pieces. His deft fingers wrapped each one in the fabric giving the finished product the appearance of an actual button. As he completed each one, he would attach it to one of Phung Tien's garments spread around the table. I could not understand why he would do that. Why would someone hide such beauty in cloth?

The answer to my question and the basis for many more came the next morning after a quick breakfast. Tran pulled me aside and gazed at me with intensely focused eyes. She was even more intense than the trip home from the beach when she had nearly drowned. There was no idle chit-chat, no laughing about the day. She stared at me and said that we needed to go.

Her matter of fact statement stunned me. I looked at her in shocked disbelief. "Why?" I asked. "We still had several days before we were supposed to return home. Why were we returning to Cho Lon so soon?" I was mid-protest, on the verge of tears, when she stopped my complaining with a look and a finger to my lips. It took quite a while for me to calm down. When my cries subsided to soft sobs, I heard the rest of the story.

"Muoi, Tho and I are not going back to Cho Lon.", she said. I had not expected this response. "What? How is this possible? We all have to go back to Cho Lon?" I was getting frantic now. "Muoi," she said, "I know that this is a surprise, but Tho and I planned this from the beginning. Phung Tien and her brother and his wife are leaving as well. We are all going to make our way to China. Cho Lon holds no future for Tho and me. China is not perfect, but it appears better than here. At the very least, I believe we will not be penalized simply for being Chinese. Phung Tien has family across the border, and we hope that they can sponsor us to a better life." She continued, "She has also hired a guide who will take us from Da Nang to the border." I stood there in shock when she dropped a second bombshell. "Muoi, we need to leave tonight."

Phung Tien's parents' activities of the last two nights made sense to me now. They knew the plan, and they were providing the means for their daughter to succeed far away in a new country. The Vietnamese government seemed consumed with seizing personal wealth for the "common good." No one in their right minds would travel in the open while carrying the fortune in gems and gold concealed in those buttons. They would risk certain arrest if they did so. I silently wondered if Tran had secreted away some gold or jewels as well. I was about to voice the question when she asked me one instead – a question that I felt unprepared to answer.

"What do you want to do?" she asked me. "You have a choice to make. You can continue with me and the rest to China, or we can send you back to Cho Lon alone." I was speechless. What could I say? Mental snapshots of all the people – my friends who had fled our hamlet flashed in front of my eyes. In my mind's eye, I could see their empty houses as clearly as if I were standing on the rooftop at home. Home. What about my family? What would my life be like without them? What would their life be like without me? What would my mother tell me to do? I didn't know. Mother was not here.

I found myself facing this difficult decision without her guidance, yet with the certainty that I needed to decide quickly. Tran needed an answer now.

Then, I remembered my secret dreams, what I had said that night after I witnessed the boy's death. I remembered my anger at his ending and that I would do anything to escape that place, the place that my home had become. The flashback had only taken a moment, but it helped me make my decision. My dreams won. I would take my chance and tie my fate with Tran's.

We left Phung Tien's house that night shortly after dusk and casually walked to the place where the train tracks left Da Nang on their way north. Our light banter gave no indication that anything was happening other than a stroll on the streets with friends. As we approached the train tracks at the edge of the city, the two men looked for the place where the rails took an uphill grade. Supposedly, that would force the train to slow down, hopefully enough for our purposes.

There was a new moon tonight, which meant the only light came from the surrounding homes and the stars. We intentionally did not carry flashlights; they might give us away. We had no extra clothing. That might slow us down. We had to do this quickly and in the dark. Our guide was already at the spot, waiting for us to arrive. Just as we heard the train approach our location, he ordered us to start moving, and then running – fast! The train would slow down on the uphill grade, but it would not stop, only slow. I realized that this was not going to be the easy boarding we had in Cho Lon; this time, we had to board this train on the run.

I sprinted along the train's path as fast as my legs would carry me. I had no idea how many others were there with me, just that there were more than our little group. Tran's brother had her on his back running for all he was worth, and, out of the corner of my eye, I saw Phung Tien and the others not too far away from them. Apart from them, I didn't see anyone. I had to concentrate on the moving train ahead of me.

I was almost at the train when I realized that I had no idea how to get on board! Then, as if God heard my pleading, people on the train appeared at the doors and windows, gesturing frantically for me and the others to hurry. A total stranger yanked me through the door. My savior threw me behind him as soon as I was clear and reached for another person needing assistance from outside. I silently prayed that others were doing the same for my friends. When the engine topped the hill and the train started picking up speed on the other side, bodies occupied every inch of the car's interior.

I took a few moments to catch my breath. My lungs burned, and my legs did not seem to want to support my body anymore. As I sat on the floor panting, I observed the activity around me. I had only thought the trip from Ho Chi Minh City had been chaotic. This was far worse. Compared to this, the other journey had been a quiet luncheon in the park. Here, sitting amidst the crowd and the nervous noises, the stench of sweat and fear attacked my senses on every side. This situation was many things, but I have to say, boring was not one of them.

When I was finally able to stand, I began to move around as best I could. All around me was a tangled sea of legs and bodies. My mind rewarded me with the unwelcome image of my opera trip with Tran so long ago. However, now, like then, I needed to find Tran. Unlike that time, there was no guard present today to assist me in finding her. The constant motion of the crowd made focusing on my surroundings even more difficult. Everywhere I looked, I saw strangers towering above me. Indistinct faces blended into each other, none of them belonging to my companions.

Instinctively, I wanted to shrink back into the shadows and hide. I had no idea where my friends were. I had not seen them since the run began. I was not sure they were on this car, or even if they had made the jump to the train at all, and if they had, how could I possibly find them in this madhouse?

I threaded my way through the swarm of legs that seemed intent on either kicking me out of the way or stepping on me. As I passed by each person, I looked upward expectantly, hoping, praying to find some recognition in their face, but to no avail. As I moved from one car to the next, I began to have a sinking feeling that Tran and company had not made the train at all. I was truly alone.

I started to panic when, out of a bunch of legs, a strong arm reached out and snagged me. My eyes followed the arm, and I found it connected to...Tran! She had seen me first. She pulled me up to her and gave me the tightest hug I could remember — one which I returned with enthusiasm.

When she finally pushed me away, we had a serious talk. She spoke in a whisper, barely discernable over the surrounding crowd. In it, she gave me a firm order - not a request - not a warning. "Muoi, from this point on in our journey, maybe even until we reach safety in China, you are not to speak to anyone but me and even then, only in a whisper." She continued, "The way we speak is a giveaway to where we came from. We in the south talk differently than those in the north."

I completely understood this. I remembered how my teachers from the north had confused us at first with their strange speech. She said one more thing. "Right now, you must understand that being from the South would not be to our advantage, especially if they discovered we were Chinese."

Now, telling a normal twelve-year-old that she couldn't talk would be an act of pure torture, and I was not normal. I lived to talk, laugh, and scream. Talking was part of my nature. Staying quiet for a few minutes seemed like forever, and this would be days. If Tran had mentioned this condition when she asked me to come, I might have reconsidered the trip altogether.

Now was a little late for that, though. As the train pushed farther and farther northward, I resigned myself to my fate and tried my best to do as she instructed. I sat and said nothing. It was funny. Even though I was seemingly locked in a silent prison, I soon discovered that listening was more fun than I had imagined! I passed the time now by eavesdropping on my fellow travelers and was surprised by what I learned. Tran was right. I identified several distinct dialects just in the people around us. Some I could easily understand. Others, I could barely identify as Vietnamese. One question still burned in my mind. one that I would have to ask the next time Tran and I spoke. What difference does being Chinese make?

I understood that life for us Chinese in Cho Lon was getting more and more difficult. Still, things had quieted down significantly since the raids had stopped, and the strong military presence in the community was now gone. Granted, we would never be able to return to our previous life, but life would continue. I asked Tran about this in one of our whisper sessions. She said that Chinese persecution was much worse here in the north. Communism was entrenched here and had been for a long time, and the people reflected the government's opinion without question. Here, regular people, as well as the military, would verbally and sometimes even physically attack us if they discovered who we were.

After reunification, China and Vietnam had become enemies. There was now much talk in the north that war between the two countries was inevitable and could happen at any time. In Hanoi, the paranoid politicians had convinced themselves that the Chinese/Vietnamese were spies for their old homeland. The government had now stepped up the persecution of persons of Chinese descent. They would do everything in their power to silence the foreign agents. I now understood the necessity of dampening our voices and praying that we would somehow pass through undetected. Fear found a new home in me.

The next two days and three nights blurred in my mind. The change from waking to sleeping became indistinct. On the spur of the moment, our guide would roust us and order us to exit the train at one of its stops and to do it quickly. We had little warning and rarely had more than a minute to get off. More and more, we would just react to the guide's voice. Once we were clear of the train's right-of-way, we would find a place out of sight and hide until a bus came along to take us to the next step in our quest.

As we passed through some mountains on one such bus, the brakes began to fail as we were going downhill. The driver panicked and ordered everyone to jump off the bus while we could, with him taking the first leap. There was nothing else we could do. Tho and I were at the bus's front, so we became two of the first ones off.

As I dropped and rolled on the road, I realized that Tran couldn't get off. She was stuck at the back of the bus with some older people who would also not physically be able to jump. In the few seconds that this thought took to cross my mind, Tho and some other men grabbed large rocks lying along the roadside. They sprinted ahead of the moving bus and placed the stones in its path, hoping to slow its progress. At this point, the bus had built up some momentum, and when the vehicle hit the first rocks, it bounced over them readily, slowing the bus only a tiny bit. Again and again, the men placed more and more stones in the path of the bus, each one slowing the bus more and more until the vehicle finally came to rest on top of the last rock. Tran and the others were safe. The excitement over, we resigned ourselves to walking the several miles to the next stop.

This process of alternating trains and buses continued for two more days. The stress stretched our strength and nerves to the limit. The longer our journey took, the more the novelty of the experience wore thin. We all asked the same question, "When would it ever end?"

I was dazed, dirty, exhausted, and worried. I looked at my friends and sensed the same growing, gnawing concern, even fear, in them…even in Tran. Already frightened as I was, the realization that they were also scared bothered me even more.

Hanoi

Late one night, we left the train for the last time. Of course, we didn't know at the time that this was the last one.

To us, this was just one more stop. I was still a little groggy from the half-sleep that Tran had rudely awakened me from, but I was awake enough to see that we had a different guide now. He told us that our old guide would be returning to Da Nang, where he would gather a new group of travelers. Our new guide then directed us to meet under a nearby streetlight. He told us to stay close together and be as silent as possible. He led our parade into a maze of nearby warehouses. I was so tired. I just stumbled along in whatever direction one of the others led me. I didn't even know where here was!

I guess that I mumbled that question aloud because one of the others answered that we might be in Hanoi. We continued shuffling in the dark from streetlight to streetlight. Our guide was ever alert for signs of other people out at this hour, anyone who might give us away to the authorities. So far, I had seen no one. As far as I could tell, the area was devoid of people. We were alone.

I am not sure how far we walked, but my legs told me that it had to be a goodly distance. At long last, our guide stopped in front of a nondescript building with no markings differentiating the façade from any of the other ones. Once again, the guide took great pains in making sure that no one was following us. When he convinced himself that it was clear, he opened a door in the structure's side and hurried us inside. The building was even darker and more foreboding inside than it had appeared outside, and my eyes took some time to adjust to the gloomy interior. When they did, I could see that we were in a large room and that the room had other people already present. It appeared that another group had come before us and was sitting, waiting in the near darkness.

They looked up at us expectantly as we entered. I guessed that the others thought we might represent the next step in their journey. When they discovered that we were just like them and would be waiting as well, they shifted their attention away. Our guide pointed us to a small, vacant space on the floor – just enough room to sit. He then gave us a loaf of hard bread to share among our group and pointed to a small fountain that we could use for water. Personally, I didn't care what was on the menu. I was hungry. I'd take anything. After we ate and drank, we dozed as we also sat and waited for what was to come next.

I have no idea what time I awoke. It had to be in the middle of the night. My friends were around me, restless in their fitful sleep. In the near darkness, I could see other Chinese faces, not unlike my own, sleeping or looking back at me - their eyes drawn to mine. Tran had removed the restriction on talking, so I was free to say anything I wanted. I tried starting a conversation with a lady sitting next to us, except she nor anyone else seemed interested in talking to me, so I just kept to myself. The sharp smell of dirty bodies too long without a shower was strong in the room. I did not doubt that I probably contributed to the overall ripeness of the situation.

No, I sensed something else, something different, something intangible about the people here. There was an uneasiness, a fear that seemed to fill the room. I guessed that we had that in common too. Our fear united us even though we had no idea where or how we were to go from here. As I faded back into sleep, I couldn't help but wonder what the fates held for us next.

I didn't have long to wait. In the dark, early hours of that next morning, our dreams of a life in China evaporated with the morning mist. Soldiers armed with flashlights and guns poured through the doors shouting at the tops of their lungs. My body refused to hear the alarm, not wishing to wake. Still, when I did, the scene immediately reminded me of when the soldiers came and destroyed my father's business. I awoke to that same terror I felt that night. A man, an officer from the way he acted, ordered us to stand, to be quiet, and to await instructions. He had a gun.

I heard a few suppressed whimpers as they emanated from the crowd. I tried my best to comply with the order like most of the others. This was doubly difficult since my current state included quivering like jelly on the inside. I watched in horror as the soldier's flashlights played slowly back and forth over each of our faces. The glaring light gave a dark outline to the tears falling from many eyes and provided each of us a deathly glow in our faces. I prayed, and I am sure others joined me in my petition for safety. From the looks on some people's faces, they anticipated the worst and had already made their peace with God.

The officer returned to the front of the group and shouted that, in attempting to escape, we were performing a criminal act, a treasonous act against the Socialist Republic of Vietnam. For that offense, we had to be held accountable. Sounds from outside told me that even more people, presumably military personnel, were surrounding the outside of the building. Their lights played against the outside windows, and their rising voices made even the thought of breaking free an impossible task.

The soldiers surrounding us shoved us roughly with their gun barrels as they herded us like cattle toward the door. There, armed guards, with their weapons ready, watched us expectantly on either side - silently willing us to dare to disobey. When someone did stumble or stray from the line, the soldiers were immediately there to jerk them back into line, doing so as roughly as possible. I was shivering as we exited into the morning air as they pressed, partly from the cold but mostly from the events around me. Tran and I limped together out into the darkened streets. I knew that we were all in this predicament together, but I could not help but feel painfully alone just then. I heard shouting coming from behind me when some fools attempted to defy the order. They refused to leave the room. When a physical struggle erupted, we feared that the soldiers would shoot them on the spot for the trouble they were causing. Instead, the soldiers simply gassed them. Soon, the guards pushed their coughing, retching bodies in line with ours. What little of the gas ventured outside made me want to throw up. I could not imagine getting it sprayed on me directly.

I tried my best to make myself invisible in the folds of Tran's skirt, having limited success. It simply wasn't large enough for me to lose myself inside of it. My mind was racing, stuck on what the soldier had said. I was having a hard time coming to grips with the truth of it. I was a criminal. Worse, I was a criminal against the state. That thought lingered for a moment before I asked myself the next question, the one that scared me most. What would they do to me? I was so frightened! I wanted to go home. I longed to be sleeping peacefully next to my sister on the bunk. How wonderful to be waking to the sound of the rooster down the alley. I wanted to do my chores and make sugar. More than anything, I wished I had never come with Tran on this miserable adventure.

My thoughts flashed back to a young man bleeding out in the traffic circle. I saw with great detail the look of smug satisfaction on his executioner's face. Each word the officer had said rang in my ears. "This is how we treat those that break the law." As my thoughts returned to the present, I lost all hope. My world stopped. I couldn't breathe. If they would shoot someone for stealing bread, what chance had I?

The faces around me said that other prisoners thought much the same thing. We all kept our eyes lowered as we processed out of the building. No one dared to look our captors in the face for fear that they would consider it a threat. Ours were the faces of the dead. Again, I saw the dead boy's body in my mind. I realized that once they killed us, the soldiers would bury us without ceremony, without honor. We would have no funeral with mourners and family speaking of how great we were. Our families would never even know what had happened to us. We would simply be gone.

The men in uniform continued to wave their rifles and prodded us with their barrels when we moved slower than they liked. With every step I took as we crept down the street, I anticipated the bullet that would end my life. When would they do it? Would they execute us privately? All they would need would be a ditch nearby to cover our bodies. That way, only the soldiers would know. Perhaps the government wanted to do it with witnesses - make a public spectacle of our deaths. That would tell the world in no uncertain terms, "Don't try this." Every moment seemed an eternity. Every step was torture. I could feel the tension continuing to build with every step we took. I did not want to die. My heart thumped in my chest so rapidly that I felt positive that it would burst, killing me on the spot. Yet, step after step, no bullets came.

After a while, I was almost at the point where I didn't care what happened, just so long as our captors did something soon. About then, we arrived at a train spur with an empty train just sitting there. That was where the soldiers stopped us. The officer with the bull horn then commanded us to board the train, with the soldiers pushing us to accelerate the process. In silence, I entered the railroad car, confident that the plan was to execute us publicly somewhere else. The officer's next words, however, stopped me in my tracks.

This had to be a dream. The leader's instructions were so surreal. How was this even possible? Somehow, in a complete reversal of his previous statements, the leader now claimed that the government wished us no harm. In fact, instead of punishing us for our crimes, they were more than happy to send us back to our homes in the south, where we could live productive lives for the state. I did not understand what was happening. What was this? Were they sending the criminals against the state home? I hated to complain, but something did not seem right.

Apparently, this entire train was for us; no other passengers would riding along with us. As the engine started up and put us into motion, the soldiers stood at attention and dispassionately watched us leave. Until that very moment, I still waited for the shot or an explosion as the officer detonated the train with explosives. I almost laughed as I considered the irony of allowing the captives to have just a small taste of freedom before snuffing out their lives. Even now, the thought that they would simply send us away was beyond my comprehension. I know that one should never question divine intervention, but did a miracle just occur? Neither I nor any of my friends wanted to challenge why; we just wanted to go - the faster, the better. The rest of the crowd remained silent, also disbelieving the sudden change of events. Even once we were safely outside of Hanoi, everyone stayed within their small groups. Each was unwilling to trust that one of the others might not be a government spy — someone who would inform the authorities on them at the slightest violation of the law.

We also stayed tightlipped on the way back, partly in fear of betrayal but mostly from sheer exhaustion. The stress of our forced march took a lot out of all of us. Even so, rumors flew swiftly through the cars in nervous whispers. When we made our first stop not too far out of Hanoi, the stories told us that the local police had apprehended those who had just exited the train. We were unsure whether to believe this or not. Still, when we arrived at Da Nang Station and personally saw the police arresting Phung Tien and her brother and sister-in-law, we knew the rumor to be the truth.

This was very confusing. Why let us go and then arrest us later? Tran thought they possibly wanted to keep the nature of our arrest quiet. Had we all been arrested at once in Hanoi, the action would have been a big deal with unwanted publicity. By letting the locals capture smaller numbers over one thousand miles, the issue's politics would simply fade away as the train passed on into the distance. Once in custody, the locals would administer our punishments with little attention from Hanoi or China.

After Da Nang, we had thirteen hours to discuss how to stage our arrival at Ho Chi Minh City and what, if anything, we could do to change the outcome. At other stops, people jumped off as the train slowed and made a run for safety, trying desperately to lose themselves among the people along the right of way. The three of us decided that this plan would be the best for Tho as well. After jumping from the train, he could easily blend in with the crowd. Once clear, he could find his way to his father's home and then find a way to let my family know what had happened to us. We all realized that there was no way for Tran to jump, and I was firm in my decision not to leave her. Tran and I would continue to Ho Chi Minh Station and let God handle what fate waited for us there.

When the time came, and the train slowed to a reasonable speed, Tho made his jump, rolled across the ground, jumped up, and threw a cautious wave to let us know he was unharmed. Only minutes later, we arrived at the station. We delayed the inevitable for as long as we could. Everyone had to get off here. This was the last stop for the train. When everyone else was gone, we made our move. As we left, we trembled, leaning against each other, unsure of what awaited us out on the loading platform.

Tran leaned even more heavily on her crutches, trying to look even more pathetic and crippled than she was. I desperately tried to disappear behind her and acted much younger than my age playing on my small form. Carefully we moved, step by step, taking our time to exit the building. With each passing moment, we expected to hear a shout to stop, but no one yelled, no one grabbed us, no one seemed to care. We left the station unmolested by soldiers or police and finally, on the open street, dared to take a deep breath. Tran and I had no idea why the policemen had spared us. The only possible explanation was that our ruse had worked, and the authorities felt that a cripple and a small child simply were not worth the trouble.

By the time we cleared the area, the hour was extremely late. There were few cabs available, and Tran was not sure about the wisdom of hailing one anyway. Instead, we walked across the district to Tran's parents' home in District 1. There we spent what little remained of the night.

Early in the morning, we headed home, still wearing the same clothing that we had left Da Nang in a week before. We were a ragged, bedraggled pair that wandered to the familiar door in Cho Lon that morning. We were so tired and dirty that San didn't even recognize me as her sister. Tho did make the trip safely to his father's home. He sent a message to our family a few days later, letting them know he was fine. He stayed there for a month before venturing out to see us in person.

We received word from Phung Tien's parents that the police had sentenced her to three months in a reeducation camp for her crime against the state. After her release, she wrote to Tran and told how her captors beat and tortured her every day. As for me? For once in my life, I was more than content to willingly do my chores, be a dutiful daughter, and put my dreams of escape to rest. I was so happy to be home.

Fig I-1
Muoi's mother and father, @1965

Fig I-2
Mother and Muoi at Con Phung @ 1969

Fig I-3
One ounce of 24 karat gold
It took eight of these to pay Hung's passage

Fig I-4
Catholic Church courtyard

Fig I-5
Light pole where boy was
executed for stealing bread

Fig I-6
Large alley as seen from
Muoi's second floor
balcony

Fig I-7
Outside entrance to Muoi's house

Fig I-8
First Floor of Muoi's house

Fig I-9
3rd floor room shared with rest of family

Fig I-10
View from 3rd floor window into neighbor's room

Fig I-11
Front row: Hoa (Tran's brother), Tran, Thanh (Tran's sister), Nhi, Unknown friend of Nhi
Second row: Lisa (Muoi)

Fig I-12
Lisa (Muoi) with her childhood friends in 2017

Fig. I-13 The Quan Family (taken some months after Muoi's mother's death)

Fig I-14
Quan family and friends in 2017 at one of their Tuesday
night dinners.

The Chance

Chapter 16

The chance

Figure 16: The escape boat, 1979

I have known many formidable people in my life. None of them have been stronger and more determined than my father. While other families flailed and sometimes fell, ours remained strong and resolute. There is no question in my mind, but that my father's ability to predict, scheme, and plan future events allowed us to survive Vietnam's reunification.

After the raid had destroyed our medicine business, he did his best to stay one or two steps ahead of the government. He seemed to anticipate every new threat that would come our way, and in so doing, predict where the next opportunity for his family might be. He was painfully aware of the border war with Kampuchea and realized that it would be a long and drawn-out affair. Of course, that meant that the army would be needing lots of new volunteers to join the fight. His firstborn son was just the right age. He had to save Hung.

With that thought in mind, my father looked for a way out for his oldest boy. Long before my trip to Da Nang unfolded. Before Tran and I had our misadventures in the north, my father was secretly at work. He made a trip to My Tho and had a quiet conversation with his brother, which revealed a chance for Hung. It seemed that a close friend of Uncle Ho knew a person who was building an escape boat near Long Xuyen, a village upstream on the Mekong. Construction was well underway.

One conversation led to another and eventually led Father to the owner of the boat. The two of them came together, where the owner explained the details.

He said that the venture had the secret blessing of the Vietnamese government. They wanted to have all Chinese people leave Vietnam but knew they could not force them out without angering China. Since they could not afford a confrontation with China, they hoped to encourage people of Chinese descent to leave the country voluntarily. If they could do so informally, they would not incur any responsibility for the evacuation. In this undercover agreement, the boat owner had promised to take Chinese persons out of the country without cost in exchange for clear passage past the Vietnamese Coast Guard.

Despite the promises, there was a cost, and that price was a princely sum, too. Twelve ounces of gold for an adult or eight ounces for a child or youth. That considerable sum would buy a single ticket on the boat. Furthermore, the price was non-negotiable. The boat owner did not doubt that if Father wouldn't pay, someone else would. Escape from the country had become a seller's market with people bidding against each other for a chance to leave. For this opportunity, Father knew that people would line up to go.

It was not entirely the owner's fault that he had to charge such a substantial fee. The bribes paid to government officials made up the lion's share of the cost. Having the Chinese leave Vietnam might be in the country's best interest, but that didn't mean officials couldn't make a profit while facilitating the exodus. For their part, the officials would guarantee that the Vietnamese Coast Guard would look the other way and allow the ship to pass through Vietnamese coastal waters without problems. They also assured that the "escapees" heading to the launch site from different regions would not have transit problems to the departure area. Part of the payment would cover the actual cost of boat construction, fuel, and supplies. A smaller portion would be his profit that would allow him to restart his life elsewhere in the West and was his due for the risks he was taking.

My father did not agree to the plan right away. Before he would commit, he found it necessary to meet with the boat owner on multiple occasions to ask questions and get answers. On one such trip, he required the owner to take him to the construction area to confirm that the boat building was well underway. After this final journey, my father relented. In his thinking, this was the only way he could assure Hung's safety.

Still, the entire scheme had to make Father think. This transaction would require a vast amount of his family's savings, savings that they had collected, hoarded, and protected. Could he turn over such a large sum to a relative stranger as well as the responsibility for his eldest son's life?

If the owner cheated him, Father could not protest to anyone. Officially, the government could not acknowledge this agreement existed. In exchange for this ransom, Hung received passage - a chance, not a guarantee of success because no one knew what would happen in the open sea, just a chance. The two men agreed; gold changed hands; a decision was made; With a handshake, they had settled Hung's fate. My brother was going to leave Vietnam.

When? That was the question. Even though the boat's construction was well underway, The owner needed to do much more before the voyage. He estimated that he would need at least a year before the ship's completion. The builders had to work on it in their spare time while still doing their regular jobs. They also could not take the chance of drawing attention to what they were doing. Even when they completed the boat, the owner still had to acquire enough fuel for the journey, which was no small task in itself. The government rationed fuel so heavily that they would have to purchase diesel fuel in small quantities. That alone could take months.

The owner assured Father that he would notify him as the time drew near. Father agreed. Until that time, the world would go on as usual, no one the wiser.

Out of necessity, Father and Mother kept these plans from me. They felt that the fewer people who knew, the better, and I honestly did not need to know. The whole thing was a huge secret, and it was as simple as that. They could take no chance of anyone accidentally revealing what was happening. Regardless of the Hanoi government's guarantees, this entire enterprise was still officially illegal. If caught, the police would punish everyone involved, including my brother. There was even a chance that the penalty would be death. My parents did inform San and My because the decision would change their duties to the family, and, of course, they told Hung. Not asked, told. No one had spoken to him at any time during the agreement process. Father had not involved Hung with the decision process. The idea had not even occurred to him. After all, the choice was not Hung's to make. That responsibility fell solely to my father. For generations in Chinese culture, that was the way. One of the father's duties was to make agreements on the child's behalf, often without the child's knowledge, let alone permission. This was one of those times.

Looking back, I have often wondered how Hung reacted to the news. I imagined that he took it hard and was probably even angry with Father for a time. Hung was already building a life here and making plans for his future. This decision meant that he would have to forego those plans and leave all of that behind. Leaving his friends would be hard. Many of them, he had known his entire life, and they were very close. Worst of all, he would have to say goodbye to his girlfriend, Oanh. Of course, he knew he had no choice in the matter. He would never argue against Father's wishes. That was not our way. There would be no chance at rebuttal, no complaining about lost things. Father had spoken. He expected Hung's obedience. Obedience would happen. Regardless of his own wishes, Hung would have made his peace with the decision and acquiesced.

In an attempt to rationalize his surrender, he would have reminded himself that the departure was at least a year away after they had completed the boat and outfitted her. A lot can happen during a year. The local authorities could find and destroy the ship, or the owner could change his mind. While he waited, he allowed his life to move forward as if nothing was happening. The plans he had started continued. His relationship with Oanh grew stronger. As he moved on, so did the whole family - those who knew and those of us who didn't. We continued to make and sell our sugar in the new house. The adults attended the committee meetings without complaint. Laundry was washed and dried. Hung worked his cannery job, and the rest of us did our chores and attended school. To the outside world, the Quan household appeared a perfect, functioning part of the Communist machine. Life was normal.

Over the next year, out of sight and out of mind, the boat took form. Unknown men clandestinely gathered supplies and fuel as the project neared completion. On occasion, Father would take a trip down to the boat site to check on their progress and guarantee his investment. There would be no chance that the owner would forget him or the agreement they had together.

The owner said that the boat would hold two-hundred-fifty people comfortably for the journey. Furthermore, they had sold all of the slots. The voyage was fully booked. He made light of the dangers of the journey ahead. In his mind, the voyage would be an easy trip to Malaysia. They would simply float down the Me Kong River and out into the South China Sea. They would then motor past the coast guard using their guaranteed passage. From there, only a day or two of sailing lay between them and Malaysia, and with Malaysia came freedom.

Soon after that last meeting, ticket holders began gathering. It would have been risky for so many people to move to a small village such as Long Xuyên. That would attract a lot of attention from the local populace and their officials - not a good idea. Therefore, the owner bribed a few local officials to look the other way. Officially, the newcomers were temporary workers repurposing an old warehouse near the departure site. The building and grounds had once been a pig farm and pork processing facility before its owners abandoned the property a few years ago. To further mask their actual numbers, the travelers moved in small groups and as individuals to their destination in Long Xuyên.

The large warehouse was perfect for the group's purpose. The structure offered shelter for all inside as well as hiding them from prying eyes. The grounds around the site were a large area extending back to the river itself. That gave them a perfect place for the boats to dock when the time came to go. There were two of them now. With more money to be had, the owner had purchased a smaller boat and pressed it into service to handle the large contingent of persons wanting to go. Following my father's lead, two cousins and an uncle had also paid to go on the trip. They were called and went to the farm at Long Xuyen one to two months early. At the same time, my brother, blissfully unaware that the builders had almost completed their task, blindly continued as he had been.

Finally, in mid-May 1979, the word came for Hung to go. The hour was late. I was already in bed asleep, and Hung, as usual, was not home. He had gone over to his girlfriend's for the evening. The message came with a knock on the grate downstairs, followed by a few whispered words. Soon, the messenger was gone as quickly as he had come. The timing was urgent. Hung would need to leave tonight.

Since neither ours nor Oanh's houses had telephones, someone had to deliver the message in person. My sister, San, rode her bicycle to deliver it. Time was of the essence. There was no time to wait for him to come home on his own. The message had indicated that the boat was mere days from leaving. If he were late getting to the launch site, he would be left behind.

While they waited for his return, my mother and father rapidly gathered a few things for his journey. Hung had an old military-style jacket with pockets everywhere. They packed my mother's ring, a simple gold band, in one jacket pocket while storing other valuable items in others. They knew that these things would come in handy for bartering after arriving at the refugee camp in Malaysia. They also put an American hundred-dollar bill into a money belt for use in an emergency. As almost an afterthought, they threw together a few food items along with some sugar wafers for the voyage itself. Altogether the bundle would have been extremely tiny for such a long journey.

When San arrived at Oanh's place, she pulled Hung aside and informed him that he had to come with her immediately and why. The announcement caught him completely off guard. I doubt that he had forgotten his conversation with Father a year ago, but I am sure he had hoped that he would have more time to get his affairs in order before he left. Hung invented some family emergency to mask his sudden exit. Oanh was, of course, oblivious to what was happening. I am sure Hung was pained that he couldn't tell her the truth, but she couldn't know. He, her boyfriend, her love, was going to disappear that night, and he couldn't even tell her goodbye. The next days would be miserable for her.

I never awoke when Hung finally returned with San around two a.m. He was still bewildered by how quickly things were happening. Nonetheless, he took the things my parents had assembled, stuttered through his goodbyes, and then sprinted the two blocks to the bus station. There, he caught the four-a.m. bus to Long Xuyên.

The twelve-hour ride southward would have given him a lot of time for thought and reflection. I have wondered how conflicted he must have felt as he started on this new path in his life. The future he had dreamed of and had planned for was gone. The new one was unknown, a misty cloud hiding what life held in store for him. If successful, that future held promises that he could not imagine. If the voyage failed, he would disappear from the face of the earth, swallowed up with the countless refugees who had died in their own attempts. Regardless of the outcome, his leaving had a real cost for him. He had turned his back on his friends who would never know which of the two fates had befallen him. What would they think? What would Oanh think?

Blissful in my ignorance, I didn't even realize he was gone. Not only that, I didn't miss him either. I know that sounds terrible, but then again, no one around me seemed to miss him at all. Of course, their omission was intentional. There was no casual talk about him at meals. There were no questions about where he was or when he would return. He seemed to have vanished from our family. Part of this is understandable. After all, Hung was almost a legal adult with a good job and a life of his own. Most of his spare time, he wasn't home anyway. They assumed that he was out visiting his friends or even staying over at the new house, closer to his cannery work. His absence around our house was typical, not unusual at all. There were so many people in our house; it seemed impossible to keep track of everyone - even a brother. We all ate at the same time, but often in different locations, some at the table, but most on the stairs. Over two weeks passed before I discovered, quite accidentally, that he had indeed left us and why he had gone. That was also when I found the universe had other plans for me as well.

Chapter 17

A twist of fate

Figure 17: Boat with plank on the Me Kong near Long Xuyên, 2017

I have noticed that regular, ordinary days are the ones that end up having the most impact on people. On those days, fate seems bored and wants to play games with us and is often offended when a day seems too typical.

I will never forget the perfectly normal morning of Thursday, May 24th, 1979. The day was absolutely gorgeous. Beautiful in a way that only a day with no school could be. That morning, the rooster's first call was practically melodic as it cheered me. Why? I knew that in a short while, the sun would again illuminate the sky, its rays lighting the way while still leaving the alleyways somewhat chilled from the overnight hours.

So, while the roosters crowed and the neighbors' music once again began to reach their bombastic heights, I rejoiced in the knowledge that this was to be a day entirely dedicated to playing. A day like this seemed to scream for play! I glanced disdainfully at my school uniform and Communist youth shirt. Then, I grabbed the glorified rags that constituted my "play clothes." Once appropriately attired for the day ahead, I shot down the stairs and into the alley to meet my friends, not forgetting my allowance, of course.

The morning was rapidly living up to my expectations. Not only were the alleyways still cool. There was even a hint of a breeze winding through them. What was the reason, I wondered, that on days like this, the colors were brighter somehow? Moods were happier. Even the adults, beginning their morning routines, seemed less irritable. Some even dared to have a smile on their faces.

Today, like most play days, I was the first one out in the alley. I ran to my friends' front doors, standing open with their parents busily working inside. Politely, I bowed to the parents, and then, shall we say, actively encouraged the boy or girl to come out. After repeating this process a few times, I had managed to assemble a group in the wider alley for a wild game of competitive marbles.

Competitive marbles sounded so much better than marbles-for-cash, or in other words, gambling. Nevertheless, that was what we did; we gambled. Throughout Cho Lon and even in Ho Chi Minh City, gambling was a commonplace recreation among the adults. Why shouldn't we children follow in their footsteps, right? Some adults like Nhi's father didn't approve of anyone gambling, while others, like her mother, certainly did.

Gambling was the subject of many of their family discussions. I am sure he was dismayed when his wife opened a Mahjong parlor on their second floor several nights a week, but he never let it show. Since Nhi and I knew nothing about gambling, we decided that we should study it. During many of her mother's evening events, Nhi and I would huddle together on the stairs. There, we could see the action taking place and could hear everything going on inside. We closely observed the patrons' actions and behaviors as they gambled. I will always remember the sound of shuffling Mahjong tiles. They sounded so much like clams being stirred in the wok when Mother cooked them. Our careful observation of the players as they set odds, threw down wagers, and won and lost money proved invaluable. Armed with this valuable knowledge, we would go forth and use the information to instruct our friends. Let the games begin!

Of course, our biggest problem was that we needed money to gamble, and, naturally, we had none. Not willing to let a small detail like that hurt our fun, we developed our own currency, empty cigarette packages. The rarer the manufacturer, say the British 555, the greater the value in the games. After the 555 came the American ones, Camel and Winston, for example, would be worth more than any of the Chinese or Vietnamese packages. We would carefully take the empty container, open it up, and rub the foil material flat. We would then carefully fold each packet into a triangular shape. That way, we could nest one package inside another for easier handling and storage. Although the papers were not "real" money, they served our purposes just as well. I promise that we fought as hard for our wrappers in our games as the adults fought for their currency in the gambling halls.

So, on this beautiful May morning made for play, I went out into the alley with my hoard of cigarette papers clutched in my fist. I had gathered them over many lucrative games and had every reason to believe that I would have many more at the end of the day. As my friends took their places, I took mine on the pavement beside them, ready for action.

In this version of marbles, every shot was a betting event. The more complicated the shot, the higher we raised the odds and the louder our voices became. The wagering became more heated, and the intensity and excitement of the game grew. My full attention zeroed in on what was happening in front of me. Nothing else mattered. A bomb could have gone off in the alley, and I would not have noticed it. A squadron of soldiers could have raced past us, and I would not have known. I was entirely in the zone.

At that moment, the game and excitement reached a fever pitch. I did not see my father, mother, and sister, My, come out of the small alley from our house. I didn't see them as they approached and then passed us. As they went toward the main entrance to the hamlet, though, they stopped. My father spoke to my mother for a moment before leaving them and returning to where we were playing. He tapped me on the shoulder a few times. Each tap gained in intensity from the one previous until finally, he had my attention, if only for a moment.

He said, "We are going on a trip and want you to go with us." Did I mention I was in the zone? I was having way too much fun for this, so I looked back down and said, "No." He told me again with a little more steel in his voice, "We are going to see Hung. You need to go." Didn't make any difference to me. I really didn't care what Hung was doing. The answer was still, "No."

There were two facts about my father that I had at that moment wholly forgotten: 1. He was not someone to whom you said no, and 2. He was someone whose temper could go from zero to one hundred in a microsecond. I got both barrels with that last "No." His teeth clenched, and his face turned a shade of red that I am unable to describe. He let me know in no uncertain terms that I was going with them whether I liked the idea or not. Furthermore, we were all leaving immediately. He grabbed my arm with a steel grip and then half dragged, half carried me over to my mother and sister.

Frantically, I attempted to grab some of my loot from my place in the circle as I loudly protested, but he would have none of that. I was unable to get even one of my precious cigarette packages. My friends said nothing. They did not want to incur my father's wrath upon them. They obviously, however, found my situation highly amusing. The looks on their faces beamed with delight, which only added to my building fury. I was so angry! What had I done to deserve this kind of treatment? I had good grades. I did all my chores – most of the time - and sometimes almost cheerfully. I hadn't even been picking on my younger siblings lately. Why was I being punished?

Of course, I kept all this righteous indignation and fury where it belonged, erupting only in the confines of my mind. As unfair as the situation was and as wronged as I was, there was nothing worth further escalating Father's wrath. The stony look on my face would have to suffice as my only outward sign of disobedience. My mood was so terrible that I wasn't paying attention when we came to the main road and turned toward the bus station instead of the new house where I assumed Hung was. There, I watched with burning eyes as Father purchased tickets for us. I couldn't have cared less where we were going.

Even as the bus bounced over the bumpy, cracked pavement that passed for a national highway, I maintained my anger. So great was my fury over my abduction and subsequent loss of "wealth" that I sulked inconsolably as we rode southward—a lot of good that did me. No one cared. No one paid me any attention at all! They just quietly talked among themselves and left me alone in my misery. That just made it worse! I was so mad! The only time I forgot to be angry when I happened to catch a glimpse of a water buffalo in a rice paddy surrounded by thatched huts instead of concrete buildings. At once, I realized that I knew this area. I had been this way several times before. We were going to Grandmother's house!

Just the thought of going to My Tho raised my spirits - just a little. Although my external facade still reflected my anger, inside, I began to think that things were starting to look up. A trip to Grandmother's house was just what I needed. My Tho was always an invitation to adventure. Maybe today wouldn't be a total loss after all. Besides, I knew that I was Grandma's favorite, which pumped my spirits up even more. Nothing like a little spoiling to take the sting out of losing all my worldly possessions. I had no idea what Hung would be doing there, but that was inconsequential.

My dream crashed, however, when the bus veered in the opposite direction of My Tho. Instead, it was going toward the ferry and the river. My much-anticipated good mood collapsed. Anger and disappointment returned with a vengeance.

As the bus pulled onto the ferry, my curiosity about my surroundings started to get the better of me. I had never been this way before, and I had to admit the new experience piqued my interest. We had never gone this way. None of our family lived anywhere around here. As the bus stopped and I had a chance to look around, I realized that the ferry promised an adventure of its own. I was amazed as the attendants loaded dozens of cars and trucks into the ferry's gaping mouth. Although the line of vehicles wanting to cross the river seemed endless, somehow, they all fit perfectly. In only a few minutes, the crew had completed the loading process and pulled up the gates. We were off...but to where?

The ferry required about a half-hour to cross the mile-wide Mekong River. I would have ample time to get out and explore a bit before having to leave. Trust me, after sitting for most of eight hours on a bus alone in my rage; I longed to run around. I quickly abandoned My and my parents to their own devices and set out on my own. There was no fear of my getting lost. The boat was large, but there was nowhere else to go except for a swim in the river, and even I wouldn't do that.

The activity on the water was mesmerizing in its variety. In this part of Vietnam, water moved everything, and today EVERYTHING was moving. Scattered across the muddy water were dozens of large ships, some even bigger than ours, and hundreds of smaller craft all heading downstream. Some of the smaller vessels had so much hay or rice that you couldn't see the boat under the cargo. It appeared as if the captain was sitting atop his load, piloting only his hay down the river. Some boats sat so low in the water that I was sure that the ship would capsize if a small bird landed on the bow.

My thirty minutes of privacy was over way too soon. I didn't have time to look, even briefly, at all the ferry had to offer. As we approached the dock on the far side of the river, a man on the loudspeaker commanded us to return to our vehicles, and, reluctantly, I complied. Only a few minutes later, we were all safely back on the bus, and the ship docked and unloaded, repeating the loading process in reverse. Then, we were back on the road. The bus went a short distance to the village of Long Xuyên, where my father made us get off.

Now, I was truly baffled. What were we doing here? We had no relatives, nor did we have any friends who lived anywhere around here. Before I could ask anyone, Father quickly hailed a *xe lam*, and we were off again. Apparently, he had made this trip before because he never hesitated in his choice of direction or transit. However, I still found myself at a loss to explain why. We were only about two miles outside of the town center when the *xe lam* dropped us off in front of a large building. My confusion grew deeper. I didn't understand this at all. I asked, "Why are we here?" "Hung is here." was my father's curt response. It seemed that he was still a little angry from my morning's tantrum and not quite ready to forgive my disobedience. I thought about his comment. It made absolutely no sense at all. What would Hung be doing here in the middle of nowhere when he was supposed to be working at home?

As I scanned the structure's interior, I saw a large cluster of people assembled near the far end. I then watched as five men separated themselves from the larger group and moved in our direction. My confusion did not improve when I saw Hung come into focus along with our cousins, Hung and Tho. Behind them were my uncles, Chau Nam and Ly Tho. What was going on here? My brother Hung did not appear to be surprised to see my parents but was a little shocked that My and I had accompanied them. I needed some answers.

We found a place to sit, and only then was I told what was going on. I had a hard time grasping what my father was saying initially. Still, as I listened and began to understand, emotions sprang up inside me that I never realized were even there. Was I feeling anger? No, I was perhaps a little upset because they had kept me in the dark, but not angry. No, I believe what I felt was envy. Jealous because my brother was going to get to fulfill my dream. He would be the one to follow my friends who had left, not me. I would be the one left behind. Hung was leaving for the magical West and all the wonders it promised. Granted, I had no concept of the dangers he would face or the uncertainties that were to come. I really didn't care to know. For me, the process was a simple one. Get on a boat and enjoy life. The only problem that I could see was that he was going, and I wasn't.

I tried hard to swallow my disappointment as I congratulated my brother on the grand adventure he was about to begin. Overall, anticipation soared through the crowd. The tension in the air was something you could almost touch. Everyone was so anxious, so ready for their adventure to begin. There was no cooking allowed in the compound, so my mother and My walked into the nearby village where they purchased some food for our evening meal. Later, while we sat and ate, Hung told us that the boat was ready and that he should leave tomorrow evening. At that moment, I realized that this was it. This would be our last night together.

That evening, we huddled together, as did all the other families gathered in the warehouse. There was little light inside, but there was enough that I could start up a conversation with a lady sitting next to us. She and I chatted for a while just to pass the time before going to sleep. All around us were the sounds of nervous people talking and playing games. Occasionally, I even heard babies crying on the far side of the room, their wails bouncing off the walls as only small children can.

Later, as the rest of the family slept, I had some time to think. For me, being here was a terrifying thought. Here we were, clustered together in such close quarters with others. Despite the bribes, we were all involved in what the government would declare an illegal activity. This situation was so familiar – so reminiscent of another group, another space, that time in Hanoi. Sleep did not come easily to me that night. I waited and watched in fear. Worried that the next part of my Hanoi adventure would repeat itself as well, the slightest sound jerked me into alertness. A flash of light across the room reminded me of the soldiers' flashlights and guns. In the end, my fears proved groundless. As the sun dawned, there had been no raid; we had been undisturbed.

That morning...the last morning I reminded myself, we went to the river's edge. There we saw the two boats for the first time floating in the area just off the shore. The plan was for them to sail in tandem to Malaysia. The crews had moored the boats side by side, adjacent to the riverbank with only rough weathered planks spanning the distance between their decks and the shore. Men were moving up and down those planks loading supplies, preparing for the rapidly approaching evening departure.

The larger boat was about sixty feet long and fifteen feet wide, while the other was substantially smaller. It sat in the water like a little boy in its big brother's shadow. Their construction seemed to be of the same dark, rich wood that I had seen used by the boats on the river the day before. The pilot's cabin was simple, a wooden box set in the middle of each ship, which hid the rear portions from my view. The larger boat had an open hatch at the front where I saw men entering and exiting.

Watercraft were a new experience for me. We had been in small boats on the river in Saigon before, but I had no point of reference for ocean fairing vehicles. However, as large as these were, I could not believe that they were big enough to hold the two-hundred-fifty bodies scheduled for this trip.

As the day continued, more people drifted into our encampment, some with family, some with none. Evening crept closer. The crowd's anticipation built to a rousing climax, becoming an energy source that would explode if not tapped soon. At long last, the owner and the captains appeared in front of the crowd. They brought unwelcome news. There would be a delay in the departure for at least a day. There was a long, loud groan from the crowd accompanied by shouts and a few curses thrown into the mix.

Complaining did no good, of course. The owner had made the final decision, and all the complaining in the world would not change that. The people debated loudly among themselves as to why this had occurred. Eventually, their emotions spent, the mob dispersed and began to settle in for the night. I was not sure that I could tolerate spending another night in that building. I feared another night of watching and waiting for the police to raid us. As if reading my thoughts, Hung had arranged for us to sleep under a tarp outside. I sighed in relief. Now there was a refuge from the angry crowds and their accompanying noise. A piece of plastic tied between two trees had never looked so good. As darkness overcame us, gathered as family one last time, a much-needed sleep came over me.

The next day, May 26th, I watched as additional people joined the already sizable assembly. I had no question that the number of people in the compound far exceeded what the boats were supposed to carry. Yet, the crowd seemed blissfully unaware of this. Their mood was festive and excited, fueled by an expectant air of anticipation. The spirit seemed to hover over the group like mosquitoes sensing blood.

The scene reminded me of a crowded market day when hard to get items were supposed to be available. People were excited to be there yet shared a fear that the merchants would run out before they got theirs. That was exactly how this situation was. People were milling about with tons of pent up energy, wanting to do something…anything, but forced to do nothing instead.

The owner and captain again called everyone together in the afternoon. They verified what most of us had already heard via rumors or figured out on our own. The reason for the one-day delay was so that they could add more people to the roster. The state officials had demanded additional gold, 200 ounces to be exact, to guarantee the ships would have safe passage. This additional sum was to pad the bureaucrats' own pockets, but what could he have told them? The government held all the cards in a rigged game.

More and more people poured into the farm, each of them promised a precious spot on the boats. There was no way to win. The owner had to take them all. If he didn't, he would anger the government flunkies, who would then disavow everything, shut the enterprise down, and arrest all concerned for planning to escape. Everyone, now five-hundred and four men, women, and children, had to leave on these two boats tonight no matter how crowded they were.

After completing our evening meal, we accompanied Hung down a dirt path to a place where someone had constructed a temporary enclosure at the riverside. A perimeter fence of chicken wire ran from the ground to the ceiling, effectively isolating the inside area. There was only one way for a person to pass inside, and a burly guard with muscles bulging stood at the opening, daring anyone to get by him. His job was simple. Allow only those with proof of passage to proceed into the second area. All others had to remain outside.

The four of us again gathered around Hung to say goodbye. He was wearing his old army jacket and cutoffs as he left us and entered the gate. Just before entering, he gave us a final wave. Then, as we watched, the crowd inside swallowed him up. As the churning mass of people inside the enclosure grew in number, they milled around nervously, unable to stand still as they impatiently waited for their time to board. Tensions rose, and tempers threatened to flare.

Once the gate guard had successfully separated the visitors from the ticket holders, he stood across the opening as a human barrier. The owner then began calling the name of each person on his roster. That person would then approach one of the two boats and board. One of the terms of boarding had been for those going to part with any Vietnamese money they possessed. They were to place the currency in a bucket strategically placed on the table near the boarding plank. The money would be worthless where they were going, and, this way, it could benefit those staying behind.

Wait! Money? That caught my attention. Maybe Hung couldn't use his money, but I certainly could. I had no idea how much he had with him, and I didn't care. Whatever the amount, no matter how small – that money was going to be mine. I quickly took in the surrounding area making up the plan even as I set it into motion. I began stealthily moving away from my parents. My sister was firmly glued to my mother's side while my father was craning his head every which way, looking for Hung in the crowd. They were oblivious to my actions and would notice nothing, so I said nothing as I deftly moved away from them into the crowd of well-wishers.

I carefully slipped around the edge of the fence. My small form molded itself into any available space while being especially careful not to raise the alarm by stepping on anyone's feet. With skilled moves honed in my dance studies, I dodged in and around people, squeezing myself into smaller and smaller spaces until finally there I was. I was standing next to the gate with only the towering guard blocking my way to my ultimate victory.

Now, I played a waiting game. I stood there, calmly and patiently, waiting for an opening. I had to admit. This guard was good at his job. He diligently scanned the crowd, eyes moving back and forth in a steely stare, daring anyone to challenge him. Fortunately for me, he, like most adults, failed to look down. He did not see any danger down at his feet. There was no threat there. He shifted his stance just a little to get a better look down the fence line. That was all I needed to make my move. In the space of a breath, I folded myself flat against the gate edge and zipped past him. Easy! I was inside. All that sneaking into the Chinese theater actually paid off! I would have to thank my aunt later.

Once inside, I became aware of the owner reading the passengers' names and remembered that I had some urgency in finding Hung before he boarded. I forged onward through the crowd as rapidly as I could, keeping my eyes open for his distinctive jacket. The gathering darkness lit only with the glow of a few dim lights made faces increasingly hard to distinguish in the crowd. I had just about given up, assuring myself that he had already boarded when, out of the corner of my eye, I caught a glimpse of his army jacket. I zoned in and quickly found myself standing beside him and my uncle.

The look on his face when he saw me was precious. He was perplexed. He could not begin to imagine how I got into the enclosure, let alone be standing here in front of him. I demanded the few pennies he carried in his hand. My outstretched hand and a threatening face honed over years of haggling and playing convinced him. His coins changed from his hand to mine. Mission accomplished.

Now that I was inside, though, I could appreciate this new vantage point. I had a much better view here than outside, and as a side bonus, I wouldn't have to slip back past the guard at the gate until everyone else had boarded the ships. I had not been looking forward to explaining to the guard how I came inside. Waiting inside eliminated that risk. I decided to settle in and watch.

So, I stayed there, next to Hung, and in front of my uncle. The owner was reading the names as quickly as he could. Someone else would check off the person's name and direct them toward one of the boats. I was sure that reading names should be a quick process, but it wasn't. Individually naming five-hundred people in low light takes a long time. What had a moment ago been an adventure quickly turned to indifference. Hung decided to move off to one side and began talking to someone over there; I couldn't tell who he was with, and, frankly, I didn't care. I just stayed put and waited.

The droning of the owner's voice was so monotonous that I soon began daydreaming to the sound of the names as they rattled on, one after another. In my subconscious, I pretended that I was making my escape. Hung wasn't there. I was the one going. I imagined hearing him call my name. There I was, walking forward, wearing my favorite polka-dot dress that Mother had made for dance. My parents waved and cheered happily to me as I got on board the boat and all the other people cheered as well. I stood smiling on the deck, waving back to them as the ship set off for the West. It was a wonderful time.

I was so self-absorbed in my fantasies that when the owner called one name, a girl's name, I didn't hear it. He waited for a few seconds, but there was no response to his call. The crowd looked around, getting restless, waiting for someone to shout out and come forward. When no one appeared, the owner called her again, this time a little louder. Once again, there was a restlessness as the crowd impatiently waited. Still, there was no response. He called her name a third time at the top of his voice, echoed by others in the crowd, hoping to draw the girl out. Everyone was more than ready for the process to continue.

Still in my reverie, I was oblivious to what was going on, but my uncle wasn't. He realized that the girl in question was simply not there. In a fraction of a second, he made a life-changing decision for me. With absolutely no warning of his intentions, he shoved me forward - hard - and shouted at the top of his voice, "What are you doing, foolish girl? Go! Go! Go! Why are you still standing here? They have already called you three times!"

His push, along with his yelling, woke me from my daydream. Only a miracle kept me from falling forward onto my face as I stumbled away from him. Once under control, I turned toward my uncle in anger. What did he think he was doing? However, as I turned, I saw everyone's eyes focussed on me, and I froze in place. What was going on here? Why were all these people staring at me? What had just happened? Why was my uncle frantically waving me away from him? He was telling me to hurry. Hurry and do what? Finally, a realization came to me. He was telling me that I was supposed to get on the boat.

My thoughts were a jumbled mess. One thing was sure. I had to decide something. What? The noise of the crowd had shrunk to a murmur after my uncle's shout. People were now glaring in my direction. Strange voices were telling me to move along. What had I done? The crowd began to separate, to create a path for me. I could barely see the loading plank at the end of the track. Should I go?

In desperation, I glanced back toward the visitors behind the gate, frantically looking for my parents, but I couldn't see them anywhere. The faces behind the fence blurred together, even more so as my eyes started to tear-up. It seemed like everyone was staring at me; everyone wanted me to hurry; they expected me to board. If I went, how would my parents know what had happened? What about my brothers and sisters at home? Would Hung get on this boat or the other one? My throat was dry, and my knees were weak. I was no longer safe within my dream of only a few moments ago; this was real.

The few tortuous seconds that had transpired from the time of my uncle's push seemed like hours, and still, I hesitated, unsure of my path. Finally, I closed my eyes and took a deep breath. I chose. I walked forward to the narrow, wobbly plank that seemed to stretch ahead for a thousand miles. I paused just before stepping on it, taking one last opportunity to reconsider my actions before boarding the larger boat.

The Chance

Chapter 18

In the belly of the beast

Figure 18: Boat on the Me Kong, 2017

Have no doubt; I am a formidable person. At home, I would usually walk several miles every day without a second thought. That was just how my life was. That night, the short distance from the shore to the ship felt like the longest trek of my life. My knees felt like rubber, and I feared they would collapse under me at any moment. My throat was dry like I had just run a long race and desperately needed water to drink. In that split second, I had two great fears. One was that I would trip over my own feet, fall off the plank, and plunge into the river below. The other was that at any moment, someone would realize I was a fraud. Someone would notice that my being here was a mistake, a mistake that needed to be corrected.

What would happen they found out? Would security throw me back onto the dock like unwanted trash? I could barely breathe as I awaited my inevitable discovery. Still, I carefully put one foot in front of the other and then did the same again and again until suddenly, I wasn't on the plank anymore. I was on the deck of the large ship.

I found the boat in a state of upheaval. People were going every which way. Where should I go? I started toward the back of the vessel when, out of nowhere, a man wearing a security shirt grabbed me by the arm and roughly pulled me over. I felt sure that he had found me out - discovered me to be a fraud. I steeled myself, ready for a toss to the dock below. Imagine my surprise when instead, he pointed to an open hatch near the front of the boat.

My reserves of courage were practically gone. Still, I tentatively edged over to the hatch where yet another security person was waiting for me. With a stern face that indicated he didn't want any nonsense, he pointed down into the interior of the boat. I looked. Only darkness stared back at me. I didn't want to go and shook my head to indicate it. There had to be another way.

The man was someone used to obedience. Sternly, he pointed down again. I stretched my neck as far as I could to see what was down there, but all I saw was darkness. I was even more convinced that I wanted nothing to do with that place. Going into the hold was one step too far for me.

At my continued hesitation, the guard's face reddened, and in an angry voice, he bellowed in my ear that I needed to get down that ladder – NOW! His voice was so loud and his face so twisted with anger that I realized that staying on the deck was suddenly a more precarious position than going down into the unknown. With a firm resolve, I started down.

After about three steps, I could see a single dim light bulb burning at the back of the room below me. The bulb swung back and forth on its cable and appeared to be the only illumination in the room. As my eyes adjusted to the dim light, I could see how tiny the room was. The area below was about half the size of our third-floor sleeping chamber in our house – about eight by ten feet. Other passengers had already positioned themselves across the rough floor. I was in the middle of counting how many were there when the guard again let out a second shout right above my ear. The sound startled me so that I almost fell the rest of the way down the ladder. I guessed I had been taking too long. I sped to the bottom, left the ladder behind me, and moved toward an open spot on the floor. No sooner had I cleared the ladder than another person appeared to take my place, with another one framed in the hatch above, ready to come down.

A steady stream of people processed down the ladder. As each one entered the space, the rest of us pushed ourselves closer and closer together until I soon understood how a sardine felt in its can. I crammed in with the others, arms wrapped around knees, knees pressed against chins, sides touching other people's sides. Only a few inches separated my face from the back of the person in front of me. Once positioned, I didn't have enough space to wiggle, let alone stand up. Getting up and moving around would be a monumental task and honestly was not worth giving a thought. Breathing alone seemed to be challenging enough. Yet, even packed together as we were, the stream of people continued to flow down the ladder until the human cargo occupied every square inch of space. People sat on top of others to create even a small amount of room for the newcomers. Finally, just when I thought they might stack us to the ceiling, the procession from above stopped.

Now, I heard a loud trampling of feet on the deck above. Many people were moving about above me. Considering our cramped situation, I felt safe in assuming that a person would occupy every possible space on the deck above as well.

Here below, the large number of bodies had caused the naturally warm tropical air to become even hotter with a humidity that made me long for the air back home after a monsoon. This was no longer the air at the riverside. That air had been humid as well, but this was different. This air had joined with the stench of fear and sweat emitted by every person here. The odor was omnipresent. There was no escaping it. We did little talking, and those who did speak spoke only in whispers. I decided that the best thing was to just remain silent for the moment.

Quite accidentally, I managed to find a friendly face in the group. The lady positioned directly in front of me turned her head ever so slightly. Even in the dim light, I managed to recognize her as the lady I had spoken to that first night in the compound when I couldn't sleep. I poked her with a finger and whispered a hello. She managed to turn a little more, which allowed us to converse a little. When she discovered who I was, she beamed with joy. I was a bit confused until she said that she had spoken with my parents.

Now she had my undivided attention. She had been nearby when my uncle pushed me forward and had watched me as I boarded the boat. From our conversation that first night, she knew that I wasn't supposed to be there. She applauded my uncle's actions yet feared that my parents wouldn't know what had happened to me. She turned back toward the fence and pushed through the crowd until she found my parents and My. She quickly told them what had just happened, how I had taken the place of a missing girl. Just as she finished, they called her name, and she had to move back to the front. She didn't have an opportunity to hear my parents' reaction.

Many years later, My would tell me how shaken Mother and Father were over the change in events that night. They had just started to look for me when the lady came to them. They could not understand how I had even gotten inside the enclosure, let alone how I had managed to be selected.

My shocked father was still partly pleased that another child had found a way out - especially at no additional cost to the family. However, my mother's panicked reaction was entirely out of concern for me. She despaired that I was too young for such a venture. I was traveling with nothing more than the clothes on my back, my ratty old play clothes at that. Most of all, she feared for my safety.

She and my father knew far more than I what dangers I would face on the journey ahead. Although no one had ever returned from an escape, many families had received mail from family members who had. The letters detailed the trials they experienced in their journeys both on the sea and in the refugee camps.

My parents knew that the dangers were genuine indeed.

They were concerned that they had not seen Hung board. They realized that there was no guarantee he and I were even on the same boat. The most upsetting part, especially for Mother, was that there had been no time for goodbyes. One moment I had been there standing beside them in the crowd, and the next, I had disappeared.

She knew that this was nothing like the train to Hanoi with Tran. There was no place where I could turn around, no chance of return if I changed my mind. I couldn't simply jump off the boat and walk my way home. For better or worse, this was a one-way trip. Win or lose; this one was for keeps.

The lady's words had reassured me. Sitting in the semi-darkness of the hold, I at least knew that my parents were aware of what had happened. Above us, I heard muted shouts as men cast away the lines tying our craft to shore. I must admit that I jumped a little as the engine roared to life and then idled like a caged beast yearning for release. Soon after, I felt the room tilt ever so slightly, and the engine's pitch and volume increase as the boat made its way sluggishly into the main river channel.

In my mind, I tried to visualize my mother and father. I saw them standing there silently waving goodbye to Hung and me as the boat pushed farther and farther out into the darkness of the river. As we progressed, they kept getting smaller and smaller until, at last, I saw them no more.

The engine's tone kept changing as the boat's speed increased. The growl it produced sounded angry as it protested the heavy load. Sitting in the perpetual twilight of the hold, I felt that I was almost one with the craft. I could sense its motion moving forward along the river. I could feel every direction change as we progressed, at every turn getting closer to the mouth of the Me Kong and our date with the South China Sea. We must have sailed for hours like this.

We now experienced the passage of time with angry muscles protesting our inability to move. I overheard some foolish optimist behind say that our voyage should surely be about over. She honestly thought that we had nearly completed the journey and that we should be sailing into Malaysia any time now.

Right about then, as if to physically slap her hopes out of her mind, the very temperament of the water surrounding us changed. We had no warning as our craft abruptly leaped from the river's relative safety and calmness and out into the unpredictable roiling of the open sea. The change was as unmistakable as it was dramatic. Our journey was not almost over. Our trip had only begun.

The gentle back-and-forth rocking movement of the river shifted to the rougher, rolling action of the sea, and what had been an almost hypnotic gentle motion exchanged itself for wildly random pitching from front to back as we forged our way through the surf and the tidal waters. The change in the water's temperament had a nearly immediate effect on the passengers and their stomachs.

Within the first few minutes, the first person threw-up. After that, a chain reaction began. As one person followed another, nausea cascaded through the entire assembly. Now, the sickening smell of vomit co-mingled with the existing unpleasant odors in the hold, creating a completely wretched stench.

I have no idea why I did not suffer from this disorder. But as more and more succumbed to the condition, the happier I found myself. I was thrilled with having my stomach and its contents staying right where they were. I just continued to sit there in the near darkness, uncertain of my future, with my fellow voyagers in misery. Sometime later, something I had thought impossible happened. Physical and mental exhaustion finally took its toll; the stress of the day faded away as I dropped into a fitful, dreamless sleep.

When I awoke, the world around me had not improved any at all. If anything, the situation was worse than before. The pungent odors that now enveloped me on all sides were beginning to affect me as well. As my stomach started to flip-flop, I realized that something unpleasant was about to happen. I understood that I needed to quickly leave this place; otherwise, I would join my shipmates in their misery.

The people around me appeared to be in a trance or drugged. None of them were very alert. One thing had not changed - our situation. Our bodies flowed from one to the next, and I couldn't find a gap anywhere. I looked around the space again, and still no exit. The only way out of the room, it seemed, was the way I came in. I looked up expectantly and saw a miracle in a shaft of daylight shining from the open hatch with just a hint of blue-sky peeking in from beyond the square opening. I now had a goal. That hatch was where I needed to be. I was positive that I would feel better out in the open air.

How to get there, however, was a problem. I could see no delicate way to accomplish my task, so I opted for the direct approach. After considerable effort, I managed to stand up. I took a deep breath and proceeded to maneuver across the human carpet that lay between the ladder and me. I did try not to step on people and inflict pain, but how can you do that if there was no place to miss them? Try as I might, I would find myself stepping on a hand or a leg, often getting a quick curse for my efforts. More than once, I fell into someone's lap! Slowly but surely, I eventually reached the ladder, and before I lost my resolve, I scurried upward toward the light - the blessed light. Somehow, I needed to make sense of my world, and the top deck of the boat was my only hope to do that.

Nothing could have prepared me for the brilliant light that awaited me at the top. Eyes, adjusted to the darkness below, were blinded by the full sun. Everywhere I looked, there was nothing but light. A moment or two later, when my eyes once again adapted, I was finally able to look around the deck.

I was not ready for what I now saw. There, surrounding me on every side, were people – hundreds of people; people stacked on top of each other like lost baggage with no space visible anywhere around them. My only point of reference was the hold down below, but the deck above appeared even worse. The view shook me to my soul. To avoid looking at them again, I turned my eyes outward and saw water - water everywhere.

I slowly rotated my body to get a better view of the horizon in every direction. Everywhere I looked, there was the same brownish-green water with waves lapping at the edge of the boat's deck. While I watched, some of the larger waves near the bow came over the deck and soaked those unfortunate souls huddled there. No matter where I looked, no matter how I strained my eyes, the one thing I could not see was land. There was no sign of home.

In the reality of that moment, I became fully aware of my situation. The repercussions of what I had done became clear for the first time. I had never known for sure what an escape from Vietnam would be like, but never in my dreams or nightmares had I thought of this.

I thought back to the last time I had attempted to escape. My current situation was nothing like the trip to Hanoi. This time, Tran and her brother were not here to help and protect me. I knew my brother was somewhere on one of the two boats, but I had no way to find out where he was. I could not even be positive which ship he was on. I stood alone on the deck, with the sea all around me, with only the clothes on my back. I was not prepared physically or mentally for a journey like this. I asked myself again, "What had I done? What made me decide to board? Was I really following a dream, or had an empty promise suckered me?

Standing here next to the hatch, I felt small, insignificant, and vulnerable. There were hundreds of people all around me, yet I knew no one except the one woman in the hold, and I had only known her for a day. She was an acquaintance, not a friend - not family. I shivered as a thought came over me. A memory from the day before I left for Da Nang flashed through my consciousness. I had thought the conversation so silly at the time, a needless worry. I had felt then that Mother worried too much. But now, staring out into the never-ending sea, my mother's statement from that day rang true in my ears. "Would I go if it meant never seeing the family again?" I had made my choice, and now her fears became my reality.

I have no idea how long I stood there listening to the lapping waves and the muted mutterings of my fellow passengers. The situation had me frozen, lost in my thoughts, and feeling more than a little sorry for myself. I wondered what I should do. In the end, there was only one choice I could make. At long last, I shrugged my shoulders and decided to go back down the ladder and rejoin the only person I even recognized. Perhaps we could be a team and face our trials together.

"Muoi!"

"Muoi!"

Over the engine's sounds, the sea, and the vague noises of the human cargo, I sensed more than heard my name on the wind.

"Muoi!"

This time I was sure. I had heard my name. My imagination was not playing tricks; someone knew who I was. Someone knew my name. But who was calling me? Who knew me? Frantically, I once again scanned back and forth across the deck, looking desperately for a familiar face, and when I came up empty on my search, I studied the mass of faces once more. There was nothing there. My ears had been playing tricks on me. They knew how much I wanted my family. My hopes crashed once again. My ears had lied. There were no familiar faces in the mass of people surrounding me.

"Muoi!"

Again, that voice! I was positive now that I had not imagined it. Who was calling? I shaded my eyes from the sun with my hand and searched again from stem to stern. I saw so many faces, so many people, scattered around the deck, but I took the time to study every one of them. If I saw a hand move ever so slightly, I would stop and peer closer at the person attached to the movement, praying that what I had seen a wave of recognition. I went back and forth multiple times until - there he was!

There, at the back of the boat, was a man swinging his arms back and forth. Attached to those arms was a familiar face. "Hung!" I screamed at the top of my lungs! I waved my arms desperately in acknowledgment, letting him know that I had seen him. Without giving a thought to what I was doing or who I might hurt, I raced over the people sandwiched together on the deck. I was blissfully unaware of the cries and curses that followed me. I did not stop for anyone until, at last, I threw my arms around Hung. I had found my brother. I was not alone. Gone were the memories of tricks and pranks he had played at my expense. Here, on this boat, he was my savior. I knew that everything would be okay now.

I finally loosened my grip and looked up from his shoulder. There I spotted something even more miraculous. Behind Hung, sitting on the deck at what appeared to be the very end of the ship, were my cousins and uncle. God had listened to my prayers. I could not believe my luck. What were the odds of all of us being together on the same boat? How wonderful!

Wait. The other boat? Realization dawned on me. I had not seen any sign of the other vessel while I had scanned the horizon. Where was the ship? I asked Hung, and he quietly told me that no one had seen the other boat since we left the dock. The original plan had been for the ships to stay together for the entire trip to Malaysia. We had been running without lights all night and hoped the other vessel was just out of sight. This morning, however, when the boat was not with us, everyone feared the worst. Hung and the others especially feared the guards had placed me on that boat and that I too was lost.

Last night as we stood on the riverbank, the crowd had been so thick that no one had been able to see which plank I had walked. My brother had been far enough away from me that he had not heard my uncle's shout or seen me move forward and board. Later, after the family had reunited on board, my uncle told Hung about me being a passenger on one of the two boats.

Another happy coincidence was that one of my cousins, Ly Tho, was on this boat's security detail. He had been able to use his position to grab this small but choice area for us to stay together. Initially, they had intended the space as a latrine (bathroom) that hung over the ship's stern. When the number of people doubled, they repurposed the area as passenger space - our passenger space. The entire area was a small space about 4x4 feet with three-foot walls standing on three sides to allow some privacy. The fourth side was the "toilet." This toilet was not a modern bathroom. It consisted of a square box frame hung out over the ocean. There was just room enough for a single person to squat – we didn't sit - and go. Of course, that was providing that he or she was not squeamish about looking down at the sea waves churning only a few feet below. Even though the limited space meant we were still very crowded, our situation was far better than the rest of those on the deck. This space would have to do because, for better or worse, this space was all that the five of us had. Although just as crowded as space outside and below, having family made our accommodations different. Finding them here had restored my confidence, and I now felt that anything was possible.

As I sat crammed in next to my brother, my head swam with everything that had occurred during the past two days. Those events had turned my life upside down. How had I come from being a somewhat normal twelve-year-old girl playing a game of marbles to sitting on the stern of a very fragile little boat on the vast South China Sea? I reflected upon my time on the roof of my house and my friends who left unannounced so long ago. Was this how their experience had been? Was this what I had wished and prayed for while looking down on the neighborhood?

As unsettling as the past had been, the situation only got worse as our first day at sea continued. The voyage would have been difficult with the planned company of two-hundred-fifty passengers. Now that the number had doubled, conditions were far worse. The boat would have been sluggish before, but now it wallowed like a water buffalo in a rice paddy; its engine taxed far beyond what its manufacturer had intended. We had over five-hundred souls on board this vessel, and the boat seemed to feel each one of them as it protested the load with its creaks.

When I first climbed out of the hold, I had noticed the water was dangerously close to the deck, but now, from my new vantage point, I could see that the water was mere inches from the edge. I sensed that if a large wave came over the boat, it was sure it to swamp us.

The crew had begun to collect materials they could toss overboard and lighten the load. Anything not deemed vital to our mission was fair game. Some persons had paid extra to bring luggage. Too bad. It went over the side of the boat. Valuables and heirlooms didn't matter either. If something had weight, it went into the water. The crew went back and forth to the hold, grabbing anything they could find that had any weight. Some people cried in protest as the crew ripped their possessions from their grasps. Those items joined the others into the sea.

I could not believe my ears. That was easy since I didn't have anything, let alone something of weight. How could people cry in rage over lost things? The process all made perfect sense to me. There could be no future in Malaysia if we all died today. We had to do everything possible for the safety of all. Finally, the last of the purloined items went into the sea, and then we held our breath waiting, hoping that the ship would rise, but the boat stubbornly did not move.

Extras now overboard, the crew looked for other things to go. Supplies of water and gasoline soon joined the floating refuse that trailed our boat. Being a prudent man, the owner had gathered more fuel than necessary just in case of an emergency. Now, we had an emergency, so the excess went over the side. From the toilet, I watched as the containers bobbed in our wake, teasing us for a bit before finally sinking below the surface. When the crew had cut our supplies to the bone, we waited. Then, slowly - begrudgingly - miraculously - the boat rose just a little, a few additional inches. Would such a small amount be enough? Who knew?

So much happened in such a short time. I was surprised to find that noon had not arrived yet. After the excitement settled, we entered into what eventually became our routine. We sat. If our muscles cramped, we sat some more. There was no alternative. I did my best to ignore them as they screamed for me to get up and run somewhere, anywhere. They didn't know that there was no place to go.

All any of us could manage was to stand for a minute or so. At least we had the latrine area over the stern. We took turns going out over the water, taking the opportunity to change our sitting positions for a while before giving one another a chance. We had nothing to eat or drink, so there was little need for the latrine's original function. With little else to do, I started people watching instead. I had gotten quite good at this on the train to Hanoi. Listening and watching had passed the time then. I hoped they would do the same now.

The way people reacted to their new life on board was interesting and kind of funny. There was so much I could tell just by watching their faces. For example, that group over by the pilothouse seemed to be taking their current position in stride, almost stoically, sitting tall. Their look said that they were sure things would eventually improve and that they were happy to wait. Until then, they would be strong and silent. Nothing could shake them from that position.

Some of the people at mid-deck were the exact opposites. They always complained about everything at the top of their voices, bitterness dripping from every word. "Nothing is right." "The crew picked on us." "The captain is lost." "We paid good money for this!" "Why did our things have to be thrown overboard?" I shut out their voices and ignored them.

Then, there was the third group over at the bow. They were the absolute fatalists. I looked at their faces, and I saw death looking back. To them, their world had already collapsed. Their hope was gone. Their eyes showed nothing but darkness in their depths. I hated this group more than either of the others.

The complainers still hoped; they had not given up. They held onto life as precarious as it seemed to be. The last group did not. Their condition would rot them from the inside like a disease, and in time, that disease would infect others. As I watched these groups on that first day, I thought, "How odd a bunch we were." Strange that we would share this journey. Yet, for better or worse, we were here, stuck with each other.

Sometime after mid-day, there was a shout from one of the crew. A smudge had appeared on the horizon. I could not see why I should get excited over a spot. Still, as I watched over the next hour, that smudge continued to grow larger and larger until, at last, the smudge became a ship, a large ship. Our boat quickly changed to an interception course. My family was so excited, as was everyone else on board. Even the fatalists showed a little sign of life stirring within them. Today was only our first day at sea, and I felt sure that rescue was at hand!

The new ship continued to grow until we could see its Dutch flag flying from its center mast. Its deck towered over us. We were like a toy boat in comparison. We all waved colored cloth and screamed at the top of our voices vying for their attention. We begged for them to stop. We pleaded for some mercy. We were so close that I could see men walking on her deck, just going about their tasks. No one seemed to see us! We were right here! Yet, not one person paid any attention to our pleas. We were not invisible. Someone had to have seen us. However, despite everything, the freighter seemed to be a ghost ship unwavering in its path. They continued to maintain their indifference as they left us behind in their wake. No one had even waved back. No one had shouted any encouragement. There had been no response at all.

At that point, my spirits fell from their mountainous heights of a moment ago to their lowest possible depths. I didn't understand. How could they have just kept on going? Why wouldn't they stop? Why, when we were obviously in need of help, was none offered? I could not understand how civilized people could care so little for our plight and just leave us to an uncertain fate.

After that encounter, I looked at our situation differently. I realized that we could not depend on anyone to rescue us. No one was going to save us. Everything was up to us now. Providing we were going the right direction – and there was no reason to think otherwise, we would be near one of the Malaysian islands sometime tomorrow or the day after at the latest. We could do this. We could endure cramped muscles for that long. Later that evening, as the sun set behind us, our reality - our world – our hope – once again centered on this small boat and its overworked, sputtering engine. There had still been no sign of our sister ship, and we feared that she now rested at the bottom of the sea. The sun let out its last light of the day. I, like the others on board, placed my faith in our pilot and our God as we continued to move forward into the endless expanse of the surrounding sea.

Chapter 19

十九

The anger of gods

Figure 19: Storm on the South China Sea

There wasn't much sleeping done that first night. The best I could do was nod off for a few minutes at a time, and I doubted the others had any more luck than I did. There was just no way to get comfortable enough to sleep. As I watched the sunrise on the second day, It reminded me of going to the beach with my family. We would get up while the sun still slept below the horizon so that we could delight in the dawn of a new day. When the sun rose, it was such a joyful occasion. Now, all the sun revealed as it rose over the horizon was empty seas, and the promise of blistering heat. The romance of the moment was lost to me.

Unable to move more than an inch or two, I remained in a near-perpetual stupor as I faded in and out of sleep. When I was fully awake, I depended on my fertile imagination and intermittent daydreams to provide entertainment. There was absolutely nothing else happening, and, despite the dire circumstances of my existence surrounding me, I became bored. I knew that I wasn't alone, either. No one was exempt except possibly, hopefully, our captain and crew. Everywhere across the deck, the malaise of the monotony was visible. The people sat limp while attempting to shield their eyes with pieces of cloth as the sun laughed at their efforts. They squirmed around as they stretched every direction they could think of to try for an extra inch of space.

There was little food or water on board. Individuals had brought small containers for personal use, but most of it was gone now. The captain had jettisoned much of the ship's stores on the first day to lighten the boat. My little group was fortunate that Mother had the foresight to include the stash of sugar wafers in Hung's sack. Every so often, we would each get one. We allowed them to dissolve slowly on our tongues.

No fancy meal ever tasted as good as that wafer. There wasn't much substance, but it staved off hunger for a bit and kept our mouths a little moist.

During the rest of the morning, I saw other small smudges on the horizon. As I remembered the Dutch ship's appearance yesterday, my hopes rose. Unfortunately, these smudges resolved themselves into a few refugee boats scattered across the glistening sea. They looked just like us, listless and quiet as the morning heat grew. Of course, I am confident that they thought the same of us as they eyed our boat across the water. They made no sound. The only noises I could hear were those of our engine as it sputtered along.

I scanned back and forth, looking for a sign of our sister ship somewhere out among this ragtag fleet, but she was not anywhere in sight. I did not attempt to wave or greet the others. They did not try to hail us. After all, we were all in the same situation; there was no point in wasting the energy on waving or yelling. We obviously could not provide any relief for ourselves, let alone aid anyone else.

I continued watching the other boats bobbing in the water. I was fascinated by the novelty of their presence, ever so much more interesting than the blank sea. Then, as slowly and silently as they had appeared, they gradually faded away into the horizon. Each of them going their own way to search toward their own unique destiny. A short time later, I began to wonder if I had seen them at all. Had they just been a mirage? A daydream? I didn't know. They seemed real, but then most mirages do. Maybe the vision was of what waited for us. Real or imagined, I longed for them to return or, in their place, something, anything, else that would break this monotonous nothingness that surrounded us.

Along about mid-afternoon, a much larger, wider smudge appeared on the horizon. We watched expectantly, but this one did not turn into a ship. Instead, a massive cloud bank exploded outward from the smudge as if conjured by a powerful sorcerer whom we had angered.

I watched as the darkness consumed the once blindingly bright day until the sky was as black as midnight on the night of a new moon. Only with extreme effort could I make out the fingers on my hand as I held them out in front of my eyes. The bodies on the deck appeared only as outlines of shadows. There had been a slight breeze that morning that had gently blown my hair from my face. That breeze had erupted into a gale-force wind that would have knocked me over had I been standing. The wind swooshed anything loose on the deck off into the even darker void beyond almost instantly. The boat rocked violently back and forth as the gentle lapping of the waves turned into giant monsters that sent torrents of water over us.

Blinding flashes of lightning and ear-shattering claps of thunder accompanied this upheaval of the sea. The thunder deafened me, but at least the lightning allowed me to see what was going on. I could see the men on deck struggling to move as they attempted to lock down the hatches to the lower areas before the waters cascading over us found their way below decks. A barely audible shout went up to grab anything that would hold water. We needed to bail as much of this water back to the sea as possible. The task was herculean. Our bailing with the few empty containers at our disposal seemed worse than fruitless. For every gallon we threw back, the sea threw a thousand more our way.

As the ship continued bucking the storm, the crew instructed those of us on deck to lock our arms and legs together. The idea was to form a human net, a webbing to hold all the people together. I am not sure who came up with this idea, but I am positive that "net" saved many lives that day. We held tightly to each other. If any one person went overboard, the sea would take us all.

Amidst the waves and lightning, as if they weren't enough, torrential rains came to beat us down. These were not the rains of home. Not even the monsoons whose water fell straight down and could fill our alley in minutes could compare with this. The monsoons were to this experience as a gentle shower was to a monsoon. I watched in awe as solid curtains of water collapsed on the deck, one after another. The deluge was like a sea god dumping giant buckets of water over us again and again. He delighted in the drowned rat expressions on our faces and our sputtering attempts to draw a breath.

Between the curtains of rain, flashes of lightning illuminated the scene. I watched fearfully as the boat's bow plunged under the water. The ship held its breath for a minute, as did I, and then miraculously shoved its nose skyward again. I was beyond wonder when I saw that our human web of flesh remained intact even as seawater cascaded across the bodies and then over the sides of the ship. The people on the deck sat with their eyes closed, trembling from either fear or the frigid water that the waves had dredged up from the depths of the ocean.

Through all of it, everyone remained clustered together, their arms and legs interlocked for the safety of all. Our vessel and our bodies were one, tied together as a single entity. If one failed, we all failed. There was nothing else we could do except ride the storm out. We were now utterly dependent on the whims of the raging storm and sea.

The boat steamed directly into the storm. Somehow, the captain had forced the boat into the wind. Had he not, the waves assaulting the bow would have gone over our sides, and we would have capsized for sure. Even so, our survival chances seemed bleak as the boat rocked and lurched in response to the storm's fury. Even the boards beneath my feet were shrieking in pain. The godlike denizens of the sea seemed angered with our presence. They appeared intent on ripping us apart board by board to assure our destruction. Only once did I have the courage to look out over the latrine box to the sea below. The sea appeared as a boiling cauldron. It frothed up and down and once even shot up to slap me in its anger. As the boat's bow went down into the waves, I could see the single propeller spinning as it came out of the water. The lightning's strobe effect made everything seem in slow motion - a climactic scene to some unnamed disaster film, totally surreal, a Salvador Dali painting come to life. I imagined a battle between gods and men, and, from where I sat, the gods were winning.

The storm was omnipotent. It drowned out every word of every prayer that dared to spout forth from my lips. Even if I could shout, my humble words would not - could not penetrate past the storm. Who was I when compared to this crashing behemoth? The constant pounding of wind and rain became expected, a new normal. I could not imagine anything else existed. Had I begged for something different to look at only this morning? How foolish I was. Did my prayer bring this onslaught upon us? Now I could see plenty. Rain and lightning assaulted my eyes while blasts of thunder deafened my ears. I lost all sense of time. My world had a new center; the storm was the only thing that mattered.

How much time had passed? Hours? Days? I reneged on my previous prayer and wistfully wished to have the brilliant sun and vacant sea once again. I longed for a gentle breeze to lightly touch my hair.

Not long after that, just as I was about to abandon all hope, just as I was resigning myself to this watery reality forever...the storm just stopped.

For whatever reason, in answer to whatever prayer, the sea gods cast their hands over the frothing maelstrom and turned it eerily calm once again. The black, strobe-lit skies evaporated into a beautiful blue dome. The lightning laced clouds moved away until the blazing sun returned to the heavens. Then, as our ears recovered, the deafening thunder turned back into the sound of our engine's thrum, again the only non-human sound I could hear.

The nightmare was over. We watched as its darkness swept away from us, growing smaller with every gasping breath we took. The storm went on to find other ships and to torment other wayfarers. Its waves of water searched for other lands to bathe in its torrents. It was now the afternoon. In the blessed heat, I watched as the water on the deck and our bodies turned to steam that danced into the sky with joy in the sun's burning light.

The human web had undoubtedly saved our lives. Now, it slowly dissolved until, once again, the outlines of individual beings appeared. We still had no way to move around, but our ability to ride out the storm seemed to fill us with renewed courage and strength – even a bit of hope and joy. I could actually hear laughter rising alongside the steam as we rejoiced together, strengthened by our ability to survive. Men reopened the deck hatches, allowing fresh air to once again flow to the people trapped below. I wondered how they had survived down there, thrown against the bulwarks, unable to anticipate the ship's movements. As frightened as I had been up here, below deck would have been insufferable.

I thought back to the complaining of yesterday as the crew threw personal belongings overboard. Hopefully, all could now see the wisdom of that act. Had they not raised the boat that morning, we wouldn't have stood a chance. The ship would have swamped. We would have perished beneath the waves. We were amazed and delighted that not one of our number had died.

Not everything was wonderful, though. The ship suffered some damage. My cousin told us that the ship's instruments had stopped working and could no longer tell us where we were. Things had happened so fast as we reacted to the storm that the captain had no way to know where the storm had blown us. All he knew for sure was that we were far off our course. Hope was not lost, however. He quoted the captain as saying, "If we keep going in the same direction long enough, we will run into something." These were not precisely the inspiring words that I wanted to hear. What if, in our wanderings, we accidentally went back to Vietnam and the reeducation and possibly prison that awaited us there? That thought sobered me up. It settled into the recesses of my mind even as a myriad of stars popped into the heavens. They cast a gentle glow over the now calm sea.

I realized then that there was an error in my thinking. Silly girl, Malaysia and the Philippines were east, and

Vietnam was west. So long as we could tell the directions, we would get where we are going, and the rising and setting of the sun and the moon would give us that. Months later, when I looked back, I realized that my fear should not have been going back to Vietnam, but the possibility that our fuel would run out and we would not reach any port at all.

Chapter 20

The deceptions of men

Figure 20: Thai Fishing Boat at Sea

The rest of the afternoon had proven uneventful. Gradually, the returned reality of our mundane existence on board replaced the euphoric high received from surviving the storm. As the sun sank beneath the waves in the west and darkness covered us with its blanket, our exhausted bodies prepared for another sleepless night.

A shout arose from the forward deck, with many more soon following each one a little louder in intensity. There, in the distance, faint lights had appeared off the ship's right-hand side, lights from another boat. What to do? Our captain hesitated in the thought. Should he expend fuel to chase the lights to their source, or should he stay the course toward the east? The ship could contain friends or foes, and he had no way of knowing which one would await them, but he also knew how dire our situation was. Our fuel levels were critical, and our bodies were beginning to show the effects of no food or drink. He realized that there wasn't a choice to make at all. He changed course to intercept the newcomer. Whether they held rescue, directions, or just ignored us, he did not care. We needed to find a sanctuary soon. Our survival depended on it.

Hundreds of eyes peered out of the darkness toward the lights as we angled toward them. When we came closer, we could see that the ship was a fishing boat with nets hanging from the masts, about the same size as our own. The fishermen on board were from Thailand and seemed quite pleased to see us.

Our captain and owner spoke with them for a considerable time. They did not speak Vietnamese or Chinese, and we did not speak Thai. Finally, using rudimentary sign language, the two captains made a contract. When the captain and owner returned to our ship, they brought the news for which we had hoped. To our joy, the fishermen said they would help us find our way to a safe port. To our dismay, they would only do so if we paid them. They would leave us to seek our fate in the sea without gold and other valuables to seal the deal. Our problem was that we had little in the way of valuables aboard. The first day had seen much of our wealth go to the bottom of the sea. Nevertheless, we dug deep in our bags and pockets for whatever we had to make the payment. When our turn came, we had to contribute as well. My brother begrudgingly gave up my mother's gold ring as the payment from the five of us. In that so many had given nothing – or perhaps had nothing more to offer, he felt a little cheated by the large payment he had to make. I, too, was saddened to see this physical memory of my mother disappear forever into the collection bag. My mother gave it to him for emergencies. I understood that, but I also hated to lose something so close to her.

I was surprised that other people showed no hesitation as they passed jewels and gold from their hands to the collection bag. They practically raced to remove their rings and watches. They had suffered two days on the water and would do anything to shorten their journey. The reward of a landfall tomorrow seemed almost too good to be true - another miracle! People wept because we had found someone willing to help us! A wave of relief washed over the ship. The ship itself seemed to sigh and relax along with its human cargo. What did the cost matter? We were saved! Our crew took our collected valuables and combined those with the remaining fuel and water from our stores. We hoped that the collected wealth would be enough to satisfy the fishermen.

The Thai crew was satisfied with the payment. After the money changed hands, they attached a towline to our bow. Then, per our agreement, the fishermen invited several security people, including my cousin, aboard their boat. They were to be our insurance against the Thai changing the deal. Finally, after everyone was in place, the line between our boats tightened, and our ships began to move as one.

The pitch of the Thai boat's engine rose as it strained to tow the additional weight. The steady thrum filled the air and grew louder under the increased load. I was so excited at the prospect of our rescue that I feared I would not sleep. I should not have been afraid. The lapping of the water, the drone of the diesel engine, and the feeling of stress leaving my body soon found me softly snoring between my brother and my cousin.

There was no way to tell how long I slept, but I would guess that sometime in the early hours of the morning, loud sounds woke me. At first, I was so groggy with sleep that I could not tell what was happening. Then, the random sounds resolved themselves into shouts and screams. They seemed to be coming from up ahead, possibly from the other ship. As more of our people stirred, different sounds pierced the night. These were the angry sounds of metal on metal—angry voices combined with the sounds of fighting. Something was happening aboard the Thai vessel. We had just enough starlight to outline the back of their boat. A minute later, we saw the shadows of people flailing as they jumped from the ship's stern into the dark sea. They splashed wildly and cried for help from us. The crew managed to throw what little floatation assistance we had in their direction while the people at the edge of the deck helped the swimmers board when they got close enough. A shout came from the deck ahead. Other people joined the cry as more people recognized the swimmers. The Thai had forced our security team into the sea!

Reports started filtering back to the rest of us as the rescue continued. The Thai had initially treated our men with care and respect. They had fed them and given them a clear place on the deck to sleep. However, later in the night, the Thai showed their true nature by attempting a sneak attack on our men. Luckily, one man laid awake, unable to sleep, when the Thai struck. He was the one who sounded the alarm that roused and undoubtedly saved the rest of the team. After a short fight, our men realized that the Thai were too organized and armed with machetes and pipes. Our men made a hasty retreat and jumped into the water.

Our captain ordered every light extinguished. One man severed the tow rope connecting us to the pirate vessel while the captain used our momentum to veer us off on a tangent. Then, he allowed us to drift. The crew herded all the women and young children below deck in the stern to protect them if the Thai returned and attacked the ship itself. I had not been in this part of the boat before. This space was much larger than the hold in the front where I had spent that first night. Each of us took grease and dirt from the floor and rubbed them on our faces. This disguise would make us more difficult to see in the darkened hold.

The captain gathered the men and older boys and prepared them to defend the ship. Each of them tied a piece of cloth to their arms, a primitive yet effective way to identify each other if they had to fight. Next, a mad search went out to find anything the men could feasibly use as a weapon. Anything with length or weight would work in this situation.

Everyone now recognized the Thai for what they were - pirates. If they chose to pursue us, we had to be ready to fight for our lives. We knew what was at stake. We would not go quietly.

The rest of the night seemed interminable. We drifted silently, afraid to breathe or cough. The gentle creaking of the ship's timbers sounded like fireworks to our attuned ears. We kept waiting for the sound of a struggle above that would indicate the pirate's return. Seconds ticked slowly into minutes, and minutes stretched into hours. Our circumstances left us with nothing but those terrible things that creep into our imaginations when sitting crushed together in the dark. Regardless of the large numbers around me, I felt alone and trapped.

Long after the break of dawn, the sea around us remained empty, and the men finally felt it safe enough to allow us up from below. There had been no sign of the pirates during the night. It seemed that the gold and jewels we provided satisfied them. They had already taken everything; why come back? When I finally came out of the hold and rejoined my family, I cast my gaze outward and saw that we were once again the only spot on an endless blue sea.

Who could have known that those fishermen, our saviors, were nothing more than pirates? The clues were there if only we had seen them. The fact that they had demanded our fuel and water supplies as part of their payment should have screamed their intentions, as should have the requirement to have the full price upfront. Men like these supposedly littered the South China Sea with their deceptions and lies. Rumors had said that whenever pirates overcame a refugee boat, they preyed upon them—milking them for everything they had. They knew that the powerless refugees would give them anything in return for safety.

The pirates would then gather anything of value and strip the vessel of its fuel and supplies. The luckier refugees would then be set adrift without fuel and water to be at the mercy of the sea, much as we were. Those people at least had a chance, a slim one, but a chance nonetheless. Pirates towed the unlucky ones to hidden ports on the mainland, where they raped the women and sold them as human cargo - slaves. The men would have a different fate. The pirates would simply kill them.

Later, when we discussed the event, most of us felt that our pirates had been fishermen like they had said. Only later, after our men were aboard, did the Thai reconsider their position and decide that piracy would pay better. As they talked below the decks, they probably thought, "Why should we take them anywhere?" The bungled attempted assassination of our people showed their inexperience and, fortunately, incompetence. Had they had guns aboard, the situation could have been disastrous. Granted, this was a terrible experience, costly in money and morale, but we were still intact. In my mind, our situation could have been so much worse. No one had died. No one was raped.

For the rest of the day, hundreds of eyes scanned every horizon. We vigilantly watched for any smudge on the horizon, any indication that the Thai were returning. As mid-day passed with no sign of them, our concern shifted to other things. Where had they led us? The Thai had towed us for several hours before we cut the rope. We had thought ourselves safe, even rescued, so no one had thought of making a note of our speed or direction.

To make matters worse, the pirates had stripped the boat of everything they thought had value. All we could do was drift along with the currents - not an encouraging prospect. The worst thing was that they had stolen our hope along with our money. All around me were people who had been crazy with joy just a few hours ago. Now, those same people seemed utterly lost in despair. They sprawled across the deck as best they could, drowsy and listless. Many looked sick; some appeared almost dead.

That is a novel thought. What if we were dead? What if this was our hell and the storm and the pirates were demons sent to torture us? What if this was our fate, to forever sail across an endless sea tormented by demons?

No. This could not be. I was tired and depressed like anyone else, but I refused to give up. I refused to believe that this was our forever. I would not sacrifice my hope. The thought of my brother and me dying never crossed my mind as I stared into the empty sea.

Chapter 21

二十一

Miracles

Figure 21: The Kua Koon, 1979

By the third morning, the combination of sun, hunger, and dehydration was beginning to take its toll on me and the others. As I looked around the deck that morning, try as I might, nothing stayed in focus. The images around me swam across my eyes, eluding all my attempts to capture them. I tried to think back to before the trip had started, but I couldn't concentrate anymore. Family, friends, home…all my memories faded into the uniform gray background of my mind. The passing of time didn't seem relevant anymore. How long had our journey been, three days…four…ten? I hadn't had anything to eat or drink except sugar wafers for so long that my body matched my will. They both had no strength left at all.

No one on board had died. That was a miracle all by itself. Even after all the trials we had suffered, all five-hundred and four souls we started with were still here. The excitement shown only three days ago by our group of adventurers had almost evaporated. I found it hard to imagine that it had only been three days since we stood on the dock. We were no longer those people. Our adventures in that short period had taken their toll on all of us. I felt confident that we only had a little time before the older and weaker members of our company succumbed to death.

Even now, as I fought to keep my spirits up, I was beginning to question our ability to survive much longer. I reminisced about those we had left behind, and a sense of sadness overtook me. Mother had been right. I might never see my family again. I tried desperately to conjure up a vision of my mother, something to hold on to, but could not keep her image intact in my mind. I missed her so. I prayed that she would instinctively understand that when she thought of me.

Another glance over the deck. All I could see was weathered bodies stacked like cordwood. Only an occasional movement indicated that we were not already a ghost ship. Out of fuel, we drifted aimlessly across the sea. I could see a dread in the hungry faces of my shipmates, and I was thankful that I had no mirror to see my own. I could almost taste the despair drifting on the breeze.

Just then, when we had all but abandoned hope, a shout came up from the pilot's box. Another streak was spotted just coming over the horizon. I remembered how a similar announcement had caused delight on the first day. Today, there was barely any reaction at all. I guess we knew that this ship would be just like that first one we had seen. I knew the crew would ignore us. In our current state, even pirates would not give us a second look, let alone investigate. The approaching ship would pass, and we would still be like this afterward. With no fuel, we couldn't approach them even if we wanted to.

The new ship grew and grew. It seemed to head straight for us on its own as if drawn to us by an unknown force. When the vessel was close enough, men on the deck looked down on us, pointing and talking among themselves. We struggled to even wave in our weakened state—no more frantic waves of cloth that had welcomed the Dutch freighter that first day.

Even as we watched, the new ship slowed its approach coming to a stop a short distance away. This thing was huge! This boat was by far the largest ship we had seen. Despite our experiences with the other, my spirits rose, just a little at the possibility of aid. A short time later, the captain of the ship called to us over a bullhorn. Were we in need of assistance? This got our attention! Did we need help! Yes!

Suddenly, I became aware that the captain was speaking Vietnamese. For just a moment, I became fearful that we would have to return to Vietnam. Then, in the next breath, I realized that outcome would still be better than what was happening to us now. The more I listened to him, though, I realized that his command of the language was not that of a native speaker. His speech was not much better than my own. He had undoubtedly picked up some Vietnamese in his wanderings.

The ship was the Thai freighter, *Kua Koon*, carrying wood from Indonesia to Bangkok. Her crew threw ropes to us to pull our vessel alongside her. Once we were in place, our people surged forward almost as one attempting to use the ropes to climb aboard, nearly capsizing our boat in the process. Some of our people had not moved more than a couple of inches since leaving the riverbank; it was miraculous that their muscles worked at all.

Another shout from the freighter silenced us. The freighter's captain ordered everyone back to their places. He promised to take care of everyone, but the removal must be orderly. If we could not comply, he would take his ship and leave. We were not sure whether that was a promise or a threat. Regardless, that settled us down in a hurry. We awaited further instructions.

The captain outlined a triage method of moving people to his boat. The first to board were the elderly. In their weakened condition, they would require the most help as well as medical assistance. The women and children would follow. The remaining men and older boys would remain on our boat for the time being. Hung and my uncle took care to ensure that my younger cousin and I boarded safely in the first group of women and children.

At that moment, I realized how many women and children were on board. When the crew had completed our transfer, only about fifty men remained on our vessel. Aboard the freighter, the crew erected a large tarp over the deck to give us some protection from the sun's rays and provided us with food and fresh water. The ship's medic provided emergency medical care for those who needed it. They then attached a tow line to our boat, which then allowed itself to fall behind the freighter. As the larger ship began moving, the rope tightened, and our boat began to follow behind.

After our experience with the fishermen, I have no idea why we were not warier of this group. They were Thai like the others. We should have been more alert to this outpouring of compassion. There had been no hint of betrayal from the fishermen initially either. Nonetheless, this felt different. They had not demanded payment of us this time as pirates surely would have. In fact, they freely offered us food and water with no promises of reward for their mercy. It was true that they had effectively separated the elderly, women, and children from the only ones who could defend us, but really what else could we do? We were people at the end of our rope. Death had been beating at our door, demanding to allowed entry.

As I sipped my water, I silently observed the change in mood around me. Only a few hours ago, we had each been making our peace with God and preparing for the worst. Now we were here - we were saved. We reveled in the shade from the sun as we ate prepared food and drank clean water. Now all the people could talk about was how remarkable our sudden change of fortune had been. Hope raised its head, not fully restored, but well on its way. If we had made a mistake in trusting them, if we had erred in our judgment, then we would have to live with that. Our only other choice had been death itself.

The freighter was gigantic when compared to the boat we had left. I watched from the stern as our boat drifted behind, looking very much like a tiny duckling trying to keep up with its mother. Because of her size, we luxuriated in the ability to stretch and walk, dare I say run, around the deck. On every face I saw, a smile looked back at me. Back on our boat, our men also enjoyed newfound space and freedom made available by our absence. The crew of the freighter had sent food and water to them even as they served us above. This was a good day.

After we had bedded down for the night, the freighter's captain went to our boat. He needed to discuss our future with the men. He advised them that Thai law forbade Thai commercial vessels from helping refugees in any form. Bringing them into any of the country's ports would be out of the question. Any violations of this law would result in the ship captain going to prison for many years.

He was honest with them. Because of the threat of punishment, he had seriously considered ignoring us and going on to Bangkok - leaving us to our fate. However, as he approached our vessel and saw our pitiful condition, he realized that he couldn't abandon us. His conscience triumphed over the law. Now, as he addressed our men, a new question emerged for discussion. What should he do with us now? In his way of thinking, he could only see one way to take care of us and satisfy the law.

He continued to explain. As we approached Thai waters, all of us would return to our boat. His crew would supply our vessel with enough fuel to reach land and more than enough food and water to last for a couple of days after we arrived. He felt optimistic that those supplies should be enough to get us to the refugee camp outside Bangkok. In return, his only request was that no one mentions his name or his ship in conversations with anyone there.

The captain's statements were not what the men had hoped to hear. They had heard numerous rumors about the Bangkok refugee camp and the poor conditions there. Stories abounded about those whose boats had cast them upon Thai shores. Some found their way to the camp, but others often fell victim to pirates and slavers. Even if we made it to the refugee camp, they were said to be severely overcrowded and underfunded.

Additionally, people, particularly women and girls, often disappeared from those camps, taken by evil men who sold them into prostitution and other forms of slavery. Everyone agreed that the Thai captain's proposal would be the worst-case scenario. The men knew that there had to be a better solution to the problem.

The solution turned out to be an act of desperation. The captain's proposal had fallen on hardened ears, so our men took matters into their own hands. They hoped that if they damaged our boat so that the trip to land was impossible, the captain would reconsider his decision. This was quite a gamble. The captain had been sympathetic once; there was no indication he would do so again.

They decided to take that risk. The men bet everything on the chance that the captain would again flout Thai laws and save them.

They put their plan into action that night, after everyone but the night watch on the freighter had gone to sleep. The men split into two groups. Some of them took makeshift hammers and clubs to the engine damaging it beyond repair. Other men used brute force to pry open already weak sections in the hull. They singled out those planks where water was already seeping inside. They knew that the damage from the night's activities had to appear coincidental or the result of the pirate's raid. It could not look like deliberate sabotage if they were to sway the captain's mind.

Shortly after dawn, as the water rose slowly and steadily in the hold, our men shouted a mayday to the freighter's watchman, begging for rescue. Rather than allowing our men to die, the crew pulled them to safety as the boat began to tilt toward the sea. As the last few men crawled over the freighter's edge, the Thai crew severed the tow line, and our small boat sank forever beneath the waves of the South China Sea.

We had endured much together on that craft. I hated to see it go this way. Some of the other passengers bemoaned the fact their few remaining belongings went down with her. Our men ignored their cries and fought the urge to smile. They stoically stood side-by-side as they watched the boat sink. They dared not allow their inward joy to show. They knew that their actions had won the better bargain for us all. Bangkok was still far away. We would deal with those problems then.

Two days later, we arrived.

On day one, we added a new passenger, a beautiful, healthy boy. Two of our women had been pregnant when we left Vietnam, and we had expected this one's birth at any time. Now, he was here. The mother had feared for her unborn child. What kind of existence would he have? Now, the world he entered was entirely different. We all celebrated the joy of his birth. After everything that had happened to us, this was a sign of good fortune, a new beginning, a new life! His mother named him Kua Koon, after the ship that had saved him and us.

I adjusted quickly to our new surroundings, relishing the sense of freedom and happiness provided by the expansive deck. The captain had banned us from the crew's quarters, but the entirety of the deck was ours to explore – my playground. I never worried about what would happen when we got to Bangkok. I had seen more terrible things over the past week than most people did in a lifetime. Today was a gift from a benevolent God. What would happen tomorrow? I didn't know, and I didn't care. That would be for the fates to decide.

So, I spent the day enjoying the present. Faith had gotten us to this point. How could faith not continue leading us in the right direction? Blissfully, I ran barefooted across the wood stockpiled on the deck, loving the simple act of moving about, something I would never take for granted again. In the beginning, the wood planks that made up the freighter's cargo were rough, but over our days onboard, as we passed back and forth across it, we wore them smooth. Such was our joy.

The freighter crew continued to do things to make our lives with them better, more bearable. The addition of five-hundred additional people taxed the ship's facilities to the maximum. There was enough water to get us to port, and the crew would supplement the food supply with fish from the sea. The biggest issue now was sanitation. Now that we were eating and drinking, other biological functions began to "flow" naturally again.

The crew put together a makeshift shower and latrine at the stern of the freighter for our use. Marked off with tarps and plastic, it provided us with a modicum of privacy as we bathed and relieved ourselves. The crew provided a hose to wash our bodies and wash our bodily waste off the boat with saltwater.

Once, while I was washing the deck after a trip to the latrine, something glittery caught my eye. I reached down and picked up - a gold pendant! Heavy gold. What a fantastic find! Something of this size would be worth a great deal of money, more than making up for our mother's lost ring. I never wondered who had lost it. That was irrelevant. In my mind, "finders keepers" was the rule, so I kept the gold. Later, I showed the pendant to my brother. He agreed with me one hundred percent. He carefully placed the precious piece in one of the many pockets of his army jacket for safekeeping. This was to be our secret.

That afternoon, the sailors' nets captured a large catch of fresh seafood that they threw on the deck for us to enjoy, a treasure dropped before our eyes. We ate and ate until we were so full, we thought we might burst. Later that evening, I started running a high fever and began continually throwing up, accompanied by bouts of intense diarrhea. All of us had eaten the same thing, but no one else became ill, so the women thought it unlikely to be food poisoning. There had to be another explanation. That night, my brother stood a constant watch over me, fearing that I might die. He treated my symptoms with the only remedy he could remember from my mother's ministering at home, Gua Sha. This treatment involved roughly scraping my skin with a spoon or coin, scraping so hard that the blood welled up close to the surface. In theory, this treatment would allow the unhealthy elements in my body the opportunity to escape and for my body to heal itself.

I am not positive if the treatment worked or just the passing of time cured me. Nevertheless, the next morning, my fever had broken. By mid-day, I was back to my usual rambunctious self - no worse for the wear. From that day on, I saw my brother differently, more of a caregiver, protector, and friend than I had ever thought him to be. A sense of warmth filled me. One that I had not felt since leaving home. This was a good feeling.

On the third morning, we arrived in Bangkok, and the anticipated hornet's nest unleashed itself upon us. In short order, government officials found the *Kua Koon*, our new home, had violated Thai maritime law. The police boarded shortly after and placed the captain under arrest. Since we were the cause of his crime, his arrest greatly disturbed us. We had assumed, naively, that the officials would forgive his violations once the truth came out. Now, we could see that this was not the case. We worried about the captain's fate and concerned about what might happen to us next. The captain had not exaggerated about what would happen to him. We had never thought about what would happen to us.

Again, fate…God… smiled upon us.

Chapter 22

二十二

Bangkok

Figure 22: Hung and Muoi photo for immigration, 1979

The news loves a victim, and the more victims, the better. The captain's blatant violation of the law was newsworthy. Add to it a crowd of refugees on his ship, and the media swarmed us like flies to honey. In only a few hours, word of our plight blasted across radio and television in the Bangkok area. Local newspapers put us on their front page. We were big news. Since everyone loved an underdog and a captivating personal interest story, other countries worldwide picked up the story. Within days media people from all the major outlets worldwide gathered to cover the controversy surrounding our arrival.

A Chinese man who owned an alligator farm just outside of Bangkok watched the news that evening. When he discovered that most of us were of Chinese descent, he contacted the government and offered to provide us with two meals a day - a luxury! I am sure the donation was not a big deal for him, but for us, this was like having Chinese New Year every day. The food provided per day was more than most of us received at home! Soon, other charities like the Red Cross stepped up with clothing to replace our rags and other much-needed supplies. Doctors came out to the boat and gave us physicals and provided medicines for the illnesses beyond our shipboard medic's ability. One of our Vietnamese ship owners had been a member of the Saigon Lions Club before Saigon's fall in '75. He reached out to the Bangkok chapter, who also rushed to our aid and spread the word to other chapters worldwide. With clean clothes replacing our filthy rags and tasty, wholesome food filling our bellies, our situation had never been better.

On our second day in port, we welcomed representatives of the United Nations High Commissioner for

Refugees (UNHCR). They came on board to ask questions, take pictures, and begin processing our applications to prospective host countries. We had been given priority at the request of the government and the shipping company. The freighter owners were losing money every day the *Kua Koon* was in port, and the government was losing face. They both wanted the ship put back into service as soon as possible.

After a long time with an interpreter, Hung and I completed applications for all twenty available countries. Then, we stood up in front of one of the ship's hatches for our official photograph, which was then attached to our other paperwork. They photographed Hung and me together because I was so young, and they felt that we should stay together in our placement. When the young woman asked us if we had relatives who might sponsor us in one of the host countries, Hung produced a note from one of his pockets. Exposure to the water and sun over the past week had smeared and faded the printing a bit. Still, my mother's handwriting was legible. The paper contained the name and address of an uncle in the United States.

Now, in the western sense of the word, the man they reached out to was not my uncle. At home, we would refer to any close male friend of the family as "uncle." "Uncle" Le Quong The was a little of both. He was the ex-husband of my grandmother's niece – no blood relation at all to Hung or me. He had been an officer in the South Vietnamese Navy when Saigon fell in 1975, virtually guaranteeing his death as a traitor if caught by the new regime. He desperately tried to get his wife and children to flee the country with him, but she refused to leave and stayed behind in Saigon. He had no choice. He managed to escape on a naval vessel with thousands of others during the mass exodus on April 30th, Reunification Day. He hated to leave them, but there was no doubt in his mind that staying meant death. Years later, as my parents planned Hung's escape, my father got our "uncle's" name and address from his ex-wife. Le Quong The himself knew nothing about us.

The freighter continued to be our home for two more weeks. Our community presented a sizable problem for the Thai government. Offloading us to the refugee camp would indicate that they accepted and assumed responsibility for us, but if we stayed in the harbor, they reasoned, we were not *technically* in Thailand. The freighter owners compounded the problem because they needed to put the boat back in service as soon as possible. They could not offload the wood on board so long as we were there. They had buyers expecting delivery of the product, not to mention other cargoes scheduled for the ship to deliver elsewhere. In the face of a problem requiring a crucial solution, the government did what most governments do. They passed the problem down the line rather than take responsibility. They decided to bring in a large barge and anchor next to the freighter. That way, the company had its boat, and the government didn't have to deal with us. On June 6th, 1979, we moved aboard.

Life on the barge was even more carefree than the freighter had been. We each had around eight square feet of space to call our own. Amazing! The barge was so spacious. Our area was eight times the amount we had on our original boat. Additionally, the barge's presence made us even more newsworthy. As the international news services started broadcasting news items about our plight, we began to see aid coming not only from local sources but from around the world as well.

These packages included personal stoves for cooking rice and vegetables and many other luxuries. We felt the love of the world pouring over us. We basked amid all of this generosity.

Still, the most important thing for me was that I could swim in the bay whenever I wanted. The barge sat much lower to the water than the freighter did, giving us easy access. The other children and I took advantage of that feature as often as possible, diving off the barge's deck and then quickly climbing a rope ladder only to dive in again and again. What a wonderful feeling to once again have such freedom!

In addition to promoting our plight, the media's focus on us indirectly aided the imprisoned *Kua Koon's* captain as well. Whenever someone interviewed us, we praised him and his crew for our rescue, stressing that we would have died a horrible death at sea without them. We circulated a petition among ourselves for his release, which the news media forwarded to the government ministers responsible. The petition was the last straw. Coupled with all the negative publicity emanating from the international news, it caused the government to relent. They pardoned the captain for his crimes and later returned him to duty aboard the *Kua KoonL.* We were so happy to do something for this incredible man who had saved our lives.

As we settled onto our newest home, the presence of plentiful supplies gave us the ability to barter for services. For example, we had a man on board who had been a barber in Vietnam. He announced that he would cut a person's hair for one package of Ramen noodles. People liked the idea. They lined up to get haircuts with their Ramen in hand. Others formed other businesses exchanging clothing for food or food for supplies. Our little community began to thrive.

There was no question that the number one bargaining item was cigarettes. In fact, it pains me to admit that cigarette was the first English word I ever used. Whenever sailors from the mainland brought supplies on board, we would shout, "Cigarettes?" "Cigarettes?" in their direction and then tried to look pitiful in the hope that they would respond. Many simply ignored our pleas and brushed us aside. Occasionally though, persistence would pay off when a kind soul would throw one or two out our way. Sometimes, we would get a whole pack!

It wasn't long after the migration to the barge that they called my brother and me out of the group. A representative from the United States wanted to meet with us. She had exciting news. They had contacted our uncle in the United States, and he had agreed to sponsor us! Hung and I couldn't believe it. What an incredible moment! My dreams were going to come true. I was going to go to the United States! Everything I had ever prayed and hoped for was coming true. She went on to say that our processing and departure would begin immediately. When Hung and I returned to our group and shared the news, I realized that I now faced something that I had not felt since boarding the boat an eternity ago. I was going to have to say goodbye to the people I had grown to love. I was going to leave my family behind once again.

These people meant so much to me. We had formed a deep bond - deeper than the blood that ran in our veins, but, as yet, there was no sponsor for them. After enduring so much in such a brief, intense period, I could not believe that this was where our journey was going to end. When the lady from the United States came to the barge to get us, the goodbyes came hard. As Hung and I prepared to leave, we entrusted the gold pendant I had found to Tho with the instruction that he should give it to the last one left in the camp. That person would need the gold far more than we would.

As we got on the small boat taking us to shore, Hung and I were unsure how to prepare ourselves for our next adventure. Our uncle lived in a place unknown to either of us, a place with an exotic name, Oklahoma City, Oklahoma. I had been a good student, so I could find the United States on a globe, but I had no idea where Oklahoma City would be. There were so many questions! Would Oklahoma be tropical like our home? Would people be friendly? What would our uncle be like? Would there be unlimited food like the GIs had promised? What would freedom really look like in a foreign land?

We had been promised quick processing but had no idea how fast it was going to be. Almost immediately after arriving on land, the tempo of our transition sped up. My age had again been a blessing. Because I was a young minor, immigration officials once again moved us to the front of the line. Before we could even catch our breath, they transported Hung and me to a U.S. immigration center within the U.S. Embassy. There, I received another physical, including chest x-rays, to prove that I did not have tuberculosis or other respiratory diseases. Afterward came the paperwork, endless paperwork. Except for the patience of the excellent translator assigned to us, it would have been impossible paperwork. Finally, our heads spinning with the rapidity of their actions, they took Hung and me to the airport, where we boarded a U.S. military transport plane headed to Guam. From here, they told us that we would continue to the U.S. mainland.

Before this day, I had only seen planes high in the sky as they flew overhead. I had not been to the airport in Saigon; there had been no need. Even in my dreams of escape, I had never considered that I would have to fly to do so. As exciting and as adventurous as the trip appeared, I was hard-pressed to remember any details about the experience later. The whole thing had been a whirlwind ripping us from place to place.

Hung and I were still reeling from the paperwork session. The ink on our papers was barely dry as the aircraft crew strapped us into our seats, and the plane took off. Being a military flight, it was pretty much no frills. Still, this was yet another unknown for me to experience. It added to the already mountainous list of firsts experienced in the past three weeks. Even as I gathered my strength to look around my new surroundings, the day's culminating pressures managed to ruin the experience for me. I was simply too tired to be fearful, too weary for exploring, so I slept instead.

Once on Guam, we stayed on board while our transport unloaded, refueled, reloaded, and readied for our departure. There was no opportunity to look around while we were there. The jarring impact of landing was the only reason we were awake! This next leg of our journey would be the long one – all the way to San Francisco.

Things did not go as planned, however. The plane developed a mechanical problem over the Pacific that forced us down at an airbase in Hawaii for a short repair. What little we could see reminded me so much of home. There were palm trees, and the warm, humid temperatures reminded me of Cho Lon. I wondered if this was like what Oklahoma would be. In my heart, I hoped so. At this point, the crew shuttled us back onto the transport, and then we were once again off to the U.S. mainland.

When we arrived in San Francisco in the state of California, a Red Cross lady was there to meet us when we deplaned. There was a cursory customs check, greatly simplified by the fact that we had precisely nothing to declare. She then quite literally took us by the hand, drove us over the main terminal, and led us to our departure gate. She provided us with boarding passes for our next flight and made sure that we had all our immigration paperwork and x-rays. She was friendly and efficient. Before we knew it, she was gone.

Finally, for the first time in twenty-four hours, we had a chance to breathe alone. Our next flight did not leave for over an hour, so we took some time to explore the terminal before we boarded. Around our departure gate, we discovered several small shops about the size of our sidewalk shops back home. I was shocked by the variety of merchandise they carried. As we gawked at the stores, the most incredible thing was that they placed their goods where anyone passing by could easily reach out and just take it! I wasn't planning to steal anything, of course, but I could not figure out how they stayed in business. No one in Cho Lon would be so foolish.

After begging and pleading, I convinced my brother to buy me some gum with the money he had hidden in his belt. To shut me up, he agreed, although I imagine the main reason was that he wanted some cigarettes as well. Hung pulled the cash from the belt while we carefully made our selections. Then we got in line to pay. When we got to the front of the line and placed the money on the counter, we were unprepared for the clerk's reaction. She just stared at us. Had we done something wrong? We were simply paying for our cigarettes (40 cents) and gum (7 cents) with the only money we had, a one-hundred-dollar bill.

What we didn't know was how much money this was. In 1979, one-hundred-dollars would be a house payment for many U.S. citizens. How were we to know? For us, the bill was just funny looking money. The clerk had to leave us for a bit to get our change from another store. Finally, transaction completed, gum in hand, cigarette in Hung's mouth, and ninety-nine dollars and change in his pocket, we continued to our gate and on to Oklahoma. With so many things happening so far in our journey, I could not wait to see what happened when we arrived on July 5th. Whatever was waiting for us, I knew that the adventure would be exciting!

The American Airlines flight from San Francisco was a different experience from the military transport. Here, some beautiful young women served us all the snacks and drinks we wanted. I even got a set of wings to pin to my blouse! They treated us like royalty. I was amazed at how generous they were. I just wished we could have understood each other when they spoke to us. I would have loved telling them how pretty they were and how much I appreciated what they were doing for us.

Our arrival in Oklahoma City was almost anticlimactic. We had covered over ten thousand miles over the past couple of days, with our only rest being naps on the plane. We were exhausted. The jetway here looked much like the one in San Francisco as we slowly walked up into the terminal. The people at the gate looked the same as well. Even though we had no idea where here was, we were here - here surrounded by a country where we could not understand anyone — a country where everyone looked so different. Still, I felt so blessed. My future was to begin today.

The rest of our family and friends in Thailand had to wait for their chance. Eventually, Catholic Charities in Colorado sponsored Cousin Hung, also a minor. There, the Parker family fostered him until he reached age eighteen. At that time, he moved to Oklahoma to be near to us. Canada sponsored my uncle, Chau Nam. The only one left was my other cousin, Tho. He was petrified, sitting alone in the refugee camp. If no country sponsored him, he knew that the Thai government would force him to repatriate back to Vietnam. That was something that he did not want. Fortunately, before that could happen, his rescue arrived in the form of a last-minute sponsorship from Italy.

Years later, as I reflected on these events, I reminded myself just how blessed we were in our adventures. The stories I have since heard from other passengers on other ships about the hardships they endured both in the transit and in the camps were horrible. Not to mention the alarming numbers of people lost at sea, whose bones are scattered across the bottom of the ocean. I was humbled to think that we were only a smudge on the horizon away from joining their fate.

I did not know why such charity and generosity came our way. I know we didn't ask for anything; the bounty we received was given freely. I wondered how all our group survived when so many others perished. I could only say that I was and would be eternally grateful to God and to the multitude of people He guided our way.

Chapter 23

二十三

Oklahoma City, July 5, 1979

Figure 23: The house on NW 1st in Oklahoma City, 2017
(Muoi's family lived in only the left side of the duplex)

Over thirty stressful, sleep-deprived hours had passed since we left Bangkok. We were dirty, tired, and hungry. Both of us clutched plastic envelopes from the U.S. refugee office containing our x-rays and visa paperwork, along with a small bag of clothing. It was humbling to think that small bag held everything that was ours in this world. In all that time, Hung and I had hardly spoken to each other; our transit had been so rapid that every sense was on overdrive the entire trip. Everything I had encountered was new. No, that wasn't quite right. Everything I had experienced was alien. These things represented an entirely different world from mine. This place could not be the same planet. Nothing in my upbringing would provide a point of reference for this place, this new world.

Now that we were here at the arrival gate inside Will Rogers World Airport in Oklahoma City, we sat. We had no idea what to do next. We had been riding a tornado of activity, but now the winds of fate had simply stopped. Up to this point, someone else had orchestrated every move we made. At every stop, a person or persons guided us to the next point on our journey. Now, here we were. We couldn't ask for assistance; no one spoke our languages. Someone we had never met was supposed to pick us up, but for whatever reason, he was not here. Our only choice was to remain here and trust that he would show soon. We waited patiently, half sitting and half-sleeping in chairs not well designed for either function. We waited...and waited...and waited.

Every time a door opened, every time a person shouted, every time I heard a hurried walk on the tile, I would look up in anticipation. Since I had no idea what our uncle looked like, every person entering the door had the possibility of being either him or someone he had sent. I sincerely hoped that he would recognize us. I smiled to myself. That part, at least, should be reasonably straightforward. We were the only Asian people I could see in the terminal. It was a sure bet that someone could pick us out of the crowd with no problem. Of all the countless people that came and went, no one came our way or even appeared to be searching for someone. I witnessed shouts of joy as loved ones came home and tearful goodbyes as others left for parts unknown, but none of them were for my brother and me. Hour by hour, we waited.

Hung and I were hesitant to even go to the bathroom for fear that our uncle would arrive in that fraction of a moment, and we would not be there to greet him. So... we waited for our sponsor; our eyes fixed on the entry doors that represented the gateway to our new world. A gateway that only he could open for us. The afternoon slipped into evening, and in turn, evening changed to night. We remained steadfastly at our post until, at long last, no more planes landed, no more reunited families, no more goodbyes said. All the shops and airline ticket counters had long closed. Hung and I both knew there had been a mistake made, but neither of us had a clue what we could do about it. We could not read the signs. I mean, we weren't even sure that we were in the correct city. What if there were two airports in Oklahoma City? Was our uncle waiting at the other one far from here? As we sat in the empty terminal building, allowing the different scenarios to roll through our minds, we sat there terrified and alone.

As the lights in the main terminal turned off, we began to realize that spending the night here was a real possibility. While we discussed it, I saw danger lurking in every dark corner where the darkness had replaced the lights. Neither of us had ever been in such a large, empty space by ourselves. There were so many strange sights and sounds, and who knew what else lay in wait in the areas we could not see.

In our despair, fate shined upon us once more. Seemingly out of nowhere, a guardian angel appeared in the form of a Laotian immigrant. He wore a uniform that identified him as an airport employee. I had noticed him earlier sweeping the gate area and polishing the chrome after the gates had closed. He was surprised that we were still there and came to make sure we were OK. He first tried talking to us in Laotian and halting English, but of course, that didn't work at all. He looked over our documents, especially our x-rays sticking out of the top of the packet. As a former refugee himself, these identified us better than we knew. Not only did he know what we were, he knew that we were in trouble and whether we realized it or not, we also needed his help.

He was not a large man. In stature, he was no bigger than Hung, but in age, he was much older. His eyes crinkled when he smiled, and he was smiling as he tried to make his point through gestures. He seemed friendly, but, as I reminded Hung, so had the pirates at first. His gestures indicated that Hung and I should follow him. We were hesitant to do so. We didn't know him or anything about him. Even though the hour was late, and everything had closed, our uncle could still come to get us. Hung and I discussed the matter between ourselves while he waited patiently in the chair beside us. We felt no need to move away because there was no way that he could understand what we said.

What should we do? By now, this was a familiar situation for us. Faced with a decision that could dramatically affect our future lives, we had to make a choice immediately. We had no idea who this man was or what his motives were. Yet, we knew with a lot of confidence that something had gone terribly wrong with the original plans made to pick us up, and here was someone offering to help. We did what we felt we had to do. We agreed to go with him. He seemed genuinely friendly as he led us out of the terminal, through the parking lot, and over to his small car. I casually remarked to Hung that the heat outside at this hour was as hot and humid as back home, making me a little homesick. While I was talking to him, I turned my head and glanced back at the terminal door we had just passed through. That door represented everything to us. It was the only link to the world we had left behind, and we were abandoning it for an unknown future. My brother and I exchanged glances as if to say, "It can't be any worse than what we've already experienced. Can it?" With that attitude, we made another leap of faith. We got in his car and went off with our new friend.

We drove quite a distance from the airport. The airport appeared to be far away from the city, whose lights we could see twinkling in the distance. It was totally unlike Bangkok, where the base was across the street from businesses and homes, or for that matter, like Ho Chi Minh City Airport, which was also situated in the middle of town. When we finally arrived at his small apartment, he graciously made sure that we were comfortable before signaling that he was going upstairs. We waited anxiously for his return, unsure of where he was going or how long he would be gone. When at last he returned, he was accompanied by a young Vietnamese woman who was more than happy to translate for us. My

Vietnamese was still lacking, but Hung had a lot more practice back home, so he explained to her our situation and our concerns about our uncle. Much to our surprise, she knew him!

We discovered that the Vietnamese community in Oklahoma City was relatively small. Consequently, out of necessity, it was a very close-knit group. She invited us to join her family in their apartment upstairs while we tried to contact our uncle. As we were leaving, we asked her to please tell the Laotian man how much we appreciated his assistance. We would have still been at the airport without him. Once we were all upstairs, she telephoned our uncle. To our dismay, no one was home.

Was he at the airport? Had we made a mistake? There was no way to leave a message for him, so she and her husband took turns calling his number every fifteen minutes or so, always with the same result – no answer. While we waited, she and her husband made us comfortable and welcome in their home. After such a hectic three days, most of them being unable to communicate with anyone, being with them was terrific. Finally, we had people that spoke our language. A little after midnight, just when we were about to give up for the night and go to bed, my uncle answered the phone, and a confusing conversation ensued.

Our hostess gave him our names and reminded him that he was supposed to be our sponsor. My uncle protested that he had no idea what she was talking about. He wasn't anyone's sponsor. He did know a family named Quan back in Vietnam, but he had never heard of us. No one had ever contacted him about the sponsorship of two children. We were all confused at this point. Hung and I could hear a lot of talking going on at the other end, yet the woman on our end was silent. Our hostess told us that our uncle and aunt were discussing something. The current course of events was terrible. If we could not stay with him, what would become of us? Where would we go? I am confident that our relief was visible on our faces when our uncle came back on the phone and said he would be right over to get us.

Later, the firm knock on the door startled me. Only about a half-hour had passed since the phone call, and we had just been sitting around speaking quietly with the young couple. When our hostess opened the door, I could see that two men were standing outside. Which one was our uncle? How would we know? Fortunately, my recognition wasn't necessary. He readily stepped forward and introduced himself and his friend.

They loaded us into his car and took us to his house after dropping his friend off on the way. It was a duplex on N.W. 1st that he shared with our Aunt Tran, now well into her second pregnancy. Her five-year-old son, who had only been an infant when she brought him to the United States, was with her. I realized much later how small that house was, but, at the time, it seemed huge for only three, now five - and soon six people to share. We had shared a much smaller space with ten!

Over several days, we were finally able to piece together what had happened at the airport. The U.S Representative in Bangkok had contacted Catholic Charities, who called our uncle in May for confirmation. Unfortunately, this was while my uncle was at work. Instead, they talked to my aunt and told her that two children with the surname Quan, ages twelve and seventeen, were in Thailand. They also said to her that we had my uncle's name and address as a possible sponsor. The children needed sponsorship to come to the U.S. Would she and her husband be willing to do that?

As she spoke on the phone, my aunt remembered a time five years earlier. She had been a U.S. employee in Saigon in 1975 when the city fell. She and her infant son had managed to escape on April 30th and soon found herself in the same situation. She had needed a sponsor for the two of them then. They were at a refugee camp in Arkansas, distressed at finding herself and her baby alone in this new, strange land. She delightfully remembered when her sponsors took them into their home and how indebted she felt toward her sponsoring family even to this day. Since then, she worked in the Vietnamese community in Oklahoma City as often as possible, helping refugees adapt to this new country. So, when Catholic Charities called, she agreed to sponsor us without hesitation. In her heart, she was sure the arrangement would be acceptable to her husband.

Unfortunately, she worked nights, and my uncle worked days. They often did not see each other, let alone talk for days at a time. Soon, in the busy reality of life, the phone call became a lost memory amid a thousand others. She simply forgot to tell him. Over the next six weeks, Catholic Charities failed to follow-up with her on the initial conversation. There should have been paperwork to complete that was associated with sponsorship. Worst of all, no one bothered to tell them about our arrival at the airport on July 5th. None of those actions took place. Hung and I fell between the cracks of memory and the bureaucratic machine.

The night we had arrived, my aunt and uncle had been at a wedding. The celebration had lasted a long time. When they finally got home, the events of the evening had left them exhausted. When my uncle answered the phone and found out that two children were at a friend's house claiming that he was their sponsor, he was shocked. He was sure that he was the subject of a practical joke or that there had been a mistake. The tone in his voice prompted my aunt to ask what was wrong. He pulled away from the phone and told her. Immediately, she remembered the conversation from May. She started explaining things to my uncle while he was on the phone with a perplexed Vietnamese wife. The mystery solved, our uncle came to get us. Despite everything, and fortunately for Hung and me, they welcomed us into their home.

We spent our first full day in this country with our aunt at the Catholic Charities office in Oklahoma City, trying to straighten out our arrival problems. The people there were friendly. They apologized over and over again for the difficulties they had caused. The numbers of refugees coming in from Vietnam were back up to almost 1975 levels, and they were often overwhelmed. Sad to say, incidents like ours were not that uncommon. They were elated that we had found each other even with all the mistakes.

As my aunt completed the paperwork for our sponsorship, Hung and I were given three hundred dollars and a bag of clothing from the refugee fund. From our San Francisco experience, we realized that this was a lot of money - money that my aunt and uncle could use. Hung and I knew that our presence would only cause more financial strain upon them. They, however, had other ideas. They put the money into a saving account for each of us. That way, we had funds to use in case of an emergency later.

Chapter 24

二十四

Dreams vs. Reality

Figure 24: Flooded playground at Van Phat Resort on the Me Kong, 2017

A lifetime ago, I was on my little rooftop in Cho Lon, dreaming of the mystical West and how being there would change my life. I had envisioned a place where food was free for the asking and where everyone had a car, a big house, and lots of money to buy things. I was so young and naïve then. Only six weeks back, I stepped onto a boat and watched my world view shatter in response. For me, the West was no longer the unattainable goal. The dream had become a stark reality, and I soon discovered how rarely facts live up to dreams.

First of all, I found that people here worked just as hard as they did back in Vietnam. The money had changed, but everything still costs money, and the ability to purchase things was dependent on how much you made and how hard you worked. My uncle was fortunate to have a good job making cars at the General Motors plant east of the City while my aunt worked for AT&T downtown. He worked during the day and some nights when the plant was operating at full strength. My aunt worked only at night so that she would have her days open for household responsibilities. Even with them both working, they needed all the money they earned to keep their little family afloat and prepare for their future child. In at least that regard, my uncle was very much like my father.

I had imagined that all Americans lived in palaces. Well, our three-room house on N.W. 1st was a little lacking in the palace department, even by my standards. My aunt and uncle and her son shared one small bedroom, while Hung and I slept on pallets on the living room floor, which we dutifully stored out of the way during the day. The house wasn't too small; it just wasn't as big and fancy as I had envisioned. This home had much more in common with my house in Cho Lon than with my palace.

I also discovered that the G.I.s had misled us about the food. Bread did not fall from an ever-flowing cornucopia, nor did fruit and vegetables grow on street corners where you could just pick what you needed. We bought our food just like at home, and we had budgets for food and everything else we required. When the funding was exhausted for that pay period, we simply had to do without that item.

My dreams did not include making personal adjustments either. I had just assumed that everybody everywhere did things the same way. Boy, was I wrong! Everywhere that I looked, there were obstacles to overcome and adjustments that I needed to make. I had been able to adapt to change in Cho Lon, but here, there were just too many changes all at once. The task of overcoming all of them seemed impossible, almost herculean. Even though we rarely talked about the situation, I was sure that Hung felt the same way. I wondered if he ever questioned the wisdom of coming here at all. How often had he thought about his life back home and what his future would have been like in Vietnam had he stayed? After all, he had a good job, friends, and, of course, a girlfriend there. Here he, like me, had nothing and no one. We were utterly dependent on my aunt and uncle, who were still little more than strangers to us.

After Catholic Charities corrected our immigration problems, our aunt insisted that we have a proper physical along with any vaccinations needed to live and go to school here. Back home, a doctor's visit consisted of a trip to the hospital. Everyone sat in a large room with dozens of others, waiting to see a doctor. When they called you back, you went into a large ward with many examination tables. There was little or no privacy. If you were lucky, they placed a temporary screen beside the table. Even in Bangkok, our physicals had taken place in a long assembly line with other refugees. Medical staff examined us and gave us shots while in full view of everyone else. Each of those examinations took less than five minutes, and I fully expected this one to be the same. Plus, who had ever heard of someone going to the doctor when you were well?

That said, my first U.S. doctor's visit was radically different from any of my earlier medical experiences. The exam was so formal and so private. The waiting room was small, with only ten chairs. At my appointed time, they escorted me back to a private examining room with only my aunt accompanying me. The room smelled of antiseptic and medicines, and I felt weird being alone there. When the exam finally started, the doctor took forever. He poked and prodded me in places that no doctor had ever poked or prodded before. They asked me tons of questions, translated by my aunt, about every little aspect of my medical history. In the end, they stabbed me with a needle to get my blood and then stabbed me again and again with the necessary vaccinations that I needed. By the time we finished, I was exhausted, even though the doctor and nurses treated me well throughout the process.

One wouldn't think that shopping for food would be a huge adjustment, but, here again, it was a significant shift for me. The way we shopped back home made perfect sense. There was an order to the process there. Why would anyone shop any other way? I had just assumed that everyone in the world had open-air markets for food, tailors for clothing, and the larger stores for other things like pots and machines. I soon discovered that was not the case in America.

For example, my first trip to a grocery store was nothing like the markets back home. In Cho Lon, we bought 100 mg of salt in a baggie, no brand, no ingredients, just salt. Here, there were dozens of brands of salt on the shelf. They were sold in such huge quantities that my 100 mg baggy would have looked insignificant in comparison. Instead of the small bags of sugar that my family manufactured and sold, they bought five to ten pounds at a time. That was a lot of sugar! Meat and fish were pre-packaged in plastic and refrigerated. They didn't hang the fresh meat up so we could smell the freshness like home. They even packaged chickens the same way, so much more inefficient than carrying them home live in a cage. How could you know how long the chicken had been dead? At home, Hung could buy one cigarette at a time if he wanted; here, he had to buy a whole pack or, astonishingly, a full carton!

Those weren't the only items either. Where before we had gone to the open-air market to buy only enough for each day, here my aunt and I purchased food for a week or more at a time. Trying to choose from all the different brands and quantities would have been difficult in Vietnamese or Chinese. As it was, the sheer number combined with English overwhelmed my ability to comprehend. In many ways, it reminded me of the San Francisco Airport only on a much larger scale. Here too, everything was sitting on the open shelf where anyone could pick something up, look at it, and compare it with other brands. Then came the worst part – the checkout stand. We had to pay the marked price. There was no haggling over price in any American stores. That was the part of shopping that I had looked forward to the most. No haggling took away all the fun.

At least, at the house, there were a few things that did bear a resemblance to something back in Cho Lon. The chores I did here were much like the ones I had done at home. My aunt gave me the responsibility of babysitting my cousin. No problem. I had a lot of experience, thanks to my younger siblings. Plus, her son was such an easy boy to take care of, nothing like Nguu. I also did some of the other chores, like sweeping and washing the dishes. I also got to do the laundry - with a washing machine! Sometimes, I even prepared the evening meals for my uncle after my aunt went to work.

While I was working at these little things, I could almost close my eyes and, for a moment, believe I was back in Cho Lon, but then my daydream would burst like a balloon, and I would remember where I was. Every time that happened, I felt I was losing my mother and family all over again. I missed them so much.

The greatest challenge I had experienced during our journey was still the most significant hurdle now—communication. I am not just talking about English either. English was its own mountain to climb, and I would have to conquer that slope in steps, not all at once. I am referring to Vietnamese, the language of my uncle and aunt. Hung was older and had worked among Vietnamese men back home. His Vietnamese was passable, but for me, the nuances of Vietnamese were exasperating.

Granted, Vietnamese teachers had taught me for the past four years, and many of the vendors had spoken Vietnamese. However, that had only provided me with basic vocabulary and grammar, gleaned rather than learned during indoctrinations. It had just been enough to get by. My learning did not include the subtleties of usage that I now required. The fact that Chinese and Vietnamese had many shared words didn't help much either – instead, it hurt. Often, I would get confused as to what form of a word to use. More than once, I got into trouble for using a personal pronoun, perfectly permissible in Chinese, by the way, instead of the proper title and name customary in Vietnamese. My teachers had never covered the fact that using a personal pronoun in Vietnamese was rude and a sign of severe disrespect. Now, I was reminded of this often. My uncle was quick to correct me when I failed to use the right form with him.

Oklahoma weather was something else entirely. Who could have imagined such variety? When we had arrived in July, the weather was hot and humid, quite like what we experienced at home year-round. This weather seemed perfectly normal to me. I soon got over the lack of banana and palm trees and just assumed this was Oklahoma's typical weather. Imagine my shock and surprise when I learned that the weather got cold as well. I had no concept of what that even meant. The meat and milk areas at the store were cold. Was that what they meant? Then there were the storms. Back home, we had monsoons where a lot of water fell at once - straight down. Here, the rain was more like what we experienced on the boat. The rain came from every direction, seemingly at once, as it twisted and turned every which way the wind could blow – and the wind blew! Sometimes, the gales nearly knocked me over!

As fall approached, my aunt decided I needed to get a coat. Apparently, with winter coming on, I would need one. I had no idea what she was talking about. What difference would that make? To me, summer, fall, winter, and spring were just dates on the calendar; they had little effect on the temperature. Anyway, the entire clothes shopping experience blew me away yet again!

The stores were as large or larger than any of the emporiums back home. Still, once inside, the variety in both quality and price was what amazed me. I remember my mother buying bolts of cloth at the emporiums to make our clothes or going to a tailor to have New Year's clothing made. Here there were rows upon rows of premade clothes in every size and color imaginable. As I stood in the middle of all this wonder, I wanted to ask, "Why shop for a coat?" There were so many other things to choose from instead. My aunt's concern over the upcoming winter fell on my deaf ears. The thought of experiencing something other than warm weather never even crossed my mind.

Then, come September and October, fall came with cooler temperatures and even cooler rains. Then the leaves changed - another new experience that occurred with no warning. For the longest time, I thought the trees were dying as their withered leaves fell and floated down to the ground. I was greatly upset about this until my aunt advised me that they were not dead, only sleeping. She assured me that they would grow new leaves in the spring - another wonder.

If the shock of fall was not enough, winter came soon after, and I now understood the wisdom of a coat. Not only were the temperatures frigid, but the wind out of the north was almost painful in its assault on my person. We had something called a furnace in the house that my uncle lit. This was unbelievable! We had a fire in the house!

Snow, on the other hand, was an incredible first. My first snowfall started while I was walking to the store with Hung. When I saw the snow falling out of the sky, I got so excited! As the snowstorm grew in intensity and produced even larger flakes, we were both beside ourselves with joy. We laughed and ran in zigzags here and there, trying to catch snowflakes in our mouths while all the time rejoicing in this beautiful white stuff. I don't remember if we made it to the store or not.

However, more significant than language and weather was the fear I felt as my brother and I began to grow apart. I knew my aunt and uncle cared for me, and they were doing everything they could for me to succeed, but Hung was still the only person I could absolutely trust. He had proven that time and time again in our wandering as he stood by me through everything we endured. All my experiences on the voyage here had been with him. He was my rock on that journey and even tended to me when I fell ill. Every time I felt weak, he was strong enough for both of us. More than that, he was my blood, my family. He was the only part of Cho Lon I had left. Now our new lives were rapidly shoving us in different directions. With each event that pulled us apart, my anxiety grew more and more intense. At times, the pain was so great that I thought I would explode. He was my everything, and I was very possessive of my time with him.

With every turn I made, something new presented itself, another first, another adjustment. My Vietnamese was now almost acceptable, except for the times I still managed to insult my uncle. My aunt continued to take me with her when she went out. Hung found a job at a shopping cart factory a few blocks from the house and decided to forgo school, which was an option at his age. While all this was going on, I found out that my uncle had bought a new home in south Oklahoma City, and very soon, I was going to have to move.

With the closing date approaching, something very unusual happened. My uncle sat down with Hung and discussed Hung's future. This was another first. At home, Father made the decisions. Father hadn't even consulted Hung about leaving Vietnam! After their conversation ended, they had agreed that Hung should continue to stay at the duplex. The new house was miles away from here, while Hung's employment was quite close to the N.W. 1st address. He had a new friend who was also needing a place to stay. He had agreed to move in with Hung and help with the rent. I thought that this made sense. I could stay here with Hung and his friend, and everything would be fantastic.

My aunt and uncle killed that idea at once. It seemed that it was not proper for a young woman to live with two men like this. Unlike Hung, I did not have a choice in the matter. My aunt and uncle decided that I would go with them to their new home. They promised a better life for me there. The schools around the new place were some of the best in the state, and I would start something called junior high there, whatever that was.

The thought of separation from Hung depressed me terribly. This was a step too far. I didn't want to go if I could not be with my brother, and I told my uncle this in no uncertain terms. My reaction did not sit well with my uncle. He might not be Chinese, but he was not accustomed to someone talking back to him, much like my father had been. He made it perfectly clear what I would do and that I was not to question his judgment again. He did, however, give me a promise. If I completed my homework by Friday evening, I could spend every weekend at the duplex with Hung. Though not perfect, this was far better than nothing at all. Deal! Even though I didn't know what a junior high was or what form this "homework" would take, I vowed to never, ever dawdle in getting my work done.

Moving day came far too soon. As I waved good-bye to Hung while he stood on the porch of the duplex, I swore to myself that I would hate the new house that had separated us. Again, I was wrong. Things did indeed get better after the move. In fact, the very day we moved was almost magical. Everything in the house was so clean and new – and so big! There was a yard with real grass out front and in the back. There was something called a garage at the side of the house to put the car into and a sidewalk that led up to the front door. The new home still wasn't a palace, but it was a lot closer.

My uncle reminded my aunt, cousin, and me of the importance of keeping the house exactly like this - clean and beautiful. He would allow nothing nailed on the walls so that they would remain pristine. That was fine by me. I didn't care. I didn't own anything to put on the walls anyway. In my eyes, the house was gorgeous, just the way it was. The best part of all was that I had my own room with an actual bed just for me. No "toes to nose" sharing here! I had never dared to imagine such a luxury. That day, I dared to make my first American dream, a dream that someday I too would own a house just like this. My house would have lots of trees also. I would have two cars, a VW, and a van, and I would have a piano. I couldn't play the piano, but that didn't matter. I would own one anyway just because I could. The fact that the dream was far away in the future didn't concern me. I was going to make my vision happen someday. Today, I simply relished my room, laid on my bed, and allowed myself to feel like a princess in her palace.

I was still making plenty of adjustments to my everyday life, but I could now see that my life was making a turn for the better. Even though they could never be home, my new surroundings were beginning to feel homey. All the changes had come at a price, though, and at times that price seemed much too high. I often lamented over the people that I had left behind. I knew for sure that my aunt and uncle cared for me as if I were one of their family, and I loved them dearly for their efforts, but I missed my mother. Sometimes, if I closed my eyes tightly, I could still see her standing in the kitchen - smell her cooking. I longed to play with Nhi, Yenlinh, Hue Hinh, and the others in the alleyway and listen to neighbors bicker through the windows at night. In my mind, I watched Tran's smile as we shared a joke over one of my aunt's sweet drinks. I wondered, "Who was her companion now?"

I had no friends in this new world. Here, I had cloistered myself away while desperately trying to get a grip on all the changes bombarding me from every side. I dreamed of being able to run free once more, to roam where and when I wanted, but in this land of strange neighborhoods and even stranger people, my fear kept me away. In Cho Lon, I had been fearless. I was willing to try anything. Here, my fears imprisoned me. Language and customs blocked me at every turn. I simply was unable to convey my thoughts to anyone other than family. Going outside by myself would be unthinkable. I wrote countless letters home to Vietnam in my best handwriting, then confided my torments and my conflicting emotions to my diary every night.

Chapter 25

二十五

Meanwhile, back in Cho Lon

Figure 25: View of Catholic Church from roof of Muoi's house, 2017

Mother, Father, and My's trip back to Cho Lon was much longer than the one down to Long Xuyên, or so My told me later. They were all still in shock from the events of the previous evening. They found little to talk about as they bounced down the highway toward home. When they finally walked up to the house's front door, my mother was still visibly upset. My father, on the other hand, attempted to maintain a stoic façade. The rest of the family, especially Tran and San, were shocked when told about the chain of events at Long Xuyên.

Because of the need for secrecy, even Hung's leaving was news to some of them. Still, my accidental inclusion on the boat was a surprise to all. My sister San became quiet and still like my mother. When she finally spoke, her concerns were the same as my mother's had been. "I was so young, just a child!" "The trip was so far...so permanent!" She and a few others had the opportunity to say goodbye to Hung, but they had no such chance with me. I was simply gone.

After that day, our family never said anything more about our absence in private or especially in public. They couldn't risk others finding out. Other families in the neighborhood rarely commented about someone they had not seen in a while. Most respected the family's privacy and understood the need for secrecy. People came and went from homes now with shocking regularity these days. Still, now and then, some close neighbor or dear friend would ask about us. Our family's response would always be the same. "We were visiting relatives outside the city." I guess that was a more or less true statement. On our birthdays, the family would have a special meal in our honor. They wanted to keep our memory alive in their other children's minds. These events also allowed them to instruct the younger family members about their absent siblings. They had no firm recollection of us. They had been too young when we left. We were no more than a misty memory. They offered many prayers for our safety and well-being to both the Buddhist and Christian God.

My friends noticed my absence, of course. We had so many good times together, and those memories would take a long time to fade. More than any of the others, they would often ask about my whereabouts and when I would return. They mostly missed me after playing a rousing game of hide-and-seek or a trip to the swimming pool. Each time, my parents would smile and repeat the visiting family story and say they had no idea when I would be back. After some time passed, even Nhi, the closest of my old friends, just stopped asking anymore. Her parents probably pulled her aside and told her to respect Mother's privacy.

There was one positive outcome for the family. From the government's point of view, Hung and I had never left. Therefore, the household ledger still held our names. The family received food allocations for us as though we were still there. Our parents weren't trying to cheat. No one from the government ever checked, so why tell them. The increase in rations was small compensation for the loss of two children.

That was the question, especially for my mother. Were we lost? If we were OK, where were we? What had happened to us? Were we well? Were we at the refugee camp? Had we even survived the trip? Quite by accident, she received the answers from us. One of my aunts in Ho Chi Minh City spotted us in the background of a newspaper photograph. The article was part of the media coverage from Bangkok. She was so excited that she wasted no time getting to our house to show my parents. At first, my mother was speechless; she could not believe that her prayers had been answered and we were safe. Yet, the picture was there in front of her. Those were her children. Relief spread through her face and body. Weeks of tension fell off her. She was finally at peace. For the first time since Long Xuyên, she knew her children were alive and well. She could finally allow herself to hope. Her tears that coursed down her cheeks were now tears of joy.

The situation in Cho Lon worsened over the next year. Officials made no pretext about their hatred for all things Chinese and went out of their way to penalize the community. Even though escape was still illegal, what had once been a blind eye to Chinese departures was now an open invitation. All foreign peoples were encouraged to leave the country either by their own will or find themselves going under more questionable government direct action.

Every week, either through escape or relocation, more and more families disappeared from the hamlet. The new settlements out in the desert lands of the west swallowed many of them. The people called them death camps for a reason. Many people went there, and none ever returned. Their families left behind never heard from them again.

As quickly as Chinese families left, North Vietnamese families filled their empty homes with strange voices and odors. Cho Lon had ceased to be a Chinese bubble. The city had lost its character, its foundation. My father, always trying to do what was best for his family, realized that he needed to do something...and soon, or he and his family would fall victim as well. He began looking for another boat, one where they could all leave together.

Chapter 26

My Ultimate Trial:
Brink Junior High

Figure 26: The exterior of Brink Jr. High, Moore, OK, 2017

Strange that some things never occurred to me during all the trials and problems we overcame. I never really thought the whole escape thing through to the end. The ongoing drama of simply getting here had preempted any thought of what might happen later. We didn't even know until the day before we left Bangkok that we were going to the United States. We could have been routed to any one of twenty other countries just as quickly. So much energy, so many hopes and dreams went into just getting to this place that any thinking past the point of arrival seemed - well, pointless. After all, dreams are made of ideals, not reality. I was sure that part of me realized that I would have to make some changes in my habits and that some of them would seem significant. I knew that I would have to adapt to my new surroundings and American culture. My future would depend on how well I changed.

The part of that future that never crossed my mind, not even for a second, was continuing my education. I mean, how could I even think about school when attempting to weather a storm, escaping pirates, or threatened with starvation? Possible death tends to take your mind off details like that. Yet, school now raised its head - the scourge of adolescents everywhere. Ironically, even after I accepted that I would have to go to school, I never totally understood what that would mean.

A flood of new things had pummelled me since my arrival. So many things were different in the United States. Even then, I never thought that schooling would be any different than what I had experienced back home. Despite my knowledge of this country, I assumed that I would be taught in Chinese or Vietnamese. After all, I always had been. I was in for a rude awakening. Another first was about to start.

I believe I mentioned earlier that our new house was in a good school district, the Moore school district, to be precise. Moore was a growing community on the south side of Oklahoma City. It was building a new school practically every year to accommodate the influx of people. The schools had an excellent reputation, and my aunt and uncle were so excited that I would get to attend one of them.

Anyway, early one morning, I washed carefully under my aunt's watchful eye. I then put on new clothes purchased only the week before, specifically for this purpose. We got into the car, and she drove me to a large brick structure a few miles away with the letters Brink Junior High emblazoned across the wall. We went inside together, where she spoke pleasantly to the office staff in her broken English. I nervously looked over the large room while they talked, unable to understand a word they said. In no time, she had me enrolled in the seventh grade. Mission completed. My aunt looked at me, smiled, kissed me, said goodbye, and left me...standing there...in the office...of the school...alone.

I don't think she ever looked back as she walked out the door, got in her car, and drove away. I couldn't believe it! How could she do this to me? I felt utterly abandoned, standing alone in this strange new place. She told me later that she had done this same task for the children of many of the families she had helped. She had not given a thought to how the experience might affect me differently.

Now, I was not a stranger to adversity. When I had faced the possibility of a firing squad in Hanoi, I did so with barely a whimper. Threatened with time in a reeducation camp? No problem. I took the possibility without a flinch. Pushed onto a boat in the middle of the night? Courage and grit pulled me through. Facing storms and pirates? They were both all part of surviving the day. I had seen and conquered more in the past year than a hundred other girls could claim over their lifetimes. Be there no question. I was one strong, tough kid.

Yet here I was, in the office of Brink Junior High, surrounded by a sympathetic, yet perplexed, office staff. There I cried. I bawled. I wailed. The staff made their best attempts to calm me, yet I remained inconsolable. I hated myself for crying like this. I hated showing weakness, especially in front of strangers. Yet the tears fell, the sobs continued. After what seemed like forever, I managed to regain my composure, blow my nose, and dry the tears from my puffy, red eyes.

Now calmer, I reasoned to myself, "How bad could school really be?" After all, I was a good student back in Cho Lon. My grades were always exceptional, a point of pride for my parents and me. School was school, right? How different could this be? I sucked up my courage. I had not failed in my earlier adventures despite the odds. I had no reason to think I would this time. "I can do this," I told myself bravely. Then, armed with only a few words of English, I wiped the last of the tears from my eyes, blew my nose once more for good measure, and went out to face this new world of junior high.

In retrospect, I was a fool, an idiot, a moron, and a dozen other words that I didn't know yet. I had heard spoken English before in the stores and shops, and I could even understand and say a few words if I tried. Here, however, the English language surrounded me, spoken at speeds far beyond my comprehension. Besides, everyone talked at once! As I looked around, I saw all these other students who were giants compared to me. I felt like a small, lost child who had accidentally fallen into their midst, and like a small child, I tried to shrink myself further out of view. I wanted to hide. To make matters even worse, the students changed locations, not just classes, every hour! Who does that? For efficiency, shouldn't the teachers move and not the students? As they went between classes, the students packed the hallways from wall to wall, seemingly going in all directions at once. They swarmed like a hive of bees, always in motion.

To help orient me to the school, the office had assigned a student aide to check my schedule and lead me to where I went next. The theory appeared sound, but the two of us had no baseline from which we could work. She assumed a lot, and I knew virtually nothing. First, her legs were so much longer than mine, and she walked so rapidly that I had to run to keep up. When I fell back or someone passed in front of me, my guide would roll her eyes in disdain while she waited on me, the village idiot, to catch up. The sheer size of the school was overwhelming. Hallways branched off into other hallways in a labyrinth of directions. The other youth all appeared the same to me. Everywhere I looked, there were blond heads and blue eyes. Okay, maybe not everywhere, but the point was that I felt incredibly out of place. There was one thing, however, that I didn't see anywhere. No matter how I searched, there was no other face that looked like mine. For the first time in my journey halfway around the world, I felt genuinely isolated and alone. Even my brother couldn't save me here.

For the first few days...weeks, I was miserable. Most days, all I could do was sit quietly while everyone else talked, laughed, and sometimes even worked. I could not understand a word said, either by the instructor or by my classmates. Whenever they laughed, I felt sure they were poking fun at me, which only made me angrier, more miserable, and even further withdrawn. Whenever the other students jostled and pushed me in the hallway, I knew that they pushed me on purpose, not that I was so small and quiet that they didn't see me. There were only two classes where I felt competent at all, math and art. They were my safe-havens.

Art was a common language to which I could relate. My study of calligraphy back in Cho Lon under Mom and Tran was excellent training for this. In art class, my soul was set free. I could relive the joys of my early days and recreate the art of my now lost culture. My instructor was intrigued with what I was doing and approved of my work. The sketches and drawings I made gave me a sense of satisfaction and accomplishment that my other classes could not provide. I felt that I was worthy here.

I also discovered that math concepts were, in fact, universal. By carefully following the teacher's examples on the board, I could do the assigned homework easily. Numbers, thank God, were the same in English, Chinese, and Vietnamese. He would write the assignments on the board, and I would copy them down and do them. Piece of cake, right?

Again, fate proved me wrong. The first time we graded each other's homework (Yes, we did that back then.), my "cake" crashed to the ground into a million pieces. I missed almost every problem! I didn't understand. I knew that I did the work exactly as he had shown me on the board. How could I have gotten the work so terribly wrong? I was on the verge of tears again when the student who graded my paper asked our instructor why my paper had twice the number of answers as his paper did. I couldn't understand him, of course, his talking was all noise to me, but then the teacher took my paper, examined it, and discovered what had gone wrong. I had done all the problems, not just the odd ones he had assigned. I had seen the word "odd" on the board, of course, but I had no idea what "odd" meant. After explaining and finger-pointing at the problems' numbers, I learned two new English words - odd and even. Later in my study of English, I would discover that *odd* also meant strange or weird and *even* could mean level. This language was going to be the death of me!

Outside of math and art, the salvation of my education came in the form of a woman, a teacher named Mrs. Blevins. She was the reading specialist at Brink. Her job was to work with students who had reading difficulties, and people like me, students with no English language skills whatsoever. Every day, she would come and get me out of my language-based classes: English, social studies, and science, and take me back to her room. There, she placed me in a cubicle, put earphones on my head, and let me listen to language tapes. Those tapes associated sounds with pictures, so I could finally see what the word represented. What an illumination! The earphones allowed me to hear the correct pronunciation and forced me to imitate the sounds. From these humble beginnings, my language skills blossomed. I quickly moved on to first and second-grade reading books.

Mrs. Blevins made a point of understanding my home situation as well. She was concerned about where I was with English and wanted to enlist my aunt's help. However, when she called my aunt and requested that I only speak English at home, she had a bit of a shock. After a short, virtually incoherent conversation, Mrs. Blevins realized that home would probably not be a lot of help in my language development. My future learning was dependent on school and individual effort from this point forward. My determination became my only limiting factor, and I was determined to succeed. There was no question in my mind that Mrs. Blevins and her positive attitude toward me saved my life.

I attacked English as I had done with everything else in my life – full speed ahead. In my life before America, no challenge had been unmet, and now that I had identified this challenge, I intended to meet this one head-on. Every day after school, I entered our usually empty house and continued my language learning. I read the books that Mrs. Blevins had assigned, but a lot of my education came from watching *The Price is Right, Sesame Street*, and *Electric Company* on television. I followed every word and learned every song perfectly. Anytime I didn't understand something, I wrote the word or phrase down, so my aunt or Mrs. Blevins could later explain the meaning. Nothing was too silly or too elementary for me to imitate. Morgan Freeman, a regular on *Electric Company*, was my new hero. I became obsessed with English. After all my frustrations encountered trying to communicate in our travels, I realized success in this country depended upon this more than anything else.

Not everything at school was improving, however. The teasing and ridicule from my fellow Brink students were getting worse and worse. The girls in my classes, especially the pretty ones, took great delight in torturing me. They specialized in using English words you would not find in an English textbook, or in some cases, even in a dictionary, to describe my appearance and actions. I often found myself as the butt of their jokes - jokes that often involved sexual innuendos and relationships with monkeys.

Sometimes their humor was based on my ignorance of American cultural norms. For example, one of them, a pretty, blond girl who was very particular about her appearance, asked me if I had any perfume she could use. I was confused. I asked in my stilted English what perfume was? She howled in amusement, with her friends joining in her laugh. She could not believe how stupid I was not to know such a simple word. I again felt humiliated, and I know my face burned in shame. I was so sad and depressed that I hung my head for the rest of the day. Later in Mrs. Blevins' classroom, I looked up the word and its definition. No wonder I didn't know it. I had never even thought about such an item, let alone used it. As my English skills improved, imagine how delighted I was when I discovered *blond* jokes!

Early on in my Brink experience, I made a remarkable discovery. There was someone who looked like me! My soon to be new best friend was Tram. Tram was Vietnamese, and, although we were in the same year, we had no classes in common. The staff at Brink introduced us when they needed someone to translate for them. Tram became the "go-to" person for that task. She would translate my bad Vietnamese into English and then try to explain the English to me in

Vietnamese. It was a miracle that we were able to communicate at all!

Even though we didn't share classes, we soon became lunch buddies and ate side by side every day. Her friendship made me more at ease with the social side of school, which, in turn, allowed me to deal with the prom queens who continued to torment me. She was an excellent student and openly encouraged me to show what I could do and be the same. I told myself over and over that if she could overcome something, I could too. She read incessantly, so I also read, albeit a few levels below her. When, a few years later, she became the valedictorian of our high school class, there was no one prouder of her than I.

Two years after the embarrassing first day at Brink, I entered ninth grade. I left the school behind for West Mid-High, a school for ninth and tenth graders. On that first day, the confident girl who entered West was an entirely different person from that shy, crying seventh-grader. I was much more secure in my abilities now. Although my language was still a work in progress, I could generally keep up with what was going on in class. I excelled at my school work.

West was a melting pot of several junior highs, and West was where my English name of Lisa found me. My U.S. History teacher, a middle-aged coach at the school, was terrible with names. Even though he tried and tried, he just could not get his southern drawl to pronounce Muoi. Finally, in desperation, he said in his unique country way, "Y'all look like a Lisa to me. Okay if I just call you Lisa?" I said, "Sure." The name stuck. Soon, more and more people at the school started calling me Lisa, and I found myself answering them. Before I knew it, Muoi faded into the background, and Lisa stood in her place. Later, when I applied for citizenship, Lisa was the name I chose to keep.

On the way home from West one day, I was blessed with meeting another Vietnamese student, Julie. She and I became close friends as well. Julie lived in the Shadowlake addition, not too far from my house, so we rode the bus together to and from school every day. With my aunt and uncle's permission, I would often stop at her house on my walk home, where we could talk and have a snack. Julie was a year older than me and had been in eighth grade at Brink when I started in seventh.

Throughout the rest of mid-high and high school, Tram, Julie, and others who crossed my path kept me motivated to strive and improve. Their energy and encouragement meant that the girl who struggled with "See Spot run" managed to graduate in the top ten percent of her class of 700 at Moore High School. I went on to the University of Oklahoma to study and finally receive my bachelor's degree in mathematics in 1990. This accomplishment was yet another miracle in my life. As a Chinese student back in Vietnam, I doubt if I would have completed my secondary studies. University would have been out of the question.

Chapter 27

二十七

Old faces, new beginnings

Figure 27: Miriwa Restaurant – Mom and Dad

Communicating with my parents in Vietnam was a slow and tedious process. There was no direct phone service to Vietnam, and even if there was, my parents did not have a telephone. Mail service was hit-and-miss at best, and its best was painfully slow. It might take three weeks or longer to receive anything from home.

When we had first arrived, Hung and I sent an expensive telegram to my parents. We told them about our safe arrival, our aunt and uncle, and beginning our new lives. Then we waited. The days seemed to stretch out forever. Several weeks passed before we finally received a reply, and when we did, I was beside myself with joy.

Mother and Father were thrilled that we were safe and healthy and that our new family in America was treating us well. They told us about the newspaper article and photo and how it had calmed their fears somewhat. The letter went on to talk about the rest of the family and how life was going there. As I read the letter, again and again, I could hear my mother's voice in every word. Every night, I prayed to God that by some miracle, He would reunite us.

In this manner, we managed to communicate for over a year. Then came a time when we received no reply - Mother's letter didn't come. Additional weeks passed. We were so worried. What could have happened? We felt helpless, even more so knowing that we had no way to discover what was going on or what might have happened to them. Mother's last letter had hinted at problems. What was going on?

Finally, in early 1981, we finally received a letter. This letter, however, was very different from the others. This one came from a Malaysian refugee camp. In the letter, she said that life had become unbearable for my family in Vietnam.

The government charged exorbitant taxes on small businesses such as our sugar cane enterprise, leaving the family working harder and starving for their efforts. In desperation, my father struck a deal with another boat owner. Although my father could not pay anything upfront, he promised to pay the full price once they were safely in the West. The owner agreed. I find the idea amazing that my father's word would be enough to assure this considerable debt. He made good on that promise as well. Every month, he first paid the boat owner, who had immigrated to Boston. When the last payment finally came due, he and my mother went to Boston to meet him. They wanted to deliver the final payment personally and again thank the man who had saved theirs and their children's lives.

She went on to relate some details of their journey across the South China Sea. For the most part, it was like Hung's and mine, fraught with uncertainty and peril - no promises, only chances. The risks were much higher for them because there were so many more in the group. They almost lost my six-year-old sister, Le, when the U.S. Naval vessel that rescued them was transferring them aboard from their smaller boat. Only a desperate catch that snagged her ankle saved her from a watery death in the sea. The U.S. ship safely delivered the refugees to Malaysia and the refugee camp there.

It was beyond exciting to discover our family was in a camp. Still, it presented an entirely new set of obstacles for Hung and me as well. Sponsorship rules had changed somewhat. Somehow, we had to raise the money necessary to bring them the rest of the way and take care of them when they arrived. Some refugee groups would help, but we would have to do the heavy lifting. Hung still had his job at the shopping cart factory, and I, although only fourteen, needed to find one too.

I asked my friends and soon found employment as a waitress at Lee's Garden, a Chinese restaurant not far away from where I lived. Mr. Lee, the owner, was an excellent employer. He would pick me up after school and then take me home after the restaurant closed. Everything I made went to get my family back together. I spent nothing on myself.

A few months later, another friend told me about a Vietnamese restaurant looking for waitresses. She told me that the patrons paid better tips, which I could desperately use. Reluctantly, I said goodbye to Lee's and went to the Anh Hong Restaurant. I worked there for a year before Hung and I had enough to pay for our family's transport to the states.

Once we had their expenses paid and our sponsorship papers completed and formalized, we needed to address the problem of housing. Every day during the weeks before their scheduled arrival in Oklahoma City, Hung and I searched everywhere for larger accommodations for our soon to be exploding family. The more we looked, the more discouraged we became. It seemed that everything larger was far too expensive for even our combined salaries. Making matters even worse, the landlords insisted on first and last month's rent and a security deposit as well- all paid in advance. We knew that quite a bit of time would pass before we could count on any wages earned by the others. Finally, we realized that we could afford nothing larger. We would all have to live, at least in the beginning, at the duplex. A duplex designed for two would now have ten.

So, in 1982, three years after Hung and I made our journey, my miracle came true. Our family was able to join us here. This time we made sure that there was no paperwork mix-up. This time we knew exactly when they were to arrive. No one made any bureaucratic errors. Hung and I got to the airport much too early and then waited anxiously for their flight to come in. He and I became like the ones we had watched with jealous stares in 1979 as we now stood impatiently waiting for their plane to unload. As more and more people came up the jetway, I became a little concerned. What was taking so long! Where were they? Then...joy! I cannot express the feelings that coursed through me as I saw them, at last, coming up the jetway tunnel. I shouted at them at the top of my voice. They heard and called back. Once, we had reconciled ourselves to forever being apart. Now, we were back together again! Our laughter and tears mixed with ever-increasing volume as we hugged in the gate area. Everyone around us stared as we all talked at once in Chinese. Let them stare. We didn't care. The Quan family was together again.

Hung and I shouldn't have worried about the duplex. My parents said that the house was perfect for now, and somehow we knew it would be. Our actual living quarters back in Cho Lon had not been much larger than this space. What mattered most was that we were together again under one roof. I moved back to the duplex from my uncle's home to be with my family. He and his wife were so excited for all of us. He even agreed to let us continue to use his address when we registered for school so that my siblings and I could be in Moore schools together. They said that they were happy to answer questions from the district if they ever checked.

The transition for my family was more manageable as well. They had spent the year and a half in the refugee camp learning many things, including basic English. They also had Hung and me and our recent experiences to assist in navigating this new land and its customs. School was not as scary for my siblings either. The school's approach to non-English speakers had improved quite a bit, which was a great benefit to my brothers and sisters. The Asian community in Oklahoma City was much larger now, giving my parents and San more people to talk with using Chinese or Vietnamese. The world seemed to be a kinder place.

We took advantage of my uncle's address and enrolled in Moore schools. A friend could take us in the morning and another one who could bring us home in the afternoon. My mother and older sisters soon found work at a Vietnamese restaurant near NW 23rd and Western, which was only about three miles from the house, an easy walk. At the end of every day, they gathered the "throwaway" food and brought the bounty home with them. Among the throwaways would be chicken wings – lots of chicken wings. In 1982, chicken wings were not worthy of a place on a restaurant's menu, let alone as an entree. As a result, they became a large part of our diet. My father had recipes that could make chicken wings into a gourmet meal. School and work consumed every aspect of every day. At night, exhausted bodies littered the floor on makeshift pallets, tired but happy in our new life together.

In 1984, an opportunity came our way that would change our lives forever. A Mexican restaurant on NW 23rd near Classen had failed and was up for sale. We paid no attention because we could not afford to buy it, but providence stepped in once again. The owner of the Vietnamese restaurant where my mother and San worked offered to buy the business and rent the facility back to us monthly. We would pay the rent, take care of any remodeling needed, and staff the restaurant.

We realized that this was an enormous job but also that it represented an even greater opportunity for us. Every day after school or work, we traded our school clothes for work clothes. We started the remodeling of the new restaurant almost immediately. Everything involved with the remodel we did. We tore out walls, mounted sheetrock, did all the carpentry, and painted everything inside and out. Every nail and splotch of paint had our sweat and blood enmeshed. We claimed everything. Around nine at night, we would go home, prepare our dinner, do our homework, and go to bed - knowing that tomorrow promised nothing but to be a repeat of today.

Mother had a gift for visualizing changes to the new restaurant. She had a knack for knowing precisely what to do. Mom would tell us to remove a wall because she knew the restaurant would be better without it, and she was always right. She instinctively knew just the right colors for paint and carpet. With her vision and constant supervision, our family's restaurant continued to take form until finally, we reached a point where we opened. We had to open. We had no more money to spend on construction. Ready or not, we needed income now.

When *Miriwa*, our restaurant, opened, we - all of us – took ownership. We could see every nail we pounded and every paint spill we tried to clean up. We all took pride in our efforts to make this wonderful thing happen. After opening, we did everything. We waited tables, cooked the food, and cleaned up at the end of the day. Mom was the main draw that kept people coming back. She welcomed every customer with a warm smile, making them feel at once part of her family. I was reminded of back home in Cho Lon where she would ask a visitor, "Have you ate yet?" Mom had a fantastic knack for tasting a dish once and determining what the ingredients were so that she could make a duplicate. She was very selective about what appeared on our menu. Only the best was suitable for our restaurant to serve. Her enthusiasm was contagious with both staff and customers, and the restaurant succeeded beyond our wildest dreams. The success allowed our family to grow and prosper to the point that we could at last buy a larger home.

Naturally, there were many hardships during those first four years together. Money was often short. We would have to give up our time with friends to support our family. Almost every night, we would collapse in exhaustion after school and work. All of that aside, we were happy because we were together. Nothing would pull us apart again.

Chapter 28

Full circle

Figure 28: Main road from Ho Chi Minh City to Cho Lon, 2017

The summer of 1989 arrived in due course. Ten years had passed since a wide-eyed little girl had come to the United States afraid of her own shadow. The woman who now appeared in the mirror reflected little of that girl. I was no longer insecure, no more in doubt of my abilities and talents. I had accomplished more than my wildest teenage dreams. I had worked hard at my studies, and that work had paid off. Next fall, I would be entering my final year at the University of Oklahoma as a mathematics major.

As a special treat that summer, my older sister Sandy (San) and I decided to go on vacation to the British Protectorate of Hong Kong, a sort of girls' trip. The restaurant was doing a booming business and making lots of money. For the first time in what seemed like forever, we both felt comfortable leaving the family and our business for more than a day or two at a time. Somehow, Hong Kong, a place we had never been yet so close to our roots, seemed like the right place to go.

At twenty-three and twenty-six years of age, we were two independent young women out to conquer the world or at least see a goodly portion of it. We were full of life and more than ready for a little adventure. Hong Kong would be perfect! Even more exciting, we would be making our first trip ever as U.S. citizens, and our new U.S. passports were burning a hole in our pockets, begging for use! We were ready for anything life threw at us, so long as life didn't throw anything too hard.

Hong Kong was stunning, everything that the brochures promised and more. We went everywhere. We did everything. We saw everything. We walked along the Tsim Sha Tsui Promenade and gazed at its magnificent views of the city skyline and Victoria harbor. Of course, all the incredible shops up and down its length didn't hurt its appeal at all. We went to magnificent temples and markets – lots of markets. We even touched on a couple of museums as well.

I loved being able to use my native Cantonese again. The way people looked at me, though, made me wonder if I might be a bit rusty. More than once, I noticed a clerk carefully mulling over his answer to my question. Despite my attempts to maintain my native language, I feared that I manage to attach a bit of an "Okie" accent now. Regardless, Sandy and I had a wonderful time, and like all beautiful experiences, we never wanted that trip to end. Yet, as our departure time rushed forward to meet us, we discovered that Hong Kong had yet another surprise for us - one that would drastically change our plans.

One of our last afternoons, we were strolling down the promenade arm in arm. The day was gorgeous, a perfect day for enjoying all the sights one last time while jointly bemoaning returning to work and school. Close to the end of the walk, we stopped dead in our tracks, speechless at what we saw. There, prominently displayed in a travel agent's window, was something that neither of us ever imagined we would see. There was a poster promoting the beginning of commercial air transport between Hong Kong and Ho Chi Minh City. The maiden trip was only a few days away!

The Vietnamese government had terminated all commercial carriers from the West after the April 30th reunification. Some believed that the Communists would never permit contact with the West again. Sandy and I became so excited at the thought of revisiting our friends and family that we immediately went in to talk to the travel agent and then the tour operator. They were both more than happy to echo our excitement at the chance of selling two tickets. They both assured us that there would be no problem with our reentry into Vietnam or our return to Hong Kong, but again they were selling something, so we were not as positive as they.

The U.S. Consulate in Hong Kong was not as optimistic in its response. They were totally against the idea. The official reminded us of some serious concerns we needed to consider before undertaking such a venture. Over and over, they lectured us that such a journey would be at our own risk. The United States had no agreements with the government of Vietnam that would guarantee our safety. We would have no Embassy or Consulate to back us up if we got into trouble while on Vietnamese soil. We listened politely, but we were undeterred.

Finally, we had the most challenging conversation of the day, a lengthy and expensive transcontinental chat with our mother back in Oklahoma. She was also worried about what kinds of problems we would face and repeated several of the same arguments that the Consulate had mentioned. After all the conversations and all the warnings, Sandy and I sat down. We talked seriously about whether to take the trip. In the end, our emotions won out. We fought down all the warnings and concerns. We were going back to Ho Chi Minh City and Cho Lon.

We only had a day to prepare for this spur of the moment adventure. We had to change our return flights from Hong Kong and make plans for stowing some of our luggage at the hotel while we were gone. The extra time allowed us to rethink some of the concerns that people had shared with us.

We admitted that this journey was indeed a scary proposition. Both Sandy and I had left Vietnam by illegal means. There was a chance that the authorities would arrest us on arrival rather than accept our new citizenship. After all, the United States and Vietnam had not had formal relations since Saigon's fall in 1975.

Then there was the question of money. Would we be able to spend our U.S. dollars there or even exchange them for Vietnamese dong? The one thought that bothered us the most was that if anything happened to us in Vietnam, there was a chance that no one would ever know or be able to find out what had become of us. Even with these substantial risks ringing in our ears, the overpowering desire to return to our homeland was greater. We left the next day.

After all our worrying, our evening arrival at Ho Chi Minh Airport was decidedly anti-climactic. Despite the advertising campaign promoting the tour, the flight from Hong Kong was only half full. I guessed that we weren't the only ones concerned about the reception this flight would receive. Others wanted to see how this flight came out first before they tried to go themselves. The terminal receiving area's customs process turned out to be very casual and relaxed, not what we had expected at all. I guessed that the officials on duty had been instructed to make us feel welcome, which they did. There was one time when the passport officer asked us to contribute to his "coffee fund." We knew this was a blatant attempt to get a bribe from us. We politely refused and, after receiving a scowl from the official, he stamped our passports and shuffled us through anyway.

Currency exchange was next, and I was a nervous wreck as we waited in line. I shouldn't have worried. Not only did Vietnam accept U.S. currency, it welcomed our dollars. In the end, the only thing frightening was how much our U.S. dollars were worth! Each dollar equaled over 20,000 Vietnamese dong. We did our best to hide our surprise and our purses as we left the exchange desk as newly minted "millionaires." Things were looking up.

We exited the terminal building. The rest of our tour group obediently followed its leader onto a bus and headed for their hotel somewhere in District 1. Sandy and I received some questioning looks when we stayed behind, but we assured them that we had other accommodations and vowed to rejoin them for the return flight in a week. I almost hated seeing them go. I didn't know any of them, but their presence was a little bit of familiarity. After they left, I suddenly felt very alone there, standing in front of the terminal even with Sandy by my side. So much seemed the same, but I was sure many things had changed as well, and I remembered that change was not necessarily a good thing in this country.

We had no one waiting for us, of course. We had told a small lie. No one knew we were coming. Only a day earlier, we hadn't known! There was no way to call or communicate what we were doing with our family here. We did, however, know our destination very well. We hailed a three-wheeled motorcycle cab, situated ourselves and our bags on board, and directed the driver to a street in Cho Lon that we knew quite well. We clutched our suitcases and held on for dear life as the motorcycle accelerated to a high rate of speed, such that we had not experienced since leaving here. The cab wove in and out of the late evening traffic with little regard for safety. I laughed that at least this aspect of our homeland had not changed over the years. The only speed was still faster. Agility was more important than traffic laws. Laughing at ourselves, we sat back and proceeded to enjoy the ride.

I kept getting a feeling of déjà vu as the driver navigated the boulevards. The surroundings were so surreal. Everything around us still had that same feel, that same smell of home. We watched as familiar streets passed by one by one, seemingly unchanged from the day we left. Even the same awnings swayed in the wind over the stores. I felt as if we had gone back in time. 1979 seemed frozen here.

Sandy and I looked at each other knowingly. I know we had the same thought at that moment. We felt eerily strange that after all the trials and dangers we had endured to escape this place, here we were – back where everything started, and of our own free will as well. Slowly, I allowed fear and apprehension to seep from my body. I was just beginning to relax when I glimpsed the Catholic church's familiar steeple rise in the distance, getting larger with every second that passed.

That was when a new concern grabbed me. Sandy sensed my change and asked what was wrong. I told her that I was worried about how our neighbors, friends, or even our family, would receive us. We were the ones who had left. We had deserted the rest and forced them to remain here.

We were confident that our old house was still there. My father had left it entrusted to my aunt, who still lived there with my cousin, Tran. They had thought hard about coming with my family to the United States, but in the end, they decided to stay behind in Cho Lon. They reasoned that if everyone left, the government would confiscate the house. They wanted to be sure that, for whatever reason, the family's escape plan failed, there was a home waiting for them here.

We had corresponded back and forth with my aunt and cousin several times since my family had arrived seven years ago. All those communications had been in writing, of course, but the messages had been friendly. Hospitality being so much of the Chinese culture, Sandy and I felt confident that we would find a place to stay there. The question was, would they welcome us or think of us as unwanted stepchildren encroaching on their home. Then there were the others in the neighborhood. We had gone while they had remained - stuck here. Would they resent us for that?

The taxi dropped us off at the familiar alley by the church. We paid the driver and then stopped and gazed unbelievably at the entrance to our hamlet. There in the shadows was my aunt's drink cart still chained to the wall just as I remembered it from so long ago. My déjà vu became even stronger as we moved slowly forward, pulling our suitcases behind us over the broken pavement. The racket they made was thunderous for this hour, especially compared to the relative silence around us.

Now, my fears were tested. Heads began popping out of doorways and windows to see what the noise was. There were shouts of anger at the interruption to their evening; some even came outside to investigate. There we were, standing in the alley, not sure what to do next, surrounded by a crowd. Then, one of the women shouted out when she recognized Sandy. The mood of the group changed immediately. Angry calls for disturbing their rest changed to happy shouts of joy that San had returned. The chorus became even louder when they realized that the young woman with her was Muoi - me! The women could not believe that I was she. Just as in the old days when the soldiers raided the hamlet, the voices passed from house to house - not a whispered warning this time, but a triumphant "San and Muoi are back!"

All of the excitement successfully spoiled our impromptu family reunion. When, at last, we came face to face with our aunt and cousin, we found that we had not even begun to tap our happiness, and we could not contain ourselves! We hugged and giggled like schoolgirls. Tears of joy rolled down our cheeks while we all talked at once. More and more neighbors joined in as the news spread, and soon, there was a large crowd standing just outside our house. They rejoiced in our presence. Of all the people who had left over the years, no one had returned.

My aunt did not want to leave us, so she had a friend alert the neighborhood commissar that we would be staying with her. It seemed that things here were not as free as they appeared. We knew we were home when my aunt voiced that her biggest concern was that she had nothing prepared for us to eat.

When I awoke to the rooster's crow the next morning, the sense of time standing still was just as strong as the night before. I was sleeping on the same bunk bed on the third floor. The impressions on my body were bright red from the perforated metal that had been below me. The only difference was that I didn't have to share my bunk as I once did. I went to the locker where my clothing had always been. I almost expected my uniform to still be there from ten years earlier. I was more than a little disappointed when I found the locker to be bare. As I hastily dressed and headed downstairs, I caught myself absent-mindedly checking the table for my daily allowance. Of course, it wasn't there either.

Tran and I walked around the hamlet that morning. While we strolled, some of the magic of yesterday evening began to fade in the light of day. Were the alleyways always this narrow? The paint on the doorways looked dingier and more faded than I remembered. The cars, mopeds, and motorcycles on the main road fouled the air with the stench of their exhaust. Their engines were so loud that talking in a normal voice was almost impossible. I overheard neighbors arguing over insignificant things like, "You swept your dirt into my doorway." and, "You play your music too loud!" The sights and sounds of this new day assaulted my eyes and ears. This was not right. They were not as they used to be.

My concerns grew until I finally decided to ask Tran about them. She looked at me strangely and frowned. She was confused at my question. In turn, her response confused me. She said, "Nothing has changed. Things are the same as always." I begged to differ with her as I pointed out the rooms' minuscule size. I mean, the existing third floor couldn't accommodate my entire family. It was smaller than my private bedroom in the U.S. Surely, someone had narrowed the alleyways during the past decade. When we had played here, I knew they were much larger. Road noise was much louder than before.

Again and again, for every point I raised, Tran assured me that no one had changed any aspect of the house or the alleys since I had left. The neighbors were just as contrary as they had always been. The roads still carried the same amount of traffic and, if anything, were quieter now. I was sorely mistaken.

I shook my head. I knew that I was right. I noticed more and more examples of change as we wandered farther out into the surrounding area. The vendors had pushed their stalls forward until they were right up to the street. That couldn't be right. Shopping wouldn't be safe. The traffic surged around us, going every which way, especially in the traffic circles. One risked death just crossing the street. We had to walk in the shadow of a car to negotiate our way around one of them. I also noticed how much smaller the market was from my memories. In my mind, I remembered that the area had been at least twice this size in my youth.

I could tell that my comments were beginning to bother Tran, and I didn't want to cause her any more distress than I had. We changed the topic as we slowly walked back to the house. We talked about the fun we had shared and the times we caused trouble for the rest of the family. We laughed over the good times and hardly mentioned the bad. She asked me about America and my life there. She was fascinated when I told her about university and how my studies were going. Two things that didn't come up in conversation were our failed trip to Hanoi and the dangers of my boat journey. Some memories needed to stay buried, at least for now.

As word of Sandy's and my arrival trickled throughout Cho Lon, more and more family and friends showed up at the house. Their appearance reminded me of how fast information got around here, even without telephones. I saw Nhi for the first time in ten years and was amazed at how she had changed. She was a married woman now, and her first child was by her side. My other friends had also gone on with their lives. Each of them now had a family of her own. I must admit that I felt a little jealous since I didn't even have a boyfriend.

I had bittersweet feelings as I saw how life had continued here without me. Of course, I realized that my life had changed also. Part of me even understood that my circumstances had changed much more than theirs had. They were still going along the paths set in place by their ancestors while I had forged an entirely new one. The fact that I had returned at all represented a significant change in my life. I was still disappointed. I guessed that I had expected Cho Lon to stay frozen in time.

For the next few days, we visited other family and friends. We had a wonderful time reconnecting with this lost part of our lives. Despite my earlier concerns, everyone was so welcoming and friendly. Everyone was so wonderful, San and I decided to do something special for them - a party. We would throw a gala for all of them on our last evening in Cho Lon.

The very next morning, we went to a neighborhood restaurant to put our plan into motion. We felt that it was a large enough venue for everyone to fit easily, and the proprietor readily agreed. The real question was could we afford the price. We knew we would have to pay in cash, and though we were "millionaires," the costs would add up quickly. After describing what we had in mind to the restaurant owner, we waited patiently as he prepared an estimate for us. While he was doing that, Sandy and I discussed what we could drop from the proposal and still have a good party.

The price he gave was unbelievable! We had a hard time maintaining a straight face. We didn't even haggle, which was impressive. He agreed to provide the restaurant space, food and drink, a live band for entertainment, and a videographer for only $360! What an incredible bargain! Back in Oklahoma, the cost of the band for my junior prom had exceeded that! We couldn't sign the agreement fast enough. After all, we didn't want him to change his mind. All that was left to do was getting the word out to all our family and friends.

Why was the cost so low? Money was all relative. For us in 1989, $360 represented about two weeks' wages. Here in Vietnam, that sum would take a lot longer to earn. In actuality, $360 was significantly more than two months' salary for the average Vietnamese worker. With the cost of raising a family, such an extravagance as a party like this would be an impossible luxury for regular wage earners.

Nonetheless, with the price so low, Sandy and I braced ourselves to be underwhelmed on the night of the party. The reverse sticker shock worried us. We were afraid that the promises made to us might fall short of our vision for the evening, but we shouldn't have worried. The party was everything the restaurant owner promised and more. The event was an enormous success with our friends and family. All of them came. We ate, danced, and sang for hours on end. The food was fantastic! Everyone ate their fill, and many even took some home for the next day! We never wanted the night to end. This event would be the talk of the hamlet for years to come.

However, all good things must end eventually, and so with the party. As we were leaving, a line of boys on motorcycles, all students of Tran, waited outside the restaurant. Each of them was anxiously vying for the right to give Sandy or me a ride home. The attention flattered us but left us more than a little flustered. Who would we choose! How could we select an escort from all these clamoring boys! I am sure that I blushed a little at so much attention. Although I am not sure who San rode with, I safely chose a family member. I didn't want to cause any hard feelings, but the slighted boys looked very discouraged as we sped off.

The next morning, we were a sad pair of girls as we started gathering our things and preparing to say goodbye. As difficult as the decision was to come back to Vietnam, leaving was an even harder one. Hugs were tight, and tears flowed abundantly. Sandy and I both promised to return soon and to bring others with us. As she hugged me, Tran told me through her tears that at least this time, she had the chance to say a proper goodbye. My vision blurred as tears crept into my eyes as well.

Before we left for the airport, I excused myself to make one final stop. I went back to my place of youthful solitude - the roof for one last look around. Standing there, I saw the metal sheet where we had dried the Chinese medicine now rusted with disuse. I clearly remembered carefully placing the small discs on the metal and picking them up after they dried. The Catholic Church was still there, of course. The doors had reopened to its parishioners in 1986. It seemed that the Communists now saw a need for the stabilizing influence of faith. My Catholic friends had been correct in that their beliefs had persevered. I was disappointed as I noted that we were no longer the tallest building around. Newer, taller buildings had sprung up on the main roads and now blocked my view. Everywhere I looked, the paint was drab and chipped. The world was different.

In my mind, I wondered how my parents had ever survived here with eight children? How had they managed to evolve alongside their country with such turmoil around them, changing their source of income seamlessly from

Chinese medicine to sugar reseller and finally to sugar manufacturer? Even in the refugee camp, my siblings had told me how hard my parents had worked to support them - always looking out for what was best for the children – for us. My mother had once told me that "it is easy to look ahead when the worst was behind you. Only good times could be ahead." That philosophy, coupled with grit and determination, allowed them to succeed against impossible odds both here and in the country I now called home - the United States.

Here in Cho Lon, despite Tran's insistence to the contrary, a disease seemed to have its grip on the surrounding city. Everything appeared the same on the surface, yet everything changed so drastically when I dug a little deeper. Apart from the party last night, everyone seemed quieter. Everywhere in the hamlet, I found new neighbors inhabiting the homes of old friends. A type of malaise seemed to drape itself over the neighborhood and the city, but somehow I was the only one to notice or care. How could they not see the change? How could they not be afraid of what was happening?

Just then, as I lamented the fate of my beloved city, a noise reached my ears. The sounds of children playing in the alley below found their way up to me. From the sound of it, they were actively engaged in a game of tag. Their screams and shouts of joy echoed up the walls and found their way into my heart. There was a part of me that desperately wanted to run down and share in their games, to kick off my shoes and run haphazardly through the alleys playing tag or hide and seek or crawl on the ground with marbles.

I smiled and remembered when we went to the market yesterday. How I laughed as I haggled over the price with the vendor, even though I could have easily paid the asking amount. We both got what we wanted at a fair price. I remember cringing and saying a silent prayer as we walked past the light pole with the five lights, the one where the thief had met his fate on that market day over ten years ago. I could still see his dead eyes burning into my live ones as we passed. I shuddered at the thought and again felt the chill from that experience. I suffered a touch of sadness when I discovered that my birthplace was no longer a place to bring babies into the world and housed offices instead.

At that moment on the roof, I realized that Vietnam, that Cho Lon, was not my home anymore. This place had not changed at all. I was the one who had changed. This was Muoi's home, Muoi's world. This place was full of her memories – her life. In these alleyways were the joys of her youth, and there they would never die. Those memories would live forever in the joy of children playing in the alleys and the churchyard. At that moment, a pang of sadness welled up from the bottom of my soul. It was a sadness that found itself climbing into my throat and eyes until I finally released it in a long heartfelt sigh.

This was Muoi's world...

I am Lisa.

Afterward by Bruce Baker

After that fateful trip with Sandy in 1989, Lisa and her family continued to prosper in their adopted home. She earned her degree in mathematics from the University of Oklahoma in 1990. Lisa then continued working for the family business, helping to assure that Miriwa remained a resounding success. There, while waiting tables, she met a young medical student from Taiwan, Paul Cheng. She and Paul later married and raised three beautiful children: Mika, Miki, and Michael. Each of them is immensely talented. All three attend Oklahoma University like their mother.

After becoming a U.S. citizen, Lisa's father tried to get her aunt and cousin from Cho Lon into the U.S. under the Orderly Departure Program (ODP). This process is a long and arduous one, often taking over a decade to complete the paperwork and get the necessary visas. This wait proved too much for her aunt. She died before Lisa's father finished the process. The U.S. eventually turned down his petition for Tran because my cousin was too distant a relation to fall under the program.

Lisa's mother, Xu Huynh, who had always been Lisa's guiding light, passed from this life in 1998 after losing her battle with cancer. Her father, Quyen Quan, followed her in death in 2009. Their legacy, their children, lives on. They passed their lessons of determination and resilience to their offspring, who are now giving them to their children and grandchildren as well.

The rest of the Quan family continues to thrive. Each has an area of expertise in which they excel. Although Miriwa closed its doors after their father died, a new enterprise, Pho39, opened in 2017. Billy (Hung) does most of the cooking with everyone else helping as much as they can - waiting tables, mopping floors. Mika claims that this is their Miriwa, and they must treat this restaurant in that way - with respect and diligence.

Lisa's cousin, Hung (Mike), lived in Colorado for a few years before moving to Oklahoma City. Her other cousin on the boat, Ly Tho, still lives in his sponsoring country of Italy. In like manner, her uncle, Chau Nam, remains in his adoptive country of Canada. Mike filed for ODP for his family once he was eligible. Unfortunately, his father, Lisa's Uncle Ho, did not live long enough to see his son again. Still, Mike and the rest of the family, his mother, and three of his siblings were reunited when Mike sponsored them to come to the United States.

The entire Quan family tries to get together every Tuesday night to share a meal at one house or another. Not everyone can be there every Tuesday, but as many as possible are there. I have been delighted to be able to join in on many of these events. Anywhere from forty to fifty persons usually show up. Food is plentiful. Laughing is contagious. Love abounds. During the school year, the children help each other with homework while the adults converse. The spirit that pushed this family upon America's shore is very much alive in their children. Theirs are the family values that defined their parents and should inspire us all.

Lisa took over a travel agency, Airway Travel, in 2001. She specializes in Asian trips, especially for those who find communicating in English difficult. In a time when travel agencies are an anachronism, hers stays busy. In the times that I have visited her, there have always been people waiting for her to help them. She even opened a branch agency in Ho Chi Minh City. That way, travelers have a place to go if they have problems while visiting family and friends in their homeland.

Lisa goes back to Vietnam often, as do many members of her family. Tran still lives in the house in Cho Lon and still tutors students there. Every time Lisa returns to Vietnam, she always brings an extra suitcase filled with things to make Tran's life a little more enjoyable. Even though she is in her 60s, Tran still climbs the stairs every day to cook, sleep, and do other things. Sometimes her brother's wife stays with her to help, but often she is on her own. Tran was able to come to the United States for a visit in 2018. During her stay, her American family gave her all the experiences she could imagine and more. I got to visit with her again at Steve's house at one of the Tuesday meals. She was still full of life and as irrepressible as ever.

Looking back on my visit in 2016, I remembered how Lisa's personality changed as we approached her old hamlet from our hotel in District 1. The years seemed to melt away as she excitedly pointed out landmarks from her youth: the place she was born, the site of her old school, and the street where the market was. I then saw the church, just as she had described, rising ahead of us. As I watched, she once again became Muoi, and the excitement in her voice gave me a glimpse of the twelve-year-old who took her chance and came to America.

One Last Thing

People often use the words immigrant and refugee as synonyms rather than identifying them as two diverse peoples. True, their goals might appear to be the same but, I assure you, they are not. Although both originate in a foreign country and seek a better life elsewhere, there are distinct differences.

An immigrant plans his or her change of country over an extended period, typically years, while he or she completes the required paperwork, applies for visas, and waits for interviews. The foreign-born spouse of an American citizen waits an average of eighteen months for a visa. That is the shortest wait time for all visa applications. Depending on the quota established for your native country and your value to the United States, your wait time for an immigrant visa can be decades.

Refugees, on the other hand, react to events occurring around them at a gut level. War, famine, gangs, and persecution are some of the more common reasons. They usually love their native country, and only the direst reasons would cause them to leave it. They often flee in the middle of the night with only the clothes on their backs as unforeseen dangers appear to threaten their existence or the existence of their family. A refugee's escape typically involves other risks, some life-threatening, on the journey. No sane person would take his or her family on a long, dangerous quest across foreign lands and seas - hoping for a chance of something better, something safer for them all. Yet, every year circumstances at home demand that very sane people feel forced to make this choice for that very reason – a chance."

The Chance is a journey of refugees told through the eyes of a twelve-year-old girl whose life takes a dramatic turn when she suddenly finds herself as a refugee. In a twist of fate, she boards a boat of over five-hundred souls, including her older brother, attempting to escape from Vietnam, her home. There is no destination or promise of a better life. As Lisa's brother, Billy, said in his interview: "We did not risk death to come to the United States. There were no guarantees of anything. There were no promises. We risked death for a CHANCE."

This chance is one that all refugees take, whether crossing the sea in a boat, riding a thousand miles on a train, or walking a hundred miles over a barren wasteland. They don't expect guarantees, only a chance to live in a place where death or destruction is not the only choice. Lisa Cheng (Muoi) described the circumstances as either, "You can die quickly taking the chance, or you can die slowly by staying."

My acquaintance with Lisa began when her daughter, Mika, was in my eighth grade English class at Sacred Heart Catholic School in Oklahoma City. My class was studying the plight of Cambodian refugees after the Vietnamese war in Literature class when Mika told me that her mother had also escaped - from Vietnam on a boat. Intrigued, I contacted Lisa to see if she would consider speaking to the class about her experiences. I knew that many refugees preferred to keep their experiences - their horrors, private, but I hoped she would say yes.

To my delight, she agreed. Her story, this story, was captivating. Her and her brother's experiences while coming to this country were the plots of fiction, yet somehow rang true. When I retired from teaching in 2016, I again approached her about telling her story, her life experiences to the world. This book is the result.

I had no idea what I was getting into, especially when I had to deal with my concept of Asian life. Things that were normal to Lisa were alien to me. My world view was too restrictive; I kept trying to put a Western face on an Eastern world, and the Eastern world refused to fit. Lisa had to teach me, slowly and patiently about custom differences, world history, as well as a radically different concept of family, life, and language.

Although Lisa, her husband, Paul, and their children all spoke English well, many other family members did not. Throughout the research part of this project, I leaned heavily on Lisa and Mika to translate their relative's testimonies when they could not adequately convey their thoughts. When I still could not fully comprehend her experiences in Cho Lon, Lisa's solution was simple - "Let's go to Vietnam!" So, we did.

In Vietnam, I saw firsthand the things she had described. I saw the home she grew up in, the same house where her cousin Tran lives to this day. Although the hamlet had changed in some ways, in others, it was the same as the home she knew over thirty years earlier. I went to the markets and the shops. I drank the sweet drinks. I attended Mass in the church behind her home, where she had gone daily with Tran. I walked the streets of Cho Lon, which still reflected the French's influences from one hundred years before, and saw the traffic of a population that had long outgrown its infrastructure. Most importantly, I experienced the warmness and openness of her Chinese-Vietnamese family. The love there was palatable, and they shared it freely with me, a stranger, an alien.

Before leaving Vietnam, we went to a spot on the Mekong Delta, where her boat had departed thirty-eight years earlier. I had thought of Vietnam as such a small country, yet the journey still took close to a full day from Ho Chi Minh City to our destination at Long Xuyen, 190 km. (117 mi.) away. The roads have improved much from 1979. I can only imagine how grueling the journey must have been then. Billy told me his trip was "one rough ride," and I believe him.

While we were in Long Xuyen, we found a boat of the same design as Lisa and Billy had taken. I could not believe how small! Even now, I have difficulties visualizing over five hundred people on board. We spoke to a woman who had lived her entire life at the riverside. At first, she denied knowing anything about an escape boat in the area back then. Later, after some coaxing, she finally admitted not only the boat but the relative that had been on board. Even after almost forty years, people are afraid to discuss these things.

Fear and trepidation run the length of Lisa's story. Many times, a slight change of fortune could have spelled tragedy for all those with her. Many other voyagers on many different boats did not have a "happy ever after" moment. Even though no one has an exact number, some estimates show at least 500,000 men, women, and children lost their lives trying to make the same journey Lisa and Billy made. Of those who did survive, many have stories that make this one sound tame in comparison. Stories that still wake them in the middle of the night in fear.

After our trip to Vietnam and hours and hours of interviews and transcriptions, I discovered the roadmap of an extraordinary story. The story of a carefree young tomboy of eight enjoying life to the fullest in 1974 and ending on her Cho Lon rooftop in 1989, ten years after she escaped. *The Chance* is the saga of that strong, independent, young girl and the determined, decisive woman she became.

Bibliography

Bailey, Mark, and Keven McAlester. *The Last Days in Vietnam*. American Experience/PBS, 2014.

Burgess, John. "Pirates Plaguing Vietnamese Refugees." *The Washington Post*, WP Company, 2 Sept. 1980, www.washingtonpost.com/archive/politics/1980/09/0 2/pirates-plaguing-vietnamese-refugees/ad8d9a2e-d502-4a98-bd45-e742e7781347/?noredirect=on&utm_term=.1e86c6f55184.

"Cambodia History Timeline." *World Atlas*, Worldatlas, 2018, **www.worldatlas.com/webimage/countrys/asia/cambodi a/khtimeln.htm**.

Dorgan, Michael. "XIN ÑÖØNG QUEÂN TOÂI (Forget-Me-Not)." *Thai_Pirate*, Mercury News, 10 June 2005, **www.vietnamexodus.info/vne/forgetmenot/documents/ thaipirate.htm**.

Doyle, Kevin. "Vietnam's Forgotten Cambodian War." *BBC News*, BBC, 14 Sept. 2014, **www.bbc.com/news/world-asia-29106034**.

Drainie, Bronwyn. "Pirates and Sinking Ships: One Refugee's Story - CBC Archives." *CBCnews*, CBC/Radio Canada, 29 July 1979, www.cbc.ca/archives/entry/pirates-and-sinking-ships-one-refugees-story.

Hills, Carol. "A Journalist Remembers the 'Quite Eerie' Calm after the Fall of Saigon." *Public Radio International*, PRI, 1 May 2015, **www.pri.org/stories/2015-05-01/journalist-remembers-quite-eerie-calm-after-fall-saigon**.

Hoang, Carina, editor. *Boat People: Personal Stories from the Vietnamese Exodus 1975-1996*. Beaufort Books, 2013.

Letwin, Brian. "A History of Vietnamese Banknotes." *Saigoneer*, 9 Sept. 2013, saigoneer.com/saigon-culture/980-a-history-of-vietnamese-banknotes.

"Maps of Vietnam." *Maps of the World | Maps of World Regions, Countries and Territories*, IVMH.NET, 2016, **www.maps-of-the-world.net/maps-of-asia/maps-of-vietnam/**.

Smith, Colin. "The Fall of Saigon as Witnessed by COLIN SMITH." *Daily Mail Online*, Associated Newspapers, 1 May 2015, **www.dailymail.co.uk/news/article-3063381/Saigon-Apocalypse-40-years-ago-week-COLIN-SMITH-witnessed-fall-Saigon-says-came-ways-horrifying-war-itself.html**.

Sissons, Claire. "Gua Sha: Uses, Benefits, and Side Effects." *Medical News Today*, MediLexicon International, 23 Dec. 2017, **www.medicalnewstoday.com/articles/320397.php**.

"The Vietnam Center and Archive: Exhibits - The Fall of Saigon." *The Vietnam Center and Archive, Texas Tech University*, 23 Oct. 2013, **www.vietnam.ttu.edu/exhibits/saigon/evacuation.php**.

"Vung Tau." *Vung Tau - Vietnam*, Galatourist, 2018, www.hue-hoian-tours.com/news_events/Vung_Tau.html.

Wallace, Charles P. "Nightmare at Sea: Sole Survivor Tells of Pirate Attack." *Los Angeles Times*, Los Angeles Times, 22 May 1989, articles.latimes.com/1989-05-22/news/mn-430_1_refugee-boat-pirate-attack-pham-ngoc-man-hung.

Woollacott, Martin. "Forty Years on from the Fall of Saigon: Witnessing the End of the Vietnam War." *The Guardian*, Guardian News and Media, 21 Apr. 2015, **www.theguardian.com/news/2015/apr/21/40-years-on-from-fall-of-saigon-witnessing-end-of-vietnam-war**.

Pictography

Fig 1 Baker, Bruce, *Incense Burner outside home*, 2016, Digital photograph

Fig 2 *Quan Family @ 1974*, 1974, Quan Family Collection, Scanned photograph

Fig 3 Baker, Bruce, *Market Scene in Cho Lon*, 2016, Digital photograph

Fig 4 Nguyen, Phuong, *Sand beach on the Condao island in Vung Tau, Vietnam*, 2020, Dreamstime.com, Digital photograph

Fig 5 Thoai, Huy, *Beauty architecture leads to Lord Buddha statue shining in Dai Tong Lam Pagoda*, 2020, Dreamstime.com, Digital photograph

Fig 6 Baker, Bruce, *Cho Lon House - Fourth floor kitchen/workshop*, 2016, Digital photograph

Fig 7 *Photograph of Muoi Dance Program pre-1975*, Quan Family Collection, Scanned photograph

Fig 8 Baker, Bruce, *Chinese New Year Celebration, Oklahoma City*, 2017, Digital photograph

Fig 9 Biserko, *Ho Chi Minh Poster*, 2020, Dreamstime.com, Digital photograph

Fig 10 Baker, Bruce, *The Fruit Peddler*, 2016, Digital photograph

Fig 11 Baker, Bruce, *Alligator at Con Phung Island*, 2016, Digital photograph

Fig 12 Baker, Bruce, *River scene on the way to My Tho*, 2016, Digital photograph

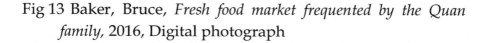

Fig 13 Baker, Bruce, *Fresh food market frequented by the Quan family,* 2016, Digital photograph

Pictography

Fig 14 Baker, Bruce, *Birdcage behind barred door in My Tho*, 2016, Digital photograph

Fig 15 Amadeustx, *DA NANG, VIETNAM - CIRCA AUGUST 2015: Moc Son Mountain, Marble mountains, Vietnam*, 2015, Dreamstime.com, Digital photograph

Fig 16 *The Escape Boat, 1979*, 1979, Quan Family Collection, Scanned photograph

Fig 17 Baker, Bruce, *Boat with plank on the Me Kong near Long Xuyên*, 2016, Digital photograph

Fig 18 Baker, Bruce, *Boat on the Me Kong*, 2016 Digital photograph

Fig 19 Krasowski, Witold, *Storm at Sea*, 2020, Dreamstime.com, Digital photograph

Fig 20 Penpun, Puripat, *Thai fishing boat at sea*, 2020, Dreamstime.com, Digital photograph

Fig 21 *The Kua Koon*, 1979, Quan Family Collection, Scanned photograph

Fig 22 *Hung and Muoi photo for immigration*, 1979, Quan Family Collection, Scanned photograph

Fig 23 Baker, Bruce, *The house on NW 1st in Oklahoma City*, 2017, Digital photograph

Fig 24 Baker, Bruce, *Flooded playground at Van Phat Resort on the Me Kong*, 2016, Digital photograph

Fig 25 Baker, Bruce, *View of Catholic Church from roof of Muoi's house*, 2016, Digital photograph

Fig 26 Baker, Bruce, *The exterior of Brink Jr. High, Moore, OK*, 2020, Digital photograph

Fig 27 *The Quan Family*, Quan Family Collection

Fig 28 Baker, Bruce, *Main road from Ho Chi Minh City to Cho Lon*, 2016, Digital photograph

Pictography

Fig I-1 *Muoi's mother and father, @1965,* Quan Family Collection, Scanned photograph

Fig I-2 *Mother and Muoi at Con Phung @ 1969,* Quan Family Collection, Scanned photograph

Fig I-3 Baker, Bruce, *One ounce of 24 karat gold,* 2016, Digital photograph

Fig I-4 Baker, Bruce, *Catholic Church courtyard,* 2016, Digital photograph

Fig I-5 Baker, Bruce, *Light pole where boy was executed for stealing bread,* 2016, Digital photograph

Fig I-6 Baker, Bruce, *Large alley as seen from Muoi's second floor balcony,*2016, Digital photograph

Fig I-7 Baker, Bruce, *Outside entrance to Muoi's house,* 2016, Digital photograph

Fig I-8 Baker, Bruce, *First Floor of Muoi's house,* 2016, Digital photograph

Fig I-9 Baker, Bruce, *Third floor room shared with rest of family,* 2016, Digital photograph

Fig I-10 Baker, Bruce, *View from 3rd floor window into neighbor's room,* 2016, Digital photograph

Fig I-11 Baker, Bruce, *Muoi, Tran, Tho, and Nhi,* 2016, Digital photograph

Fig I-12 Baker, Bruce, *Lisa (Muoi) with her childhood friends in 2016,* 2016, Digital photograph

Fig I-13 The Quan Family (taken some months after Muoi's mother's death), Quan Family Collection, Scanned photograph

Fig I-14 Baker, Bruce, *Quan family and friends in 2017 at one of their Tuesday night dinners,* 2017, Digital photograph

Made in the USA
Middletown, DE
07 July 2021